D1606343

The Illusion of Equality

Martha Albertson Fineman

The Illusion of Equality
The Rhetoric and Reality
of Divorce Reform

The University
of Chicago Press
Chicago and London

MARTHA ALBERTSON FINEMAN is professor of law at the University of Wisconsin at Madison. She is the editor of *At the Boundaries of Law: Feminism and Legal Theory.*

This book builds upon work that was presented in the following articles by Martha Albertson Fineman: "Dominant Discourse Professional Language and Legal Change," *Harvard Law Review* 101 (1988): 727; "Implementing Equality: Ideology, Contradiction and Social Change," *Wisconsin Law Review* (1983): 789; "The Use of Social Science Data in Legal Policy Making: Child Custody at Divorce," *Wisconsin Law Review* (1987): 107; "Child Advocacy and the Transformation of Custody Decision Making," *University of California—Davis Law Review* 22 (1989): 829; "Challenging Law, Establishing Differences: The Future of Feminist Legal Scholarship," *Florida Law Review* 42 (1990): 25.

The University of Chicago Press, Chicago 60637
The University of Chicago Press, Ltd., London
© 1991 by Martha Albertson Fineman
All rights reserved. Published 1991
Printed in the United States of America
00 99 98 97 96 95 94 93 92 91   5 4 3 2 1

Library of Congress Cataloging-in-Publication Data

Fineman, Martha.
    The illusion of equality : the rhetoric and reality of divorce
reform / Martha Albertson Fineman.
        p.   cm.
    Includes bibliographical references and index.
    ISBN 0-226-24956-5
    1. Divorce—Law and legislation—United States.   2. Married women—
United States.   I. Title.
    KF535.Z9F56   1991
    346.7301'66—dc347.306166
    [20]   90-11274
                                                                                        CIP

∞The paper used in this publication meets the minimum requirements of the American National Standard for Information Sciences—Permanence of Paper for Printed Library Materials, ANSI Z39.48–1984.

For the past, present, and future: for my father, Jonathan Y. Albertson; my children, Martha Ann, Amy, Benjamin, and Jonathan; and my granddaughter, Lillian.

Contents

Acknowledgments

I would like to thank my many colleagues at the Institute for Legal Studies at Wisconsin and from the Feminism and Legal Theory Conferences who have been so supportive of my work on this project over the years. I also am grateful to Murray Edelman, who has been a wonderful friend and mentor, in addition to a source of inspiration for me. I am indebted to the students whose research assistance on various aspects of the book has been invaluable: Anne MacArthur, whose contributions are most evident, worked with me for several years; Emily Van Tassel was one of my first assistants; Ellen Hauser and Amy Scarr also assisted; and, most recently, Michael Toner helped carry the project to completion. I owe a tremendous debt to Kathy DeForest, who was more midwife than typist on this book. Her patience with my technological deficiency was greatly appreciated.

CHAPTER ONE

Introduction: The Recasting of Family Law

While it is true that only women can become pregnant it does not follow that every legislative classification concerning pregnancy is a sex-based classification . . .

The lack of identity between the excluded disability and gender as such under this insurance program becomes clear upon the most cursory analysis. The program divides potential recipients into two groups—pregnant women and nonpregnant persons.

*Geduldig v. Aiello**

The instinct to treat pregnancy as a special case is deeply imbedded in our culture, indeed in every culture. It seems natural, and *right,* to treat it that way.

Yet, at a deeper level, . . . the feminists who seek special recognition for pregnancy, are starting from the same basic assumption, namely, that women have a special place in the scheme of human existence when it comes to maternity. Of course, one's view of how that basic assumption cuts is shaped by one's perspective. What businessmen, Supreme Court Justices, and feminists make of it is predictably quite different. But the same doctrinal approach that permits pregnancy to be treated *worse* than other disabilities is the same one that will allow the state constitutional freedom to create special *benefits* for pregnant women. The equality approach to pregnancy . . . necessarily creates not only the desired floor under the pregnant woman's rights but also the ceiling. . . . If we can't have it both ways, we need to think carefully about which way we want to have it.

My own feeling is that, for all its problems, the equality approach is the better one. The special treatment model has great costs. . . .

At this point, we need to think as deeply as we can about what we want the future of women and men to be. Do we want equality of the sexes—or do we want justice for two kinds of human beings who are fundamentally different?

W. Williams†

---

*Geduldig v. Aiello, 417 U.S. 498, n. 20 (upholding exclusion of benefits related to pregnancy from California's worker compensation scheme).

†Williams, *The Equality Crisis: Some Reflections on Culture, Courts, and Feminism,* 7 Women's Rts.L.Rep. 175, 195–96, 200 (1982).

1

INTRODUCTION

On one level, this book is about family policy and the changes that have occurred during the past few decades in the legal rules and processes governing divorce, property distribution, and child custody. Characterized as a crisis, the rising divorce rate which attended the passage of no-fault statutes has resulted in family law becoming an arena of social, political, and legal debates. Measures have been urged that would "protect" individuals within contemporary families from the harms associated with divorce. These measures have principally concerned the economic aspects of divorce, discussed in part 1 of this book, and custody policy, discussed in part 2.

From a broader perspective, however, the regulation of the family represented by and resulting from these new laws presents the opportunity for more than just an assessment of changing rules. The transformation of divorce law that has occurred in the past decade or so is an interesting example of the use (and misuse) of the law reform process by those attempting to give content to broader social and political goals within the framework provided by a specific set of problems. Such reformers encounter a well-developed legal rhetorical and conceptual system within which they must attempt to maneuver their reform proposals. The legal rhetoric and concepts provide both the basis for the criticism of existing rules and the standard against which proposed solutions are to be measured. Legal concepts in this context represent broad, overarching referents for reform.

During the past several decades, as in many areas, "equality" has become the normative standard in family law for reform. In the chapters that follow, I criticize divorce reform efforts based on an equality model because I believe they have had a detrimental impact on many women and children. Developments in this area illustrate that reformers can and often do create new, even more complex difficulties through the ill-considered strategies they seem inevitably to employ when using the law to attempt to construct a more ideal society. The rhetoric defines, and confines, the reform.

In suggesting that in order to do equity we must move away from equality as the grand principle in family law reform, this book does not present the popular stance regarding the context and contents of the various changes that have occurred or of those newly proposed. Close to a consensus exists among legal and other professionals concerned with the divorce process that equality-based reforms have not only been proper and appropriate, but progressive and far-reaching.

Political actors also seem satisfied. The rhetoric of the reforms has reflected the concerns of second-wave liberal feminists who employed the language of equality to mobilize women. In the legal arena, equality norms were initially manifested by the removal of gendered references in rules and statutes and the creation of a gender-neutral paradigm for reform. Women today would be hard-pressed to complain that as a group they were not well represented, since feminists were evident as actors and architects of the reform efforts. But, far from representing beneficial challenges to traditional family structures on behalf of women and children, these reforms have actually reinforced men's control within the family before and after divorce.

Equality as the Ideal

Throughout this book, I explore the tension between different, "instrumental" versus "symbolic," understandings of equality as the basis for reform. As will be developed in the following chapters, there are powerful symbolic reasons for the association of equality with sameness of treatment. There are problems that arise, however, when symbolism is the primary concern. While "rule," or formal, equality may avoid the pitfalls of protective or "special-treatment" rules, which can be used to disadvantage women as well as to help them, the application of equal treatment assumes that those subjected to the rules are in fundamentally the same position. If this is not the case, the result of applying rule-equality may be to further perpetuate result-inequality.

Rules that focus on result-equality, by contrast, are attempts to ensure that the *effects* of rules as they will be applied will place individuals in more or less equal positions. Such rules are constituted to take into account the different structural positions of women and men in our society and seek to achieve parity in position between individuals. Result-equality is a more instrumental approach to restructuring the relationships between men and women and may require that these groups be treated differently in order that they end up on the same level. However, because result-equality rules are facially unequal, they are much harder to justify. The basis for different treatment must be detailed, defended and, ultimately, accepted by those upon whom the rules operate. In the context of divorce, result-equality arguments, while available, have not been forcefully made.

Both of these concepts of equality incorporate and depend upon certain theoretical and factual assumptions about society, the role of women, and the function of law. Yet there are important areas where these underlying assumptions, and reforms that might be based on them, diverge from each other. It is my argument in part 1 of this book that, given the socioeconomic factors that typically disadvantage women in the market while simultaneously favoring their assumption of the major domestic responsibilities, result-equality should have been the objective of reforms focusing on the economic allocations made at divorce.

The symbolic aspects of equality rhetoric have dominated these reform efforts, casting debates in terms that construct rules as though the egalitarian ideal has been achieved. The assertion of equality has overshadowed instrumental concerns about the impact of specific changes on the postdivorce economic and social status of women and children. As discussed more fully in part 1, in their efforts to reform property distribution, for example, liberal legal feminists adopted the partnership metaphor for marriage as a rhetorical device by which to elevate housewives' nonmonetary contributions to the marriage to an equal status with the contributions of their wage-earning spouses. They described what they considered to be women's "victimization" under common-law property distribution schemes that tended to allocate property at divorce according to title. In seeking reform, equality, in the guise of partnership, provided the measure of ultimate fairness from which both to argue women's victimization and to fashion the solution to it. The theory was that a housewife-partner's tasks were to be equally valued with her husband's economic contribution. Through the use of such metaphors referencing dominant cultural ideals and forms, the property reformers were able to garner political support and sympathy for their equality-based proposals.

Many unacknowledged problems with this approach exist. First, only a small group of women were so economically privileged as to occupy the status of housewife. In fact, the vast majority of women work both within and outside the home, so that their contributions to the family unit could be considered to be based on overparticipation rather than equal participation. One could view them as deserving more than an equal partnership share. Further, the intended housewife beneficiary of the economic reforms may not have needed such dramatic rescue. Prior divorce law was not blind to her contribution, nor unresponsive to her economic dependence on her wage-earning spouse.

Moreover, from a result-equality perspective, I would argue that, metaphors and paradigms aside, the economic and social inequalities women as a group suffer in society are such that an equal share of assets is seldom sufficient to provide security for women and children after divorce. This is so particularly because of the obligations women typically assume during marriage and after divorce for the care of children, even under joint-custody arrangements. Additionally, any economic gains that may have accrued to women under the first round of divorce reform have been offset by subsequent changes, especially those in the area of custody. Custody decision making, also pulled within the equality maleficence, has become so unpredictable and precarious that, faced with even a small prospect of losing custody, many women bargain away much-needed property and support awards to secure sole-custodian status.

As discussed in part 2, the discourses in forming custody policy are filled with horror stories and ideals and are best understood as competing visions in a rhetorical war waged over what is desirable in the post-divorce family. In this context, it has been children who are designated as the victims, with custody reformers calling for greater state regulation of divorce to protect them. Proposals for change have been directed at both the substantive rules governing custody questions and the procedures utilized in decision making. Couched in terms of the "best interests" of children, policy recommendations in this area are designed to be symbolically compelling, a phenomenon that has operated, in large part, to place these reforms beyond criticism.

The interests of other family actors have also been forcefully presented in formal equality terms in the custody area. Groups stressing "fathers' rights" have urged policy changes similar to those supported and advocated by professional political interest groups. Furthermore, there is spillover among the discourses. For example, sole maternal custody has become characterized by professional political interest groups as unfair to fathers. This politically powerful intersection of fathers'-rights discourse, waged by angry men for use against their ex-wives, and professional discourses is also reflected in (and actually appropriates) liberal legal feminist equality rhetoric. Reforms like joint custody were, in this convergence of equality discourses, presented as necessary to rectify imbalance and establish rights.

Equally important has been the claim that these new custody norms were necessary to save children from the harms associated with divorce, particularly the loss of the noncustodial parent occasioned by the designation of a sole custodian. This argument transcends the equality rhetoric because the child's "right" is designated as paramount. There is, however, an interesting intersection of children's- and fathers'-rights discourses, with joint custody emerging as the "ideal" (fairy-tale) solution for the many problems of the divorced family (i.e., "everyone wins"). Little mention is made, however, of the substantial problems this form of custody creates for primary caretaking mothers and for their children.

Another important aspect of custody reform based on the establishment of children's separation from or theoretical equality within the family has been the advent of independent representation of children in divorce proceedings. As detailed in chapter 6, the designation of children as "victims" with independent, individual rights to be weighed in the decision-making process is a substantial departure from prior law, in which parents' and children's interests were aligned. Now, by contrast, children's interests are perceived as separate, perhaps even antagonistic to parental interests, with the state substituting its personnel for the parents in order to see that children's interests are protected at divorce.

Finally, as detailed in chapter 9, the debates around custody policy have urged the resort to nonjudicial decision-makers and processes in place of those associated with the traditional adversarial system. Mediation, for example, has been characterized by the helping professions as the more "humane" alternative for divorcing families, as a process that utilizes more "informed" individuals than lawyers and judges as decision-makers. Many judges and lawyers favor these sorts of reforms, in part because their construction as "nonadversarial" has symbolic appeal, but also because of the impact such measures have on divorce practice. Mediation removes cases from overcrowded court calendars, while simple rules like joint custody are easy to apply and replace standards which are less certain and more difficult to apply, such as the contemporary "best-interest-of-the-child" test.

There is an appalling absence of criticism about the assumptions underlying these proposals. The reforms discussed in the subsequent chapters represent and facilitate heightened regulation of the family both at and after divorce. While historically conceptualized as part of a "private sphere" into which the state could legitimately intervene only if necessary, the family in contemporary law is no longer accorded doctrinal protection as an entity. Family law now favors "protecting" individuals and promoting social ends like equality between the sexes and between divorcing parents.

A close examination of these reforms reveals the exclusion of alternative feminist and pro-mother voices from these debates. Feminists who focus on family rather than market concerns as the organizing point of their work and the mothers for whom they seek to speak use a discourse which is incompatible with the dominant gender-equality ideal.

In the chapters that follow, I am decidedly critical of the legal changes and reforms. My concern centers on the impact of the various reforms on women and their children. Beyond the superficial appeal of the symbols and language incorporated in the entire spectrum of divorce discourse lies the stark reality that, after the "equality revolution," women and children continue to suffer at divorce.

CONTRASTING METHODOLOGIES AND CONFLICTING CONCLUSIONS

My approach in this book can be described as an example of the use of feminist methodology. My inquiry into family law reform has been prompted by my attempt to understand why there appears to be little relationship between women's lives and material circumstances and the specific doctrinal representations of those lives and circumstances collected under the heading "Family Law."

In my opinion, one significant distinction between my feminist approach to legal theory and the more traditional varieties is my belief in the desirability of basing law on what is concrete rather than on what is abstract. Such an emphasis on context also has had rather honorable nonfeminist adherents. For example, Robert Merton coined the term *theory of the middle range* to describe work that mediated between "stories" and "grand" theory. He described such scholarship as being better than mere storytelling or mindless empiricism, as well as superior to vague references to the relationships between ill-defined abstractions.[1] Clifford Geertz[2] and James Boyd White,[3] among others, have noted that language or rhetoric itself is specific, tied to given material concerns. As White has stated:

> Like law, rhetoric invents; and, like law, it invents out of some-
> thing rather than out of nothing. It always starts in a particular
> culture and among particular people. There is always one speaker
> addressing others in a particular situation, about concerns that are
> real and important to somebody, and speaking a particular lan-
> guage. Rhetoric always takes place with given materials. One can-
> not idealize rhetoric and say, "Here is how it should go on in gen-
> eral . . ." [R]hetoric is always specific to its material.[4]

Feminist scholarship, in nonlaw areas at least, has tended to focus on specifics.[5] Feminist legal scholarship, however, seems to be drifting toward abstract grand theory presentations. Carol Smart has recently warned that feminist legal theorists are in danger of creating in their writing the impression that it is possible to identify from among the

competing feminist legal theories one specific form of feminist jurisprudence that will represent the "superior" (or true) version. She labels this
totalizing tendency, evident in the work of many of the most well-
known North American legal feminists, as the construction of a *scientific
feminism,* and she is explicitly critical of such grand theorizing.[6]

In my opinion, grand theorizing in law, with its references to abstract
"supernorms" such as "equality" or "justice," is little more than the re-
fashioning of positivism—a recasting of the belief that there are universal truths discoverable and ascertainable, although the insights are to be
provided within the confines of the methodology of critical legal analysis. Middle-range theory, at least my feminist adaptation of it, by contrast, mediates between the material circumstances of women's lives and
the grand theories of law. It reveals in this way that law is gendered, that
law is a manifestation of power, that law is detrimental to women. Because they have previously been hidden or ignored in consideration of
laws that regulate women's lives, conclusions are best supported by referencing and emphasizing women's lives. In the following chapters, I
place the rhetoric and the reforms of family law in the context of the inequalities of the circumstances of those women's lives.

Several other theoretical assertions or beliefs about feminist methodology, in various permutations and in combination with the lessons
learned from concrete narratives, provide the ingredients for my analyses of family law reform. These assertions form the basis for my consideration of these reforms and the foundation for my critical perspective
about their contents and nature. They are assertions that challenge existing paradigms and have methodological implications.

First, feminist scholarship should be critical. The critical stance
should be gained from adopting an explicitly woman-focused perspective, a perspective informed by women's experiences. Feminist theory
can *not* be "gender-neutral" and will be explicitly critical of that paradigm as having historically excluded women's perspectives from legal
thought. "Gender-sensitive" feminism, however, should not be viewed
as lacking legitimacy because of an inappropriate bias. Rather, it is premised on the need to expose and correct existing bias. Gender-sensitive
feminism seeks to correct the imbalance and unfairness in the legal system resulting from the implementation of perspectives that exclude attention to the circumstances of women's gendered lives, even on issues
that intimately affect those lives.

Recent changes in the family law context are illustrative of measures
that deny the existence of women's gendered lives. As developed in
chapter 3, for example, measures promoted in the 1970s sought to im-

pose a fifty-fifty scheme for the distribution of assets, consistent with the partnership metaphor by which liberal feminists chose to character-ize marriage. Liberal feminists adopted this metaphor because of their uncritical acceptance of the necessity of establishing "equality" through sameness of treatment. However, in light of the social and economic in-equalities women experience, one-half of the accumulated assets is sel-dom sufficient to provide adequately for them and their children after divorce. Similarly, as detailed in chapter 5, within the context of child-custody determinations, there has been a retreat from the historic pref-erence accorded women under the "tender-years" doctrine, an eviden-tiary presumption under which women, unless "unfit," received custody of their children, in favor of custody norms, like joint custody, based on rule equality.

But feminist analysis, when it is recognized at all in legal thought, is often seen as marginal. Further, there is a tendency in traditional legal scholarship to view the status quo as unbiased or neutral. As a result, this is the logical place for feminist analysis to begin—as an explicit challenge to the notion of bias, as contrasted with the concepts of per-spective and position. Chapter 7, which considers the uses of social-science conclusions in legal policy-making, is intended to demonstrate through the use of feminist methodology that what is often accepted as objective "fact" is not neutral. Conclusions constructed by social scien-tists or by legal policymakers and marketed as objective observations are often produced in quite biased manners, frequently contain political preferences and assumptions, and can certainly not be considered more "correct" than the information or interpretations which challenge them. There should be no refuge in the status quo for any of us. Arguments based on traditional beliefs and perceptions must be reconsidered given the realization that law has developed over time in the context of theo-ries and institutions which are controlled by men and reflect their con-cerns. This is no less true in family law than in other areas. Historically, law has been considered a "public" arena, and its focus has been on pub-lic concerns. Traditionally, women belonged to the "private" recesses of society, in families, in relationships controlled and defined by men, in the legal silences. The family has now been explicitly moved into the public arena of regulating policy. The policies, however, indeed the very terms of discourse, continue to be fashioned by a largely male elite within the context of historically bound institutions that reflect and val-idate only their experience and perceptions.

A second belief about feminist legal methodology that underlies this book is that it is necessary to evaluate critically not only outcomes but the fundamental concepts, values, and assumptions embedded in legal thought.[7] Results or outcomes in cases decided under existing legal doctrines are not irrelevant to this inquiry, but criticizing them is only a starting point. Too many legal scholars end their inquiries with critiques of results and recommendations for "tinkering"-type reforms, without considering how the very conceptual structure of legal thought condemns such reforms to the mere replication of injustices.[8] When, as is so often the case, the basic tenets of legal ideology are at odds with women's gendered lives, reforms based on those same tenets will do little more than the original rules to validate and accommodate women's experiences. As will be evident to the reader of chapter 3 concerning economic decisions, for example, the assumptions and beliefs underlying reform must be critically evaluated and carefully fashioned to avoid the perpetuation of problems. Chapters 8 and 9, in particular, detail the importance of the rhetoric and professional ideology of nonlegal actors, such as social scientists and members of the helping professions, in custody policy-making.

From my perspective, feminism is a political theory concerned with issues of power. Feminist methodology challenges the conceptual basis of the status quo by assessing the ways that power controls the production of values and standards against which specific results and rules are measured. Law represents both a discourse and a process of power. Norms created by and enshrined in law are manifestations of power relationships. These norms are coercively applied and justified in part by the perception that they are "neutral" and "objective." An appreciation of this fact has led me to focus on the legislative and political processes in the construction of law rather than merely on what judges are doing. It has also led me to concentrate on the social and cultural perceptions and manifestations of law and legality at least as much as on formal legal doctrinal developments.[9]

Implicit in my assertion that feminism must be a politically rather than a legally focused method or theory is a belief about law and social change that assumes the relative powerlessness of law to transform society as compared to other ideological institutions of social constitution within our culture. This belief separates me from the liberal legal feminists, whose resort to law to establish egalitarian relationships within the family and the workplace led to many of the reforms discussed in this book. They viewed law as the instrument of social change; I, however, believe that law can reflect social change, even facilitate it, but can seldom if ever be used to initiate it.

No matter what the formal legal articulation, the implementation of legal rules will track and reflect the dominant conceptualizations and conclusions of the majority culture. Thus, while law can be used to highlight the social and political conditions it reflects, it is more a mirror than a catalyst when it comes to effecting enduring social change.[10] This has been one of the problems with equality-based family law reforms. Egalitarian relationships may be an ideal for some, but they are not in most instances "real" for women and men in our society. The establishment of equality-based rules has not benefited women; it has, in many instances, operated to their disadvantage.

I intend this book as an example of feminist legal scholarship—to be critical, to be political, to be part of ongoing debates about family regulation. This book is concerned with methods and processes that comprise law and is about law in its broadest form, as a manifestation of power in society. It recognizes that there is no division between law and power. Law is not only found in courts and cases, in legislatures and statutes, but also in implementing institutions such as the profession of social work and in the rhetoric of nonlegal scholars. Further, "law" is found in discourse and language used in everyday life reflecting understandings about what constitutes the law. It is evident in the beliefs and assumptions we hold about the world in which we live and in the norms and values we cherish.

In my concluding chapter, I argue for the abdication of equality. I believe women and children will fare better under legal rules which reference their material and emotional circumstances, not grand theoretical abstractions. My "solutions," if they can be labeled as such, are not appeals to grand concepts such as equality or justice. They are based on my belief that we as a society should value and reward nurturing children, sacrifices made for others, and the future that is represented by the children who have been lost to equality.

In regard to the law of the family, children have been forgotten, passed by. One of the central assumptions has been that the concept of family is dependent upon a relationship between man and woman, legally privileged. Formal marriage is presented as the central most important relational component of the traditional definition of family. When this relationship is ended, as through divorce, we speak of the "broken" family. An alternative, equally valid, perception, such as that the basic family unit is constituted by mother and child, has never effectively emerged. A woman and her children are considered an *incomplete*, a deviant, family—one of the "single-parent" families identified as sources of pathology, generators of problems such as poverty or crime.[11]

The centrality of this relationship between men and women has been what defines other family relationships, as in the historical characterization of children as "legitimate" or "illegitimate" depending on whether or not their parents were married. The significant reference in defining the child is to the status of the parents' relationship. While such children today are more apt to be labeled *nonmarital,* the focus is still the same—on the adults. It is problematic that our notions of family are culturally dependent upon and focus on the formal relationship between man and woman. Privileging that tie as the primary one inevitably means that the focus at divorce will be inappropriately on doing justice between the adults involved, severing their tie in some rational and justifiable manner. As with all laws, divorce rules symbolically reflect more than what is considered to be appropriate legal policy. The norms and standards expressed in specific rules also stand as eloquent statements about society's views on the nature of family and marriage. It is little wonder that, given our focus on the adults, equality has become the dominant conceptual framework for marriage dissolution in the latter part of the twentieth century. It is also little wonder that within the confines of equality rhetoric, assets of the family, including children, have become prizes, providing an arena for competition between husbands and wives, mothers and fathers, at divorce.

Other changes have further fostered occasions for this male-female competitiveness. Family law is an area in which tensions generated by perceived changes in the position of women are clearly felt. The family is the "sphere" to which women were historically assigned, and public institutions worked to reinforce male dominance and control in the market and in the home. At divorce, men often seem to seek to assert in explicit ways the power they implicitly enjoyed within the context of indissoluble marriage and the advantages of traditional patriarchy. They must do so in a society which has evolved a system of easy access to divorce and provided some economic security for women, giving them the option to end a relationship and not fear that their own or their children's economic futures would be total impoverishment. The patriarchal definition of family has not been displaced, however. It continues to affect reform and rhetoric in the area of divorce.

What I have attempted to do in this book is to take seriously the women-focused, concrete concerns of feminism and to consider family law as it affects women's lives both in a symbolic and a practical sense. This work is intended to challenge the patriarchal norm of the male-defined and male-headed family with heterosexual union at its core. In doing my work, the task of making my analysis concrete has been essential to explicating the position of women and children. I am critical of resorting to abstractions such as "equality" for making hard decisions, and have questioned the desirability of rhetorical, symbolically pleasing changes which can harm women, such as some of those produced by the campaigns to make legal rules and language gender-neutral. I have considered it essential to the integrity of my work to anchor and inform my theoretical perspective by an appreciation of the gendered society in which we live.

Considering family law in the 1990s demands an approach that includes not only assessments concerning the real-world circumstances of the majority of women, but also an appreciation of the ways in which male power is both the thing to be confronted and controller of the forums in which any confrontation must take place. Men have been the validators; their institutions, of which law is one of the most powerful, have controlled the terms and content of the discussion so far. This book is an attempt to broaden and reshape the debate.

PART ONE

Equality Rhetoric and The Economics of Divorce

T W O

The Family as a Site of Rhetorical and Ideological Contest

Divorce law reform, despite feminist critiques, will probably be counted a success. Those who promoted the reforms have largely succeeded in dictating the terms of their evaluation. By those standards, most of the changes have had their intended effects: less fraud and hostility in the divorce process, greater equality in the division of assets, and more opportunities for fathers to remain involved with their children. The unanticipated consequences are perhaps not so much adverse effects as incomplete achievements, magnified by the habituation of Americans to divorce which has multiplied its adverse effects on women and children. The changes . . . were not intended to perfect the lives of divorced women and their children. While recent reforms perhaps have not worsened their situation, they also have not sufficiently improved it.

H. Jacob*

The Changing Family

In recent years, increased political attention in the United States has focused on the family as an institution in a state of crisis. Because the family is viewed as an institution in a transitional stage, it is the subject of rhetorical and ideological struggles within the political system.[1] In this regard, advocates of various reforms assert that while the stresses of modern life, particularly the high divorce rate, will certainly damage the family, their proposals may save it.

Discourses concerning the family are highly emotionally charged and fraught with symbolism. Discourses about family law and family problems also tend to be superficial and are often motivated by concerns other than understanding or remedying the "crises" of the contemporary family. Revealing the assumptions which underlie these reform efforts will show the extent to which tensions and conflicting attitudes among various segments of society exist concerning the institution of

*H. Jacob, *The Silent Revolution,* 164 (1988)

17

the family. In resolving these tensions, legislators, judges, and legal scholars have accepted the newly created legal vocabulary concerning family relationships, fashioned in part from existing doctrines or legal constructs and in part from more contemporary discourses, such as those of the helping professions and of liberal feminists, concerning the appropriate means of regulating the "changing" family.

Setting the Stage

A brief introductory discussion of prior family law and the nature of the reform efforts is useful. Before the modern reforms, divorce seldom occurred and, if allowed, was based on the notion of spouse "fault." In addition to providing a justification for dissolution of the marriage relationship, fault also functioned as an allocation device regarding children and marital assets, with the "innocent" spouse receiving custody and economic subsidy through property distribution, child support, and alimony.[2] The tender-years doctrine, under which mothers, unless "unfit," were typically awarded custody of young children, was compatible with the fault system, even though it reflected a preference for women as custodial parents. Alimony and property distribution were more than a penalty or compensation for a husband's "marital misconduct"; they were also awarded in recognition of women's and children's economic dependency.

Under this earlier view, marriage was a status relationship, evidencing the unity of husband and wife, with children's interests aligned with the interests of their parents. The entity, as such, was accorded protection as a "private" sphere, to be relatively free from direct state regulation and intervention. The ties between the adults and among the adults and children were not easily broken. The family unity was, at least theoretically, strengthened by the legal doctrines limiting divorce to cases where one partner was at fault.

Marriage has now been transformed from this common-law conception into the modern view of a voluntary, perhaps temporary "partnership."[3] These contrasting visions of marriage are commonly presented by legal scholars as representing steps in a progressive recasting of the legal nature of the marriage relationship, often described as a movement from status to contract.[4] The contemporary emphasis on the individualistic or contractual aspects of marriage formation has had an impact on the evolution of rules governing dissolution. Marriage is seen as a contract dissolvable at the will of either party. Unilateral access to divorce, however, has revealed the need to consider the rules governing the distribution of accumulated assets and liabilities at termination. Generally, this reassessment can be characterized as involving the gradual replacement of individual choices concerning the economic terms of marriage relationships, reflected in formal designations of ownership (title) or in explicit contractual provisions, with standardized, protective formulas imposed by the state at divorce. This form of a protective role for the state is more interventionist and reflects a major shift in the nature of the state's relationship to the individuals involved in a marriage relationship as well as a departure from traditional assumptions about the institution of marriage.[5]

Earlier legal rules regulating marriage and divorce reflected the belief that marriage was a basic social institution in which the state had a profound interest, and therefore its formation, organization, and dissolution were appropriately and closely regulated by the state.[6] Dissolution of the relationship was only permitted for state-defined reasons—acts constituting "fault." Currently, marriage is viewed as an institution existing primarily for the benefit of the individuals involved—to promote their happiness, not to perpetuate social ends. This changed perception of the purpose of marriage has led to a shift in the focus of state regulation. The state has abandoned, to a great extent, its concern with the formalities attending entry into marriage and the designation of acceptable reasons for divorce. Instead, the regulatory manifestation of state concern at divorce now focuses on the internal aspects of family life, with the need to protect individuals. Such protection has been identified with the goal of achieving gender equality by imposing egalitarian standards through formal law.

Equality operates as the contemporary justification for state regulation; while there is less concern with the formal establishment of "family" relationships, there is a correspondingly greater concern with the quality and legal implications of those relationships once they are established. Thus, while access to divorce was made easy under no-fault reforms, regulation of the family has in fact escalated, as the state's concern now centers on ensuring "equity" and "justice" between the spouses in dividing up their accumulated debts and assets and in awarding custody of their children.

This shift of state regulatory focus is consistent with the view that marriage is a voluntary and, therefore, perhaps temporary union of equals which either one may terminate at will if it does not satisfy his or her desires and needs.[7] Moreover, this shift in the societal understanding of marriage is reflected in the adoption of "no fault" divorce and of new rules governing the allocation of economic benefits and burdens and child custody.

Legal Regulation of Divorce

During the 1960s, serious and substantial reforms of the divorce system were undertaken. Initially, no-fault statutes were passed which eventually had the effect of making divorce so freely available that marriage became legally terminable at the will of either party if it did not satisfy a party's needs and desires.[8] More recently, reforms have been directed to other areas of family law, including property distribution and child custody. Instead of leaving these decisions to existing common-law title concepts, tempered by considerations of fault and judicial discretion, or designing rules to give preference to the prior lived economic arrangements of spouses, reforms were devised by which marital assets and children were "ideally" allocated on an egalitarian basis. The ideal is embodied in rules such as the presumption of equal division of marital proceeds and the preference for joint custody.

It is not surprising that the movement away from a fault-based system undermined spousal fault or misconduct as a potential allocation device in property and custody questions, but this alone does not explain contemporary egalitarian reform efforts. An essential conceptual and rhetorical aspect of changing family policy has been the successes of second-wave feminism in the legal arena and, in particular, its adoption of the language of equality, with its paradigmatic ideal of gender neutrality as the basis of proposed law reforms.

THE EQUALITY IDEAL

To a large extent, contemporary equality discourse parallels early feminist agitation during the nineteenth century. Both movements adopted a same-treatment approach to equality issues, consistent with the resilient ideal of equal treatment of individuals throughout American history. There are those who support the notion of equality as sameness of treatment, while others favor equality of *result,* a focus that might well require the development and application of different rules. These alternative theories of equality depend on whether or not, in the first instance, the individuals in question are or are not considered to be similarly situated.

In the public sphere, gender-equality rhetoric informed proposed measures designed to counter the "victimization" of women, exemplified in their portrayal as inferior. Feminists in these endeavors appropriated the logical and legal legitimacy of rule-equality discourse, proposing equal-treatment solutions as remedies to women's oppression.[9]

Equality became a banner under which early feminists organized reform efforts to demand access to political and public institutions.[10] The latest manifestation of adherence to this conceptualization of equality is the recent movement behind the Equal Rights Amendment.[11]

Rule-equality measures may be appropriate when individuals are in situations that are relatively straightforward and comparable or when their social and economic attributes are similar. But, historically, problems arose in applying this model of equality to gender issues because the notion of "equality" had to be integrated with complex, conflicting, deeply held assumptions and beliefs about whether women had different physical, emotional, or social characteristics than men which should be recognized or accommodated by law.

The ideal of formal equality has at times been rejected in order to confer "protections" designed to adjust for differences. For example, at some periods in our history, there has been general agreement that significant differences existed between men and women which justified different treatment.[12] An example of this is nineteenth-century protective labor legislation requiring that employers treat women unequally in terms of hours they could work, in order to protect them from being victimized by existing working conditions assumed to affect them differently and more severely than men.[13] Today such "protective measures" are still at issue, as recent attempts to curtail the exposure of women of childbearing age to chemicals potentially harmful to the fetus illustrate.[14] By and large, these forms of different treatment have been opposed by feminists, held up as the likely evils of anything less than a same-treatment model of equality. However, those who have argued for result-equality have increasingly done so by asserting that formal rule-equality measures will simply perpetuate inequality if applied to individuals who, in fact, are not in comparable situations. Today, an increasing number of feminists trained in law argue that conceptual and experiential barriers to the imposition of a pure rule-equality approach exist in the public sphere. As such, those feminists have come to see that formal equality may not be enough when we consider women in the workforce and market. They recognize that ensuring women's access to and success in these arenas might require "special" rules due to the inequality that defines women's lives and their interactions with institutions.

Such perceptions about the need for special, remedial treatment affect the current debates about needed law reform in all areas. While many feminist legal scholars continue to assert that equality can be achieved only through the adoption of rules which eliminate gender as a basis for distinguishing between people, a growing minority has pointed out that achieving the objectives of equality requires measures that extend beyond mere sameness of treatment; the rules should be explicitly developed to achieve equality of result, with the historic and contemporary disadvantages associated with gender given important consideration.[15]

Equality and the Market

Modern calls by feminists for explicit gender consideration in fashioning rules governing women in work and public situations differ from the arguments made in the Progressive Era for special or different treatment. Contemporary analyses focus on existing institutional structures and their historical inadequacies in incorporating women, not on the different, and implicitly "deficient" or "vulnerable," characteristics of women as a group. Therefore, difference of treatment is desirable not because of women's inherently different internal qualities but because of the discriminatory qualities of the institutions with which they must deal.

Under this approach, the significant question of differences between men and women is externalized. Because such arguments identify the root problem as involving the failure of institutions and do not concede an unalterable biological or physiological basis for such treatment, it follows that the disadvantages will disappear if the institutions can be changed. Thus, the protection that women are perceived as needing lies in assuring them access to these structures and the opportunity to function in them without being disadvantaged by institutional inadequacies.

This contemporary perception of a need for "protective" or result-oriented legislation has been at the base of many recent battles in the public arena. As women have moved into new market and political spheres during the last several decades, women's-rights advocates have had to broaden their focus beyond the historic more obvious manifestations of inequality for women, such as denial of the right to vote, hold office, or engage in certain occupations, where injustice could be rectified by simply treating women the same as men and conferring on them traditional legal "rights."[16] Legal and social theorists are now grappling with newly-defined and perceived problems, and some suggested solutions reflect the belief that problems are not always resolved by the application of simple rule-equality principles without reference to characteristics statistically related to gender and to the socioeconomic disadvantages of women in this society.

For example, some commentators have observed that more women work today than ever before in this country's history, but they point out that women continue to earn much less than men.[17] Furthermore, this is true even after decades of attempted and successful equality-based reforms. In this regard, social scientists have recognized that women are often clustered in a few occupations, and politically active women have moved from demands of equal pay for equal work to demands which raise difficult legal questions of "comparable worth" and "affirmative action." In addition, feminist discourse is at least beginning to show a growing awareness that even women who achieve access to "male" occupations do not "have it made," since sociological studies of businesses and professions have begun to reveal subtle forms of sex discrimination in promotions and delegation of responsibility, and differences between the genders in career choices related to family roles and responsibilities.[18]

This progression from concern with the obvious to concern with the more hidden manifestations of discriminatory or unequal treatment of women has created the need to develop a coherent concept of different treatment with which to address these problems. A difficult choice must be made between the two potentially conflicting equality models: that of rule-equality through the imposition of gender-neutral laws as a matter of principle, and that of result-equality, which seeks individualized justice for women.

This potential conflict is at the heart of the issue of affirmative action in education and employment, for example, when society is asked to formulate a rule which is not neutral and, as such, demonstrates a preference to achieve social equality or some other equity on behalf of a structurally disadvantaged group. The same conflict is also at the heart of many issues in family law, although this has not always been recognized, resulting in damage to many women's and children's interests.

Some feminists argue for affirmative (or protective) action in the public sphere as part of their response to the perceived structural inadequacies of economic institutions. In addressing the economic questions in divorce, however, they have for the most part adhered to the ideal of egalitarian marriage. In this regard, the question is why gender, perceived by feminists as fundamental in formulating idealized rules with which to construct women's dealings with employers and other outside economic forces, was not likewise perceived as fundamental in formulating the structure of rules governing relationships at divorce.

Moreover, some feminist theorists have recently suggested that the dependency embodied in the mother-child relationship is simply incompatible with the long-established liberal legal concepts of "individualism" and "autonomy" which dominate the official discourse.[19] Traditional preference in political theory, however, does not explain liberal feminists' avoidance of the hard questions families raise.

One reason for this dichotomy was certainly the traditional separation of family in private concerns from the public aspects of life. Classic liberal theory, while opposing the idea that status follows birth, for example, did not pull the family, with its historically sex-based division of rules and rights, into its ambit. Rather, the family was considered part of a private sphere and, thus, beyond the reach of political theory. Current concern with gender issues that continues this almost exclusive focus on women's market participation is in this tradition.

Equality and the Family

In general, feminist reformers are more likely to advocate vigorously the application of result-oriented, affirmative action principles in the market but call for application of a pure rule-equality model within the family context. Even within family-law reforms, the metaphors chosen by feminists place contractual aspects at the forefront, emphasizing a public and economic image. The metaphors reside in the terminology of business associations, as in the "partnership" designation for the marriage relationship. Such language reinforces the notion that marriage is a contractual, not a status, relationship.

In addition to choosing language that associates marriage with business, feminist reformers have sought to make discussions concerning the functioning of the family gender-neutral. This facilitates the removal of gender-specific rules in the family law area. Rules such as the tender-years doctrine have been virtually abolished either by legislation or by court decisions in the past several years.[20]

Concern with more subtle gender-associated inequalities has not yet evolved into full-blown feminist discourse in the family context. Affirmative action concepts have not been proposed. This, I believe, is because of contemporary liberal legal feminists' fundamental objective of ensuring women's ability to function as equals in the political sphere and in the marketplace.[21] The theme of equal access to political and market institutions was eventually expanded to include contemporary family law reforms, but only because the family was viewed as affecting access to political and economic power. As such, feminist dialogues on the family during the past few decades have centered on changing role expectations within marriage and on the notion of shared domestic responsibilities between spouses.[22] This focus was essential to break down the gender stereotypes historically associated with the division of labor in the family. The family discussion, however, has proceeded as an adjunct to the primary discussions of the ideal market functions that women could and should perform.

Traditional family role expectations had to be restructured, since women could not be expected to function as equals in the marketplace if they could not free themselves from their family responsibilities.[23] Thus, rhetoric in the family context has been consistent with and complementary to equal access issues raised in relation to the market and politics. Market and political access appear to be the primary ideological goal of the movement, and the writings of some of the more radical feminists condemn marriage as an institution. Because the primary focus has been on the market, the theorizing needed to resolve the difficult problem of what equality should mean in the family context has been neglected. Feminists have for the most part only transposed feminist market ideology onto the family law area.[24]

One reason the result-equality model was more easily implemented in public- and market-sphere reforms is the nature and characterization of women's positions vis-à-vis men in these areas. When job responsibilities, test scores, or inclinations are similar, but women continue to earn less or be excluded from participation, it is easy to see the inequality and argue for remedial measures. Terms like *comparable worth* and *affirmative action* seem designed to place unequal treatment in the most favorable and degendered light.

By contrast, women's experience in the family is not an experience of exclusion or suppressed opportunity but of overparticipation and extensive responsibility. Equality in this sphere can be understood to provide *relief* to women from the burdens of domestic life[25]—relief that would free them to take on market tasks—while affirmative action concepts seem more applicable to men, particularly fathers seeking custody. This utility to men perhaps explains why the rule-equality model has been more successfully adopted rhetorically, even though it is not actually implemented, in the context of families. The language of equality confers power and rights; these are more easily transferred from women to men in the context of the family than from men to women in the more general society.

THE POWER OF SYMBOLISM

An interesting aspect of family-law equality reform is the degree to which women who designated themselves as feminists chose to facilitate the shift toward equality rules, which took some protection away from women. There may be several related reasons why female-focused affirmative action arguments have not been made by feminists in the context of family-law reforms. First, such arguments would cast doubt on the symbolically significant ideal of family equality. If, at divorce, different or preferred treatment for women were to be demanded, it could not be justified as consistent with the goal of an egalitarian family in the ongoing marriage and would, therefore, frustrate desired social change.

Second, result-oriented arguments that women should be treated differently in the family area because of gender-related social characteristics might be transferred with very different symbolic connotations to the market. Such differential treatment in the family sphere may have been perceived as a way to perpetuate discriminatory beliefs already operating to disadvantage women at work. Thus, feminists may have feared that gender-specific rules in the family area, whether implicitly or explicitly formulated, might come to stigmatize or call into question the abilities or commitment of the "protected" sex on a wider work-related scale.[26]

Third, even if only the issue of divorce is considered, feminists may have believed that generalized result-equality rules would not help to improve the disadvantaged position of women at divorce but would actually perpetuate it.[27] While explicit gender-specific rules, such as the maternal preference for the custody of children of tender years, may assist women, who are more prone than men as a group to seek custody of their children, these rules may have been seen as reinforcing the notion that biology is destiny. On this level, perpetuating the notion that motherhood comes first for women may have been seen as making an individual woman's decision to relinquish custody to her husband more difficult.[28]

Finally, to the extent that the feminists' overriding objective was the affirmation of the ideal of equality, result-equality rules, which concede that equality does not in fact exist, may create an impression that it cannot exist. These rules may have been viewed as an admission that women as a group are dependent and as a suggestion that they will be dependent forever rather than as necessary corrective measures for institutionally disadvantaged women.

Equality Law Reforms

Liberal feminist law reformers were committed to certain feminist principles as they approached their task of suggesting appropriate family-law rules. Important in this regard was their commitment to the

concept of gender neutrality, which had already been expressed in earlier legislation that removed gender designations from many statutes in
a variety of states. Such a commitment would not permit sex to be used
as an explicit conceptual framework for family law reforms, even if feminists initially undertook the reform because they viewed the existing
law as potentially harmful to women.[29]

Gender neutrality as a feminist objective was important in the abstract because it alone was consistent with general liberal notions of
equality, and the reformers may have viewed their ultimate chances of
success as dependent on linking their rhetoric with traditional concepts
of rule-equality. In this way, they could build upon other politically successful movements within the personal experience of their constituents,
notably the civil rights movement. Whether it was a conscious choice or
not, the language used by feminists to articulate the problems of divorce and to define their solutions fit within the concept of the accepted
social goal of equal treatment in that it merely transposed the demand
for justice in the form of sameness of treatment onto the issue of the
law's treatment of women at divorce.[30]

As equality and the concurrent concept of gender neutrality have been
incorporated into divorce decision making, the old, tested, gendered rules
that permitted predictable, inexpensive decisions to be made in most cases
without protracted litigation have been set aside. As a result, one problem
confronting the new, formally degendered family-law system is the need to
create new gender-neutral factors or processes to handle the cases. The need
for an authoritative articulation of alternative standards has set the stage for
political and ideological battles.

Further, the push of the women's movement for equality in the family and workplace generated various backlashes. For example, the economic reforms concerning property divisions at divorce met with resistance. In addition, the feminist gender-neutrality rhetoric used to
promote economic reform has been appropriated and successfully employed by fathers' rights groups to force other rule-equality reforms in
the family-law area, such as mandatory joint custody. These latter
changes in particular were not beneficial to women and children. Joint
custody legislation is increasingly popular in the United States, and
some statutes permit it to be imposed by courts even if one parent objects.

There were, of course, pragmatic arguments that feminists made for
adopting a rule-equality model. In addition to supporting the idea of
marriage as a partnership, same-treatment equality can be viewed as giving real "teeth" to the platitudes about the value of women's child care

and work in the home. In addition, it is often asserted that, today, equal division of property at divorce puts women in a *better* economic position than they would have had under another conceptual system.[31] More generally, it is argued that the ideal of marriage as an equal partnership will reduce sex-role stereotypes in marriage by allowing each partner to decide on the type and timing of the contributions he or she will make and by promoting freedom of choice in marriage roles.

On a symbolic level, equality standards in the distribution of property are linked to the broader ideals of placing equal value on the different contributions stereotypically made by husbands and wives to the family and of promoting freedom of choice in marriage roles. Making equality the organizing concept underlying divorce may be considered part of a series of conscious symbolic choices about how best to ensure a more just society. This assumes, of course, that such choices and the laws they produce have an instrumental effect on people's behavior— that law can change conduct. The self-conscious insistence on symbolic statements may not be effective, however, if the message is likely to be resisted.[32]

Aspirations and symbolic concerns aside, when equality rhetoric is translated into specific rules governing distribution of the economic assets of marriage relationships and the allocation of care and control over children, the results must be measured and assessed in more than symbolic terms. Symbolic expression may be important, but as translated into legislation having direct impact on the lives of many people, the results must also meet standards of "fairness" or "justice"; in other words, they must conform to more than an abstract legal norm and reflect the actual experiences of peoples' lives. Unfortunately, in the family-law area, as a symbolic characterization, equality has taken on a life of its own and is emphasized to the exclusion of the fine distinctions in decision making that are necessary to achieve a more individualized or just notion of equality.

Consequences of Equality Reforms

In its simplest form, equality demands sameness of treatment, and differentiation in any sphere may be considered a concession of inferiority, or "unequalness." Using this concept of equality has confused the questions in family law, as it will in any analysis, because equality masquerades as an independent norm. In addition, framing the discussion of entitlements in terms of one individual's equivalence to others misleadingly suggests that one person's rights vis-à-vis another's are identical. Because discussions based on equality tend not to make explicit reference to the specific substantive rights incorporated from elsewhere, "equality blind[s] us not only to the existence of such rights but to their specific substantive content also." It leads as well to the "erroneous assumption that, if two parties are morally or legally equivalent for one purpose, they must be morally or legally equivalent for all purposes."[33]

Commitment to the equality ideal, typified by use of the partnership metaphor as the appropriate analytical construct to guide divorce policy, does not permit us to face the fact that women's and children's needs in this society have continued to be undervalued and ignored. The equality rhetoric now associated with the marriage relationship must be challenged as inappropriate for resolving the difficult questions in situations such as divorce, where men and women, husbands and wives, stand in culturally constructed and socially maintained positions of inequality.[34]

An equality view of marriage denies the reality of many women who assume, during and after the marriage, more than a partner's share in the conduct and burdens associated with household and child care.[35] Further, the partnership metaphor slips easily into equal sharing of property, children, debts, and so on at divorce. The metaphor has symbolic content that is preserved only at significant cost to many women who must suffer equality in this one area while the rest of society and culture continues to treat them unequally.[36]

To be satisfied with or to insist upon rule-equality in divorce overlooks the serious toll that egalitarian ideology may take on women who must function in an unequal world which requires that they meet greater demands with fewer resources. It also elevates a simplified ideal to the status of a rule of decision and obscures the real issues in divorce.

In this way, the quest for equality, which had been urged as necessary to rectify the social and economic inequalities women suffered in terms of market access, naturally led to the adoption of gender-neutral rules in family law. From this perspective, gender-specific rules like the tender-years doctrine[37] were increasingly attacked as sexist manifestations which cast women into unfortunate stereotypes precluding them from full market participation. Thus, divorce reform can be understood in part as a process involving the recharacterization of gendered rules in the family law arena in order to allow women to function as economic actors in the market. Women were no longer to be formally designated and identified as caretakers of children, a role that would impede equal market involvement. There was a conscious attempt to mold divorce-reform rhetoric so that it was more responsive to desired equality changes in the public sphere. Like the Equal Rights Amendment, suggested divorce reforms were an attempt to impose a standard of formal gender neutrality and sameness of treatment, giving them legitimacy and acceptability.

Examination of these new equality-based rules reveals choices about marriage and the family, as well as the assumptions which underlie our beliefs about these institutions. While the symbolic dominance of equality has functioned to mute criticism, scholars increasingly recognize that a serious discussion of law and legal reform must reflect the fact that there are real and unresolvable difficulties that emerge when discussing family law in the latter part of the twentieth century.

These difficulties are in part the result of the inappropriate imposition of the equality model on circumstances and situations that are far from equal. There are not only differences between men's and women's family lives in our society, but also differences between families from disparate economic, educational, and cultural backgrounds. Even if one believed that a unitary system of law could be developed and applied to clearly identified family problems, which potential visions from among many contenders should be selected? Which problems from among the vast and seemingly unending array should be cast as "typical" and thus provoke a search for "proper solutions?" Legal journals are filled with debates about what is the best set of rules to govern property division or custody and visitation at divorce, for example.[38]

This society is divided on issues such as the proper roles for women and men in and out of marriage; the content and extent of parents' post-divorce obligations—financial and otherwise—to their children; the amount of sacrifice a man should be expected to make to maintain an "old" family when a "new," and younger, one awaits. Which of conflicting and competing values should be given prominence? Whose image of the world (or at least that part of it we set aside and designate as "family") should prevail? There is no consensus about the many issues involved in this area of state regulation we label *family law*. Even an issue as fundamental as whether divorce should be freely allowed continues to generate some, though muted, discussion.[39]

Related to this is the reality that these reform efforts have typically reflected middle- and upper-class concerns, with images of the economically privileged floating through the literature of legislative reform and appellate cases in family law, (mis)informing lawmakers as to the common problems confronting families. The concerns of poor, nontraditional, and other "deviant" families have been left to the areas of criminal, welfare, tort, and zoning law, which have not been the targets of egalitarian reforms.

THE RHETORIC OF REFORM

A major source of divorce reform rhetoric has been legal academic writing, which is filled with debates over divorce, property, and custody. Analysis of this literature reveals that it, like legal considerations of ideal solutions to the problems of divorce, is also replete with disagreements over broad social values like the roles of women and men in society or the obligation of parents to their children after divorce.

Such scholarship seeks to place divorce reforms in their larger social and political contexts. Two recent books are particularly illustrative and reflect the existing consensus about the nature of the changes that have occurred in laws governing divorce. Lenore Weitzman titled her book *The Divorce Revolution*,[40] and in it she detailed the changes that took place in California. Herbert Jacob's new book is titled *The Silent Revolution*[41] and focuses on the "silent" method whereby the divorce "revolution" was undertaken. He concluded that these divorce reforms are part of the "routine flow of policymaking that occupies much of the time of American legislatures."[42] Both authors, and other commentators in general, assume that what we have undergone in family law is a "revolution," and then blithely proceed to address and assess the origins and implications of the revolutionary reforms.

In Search of the Revolution

The greatest difficulty with such overblown presentations of the divorce reform story may well be trying to determine just what changes constituted the "revolution." There is an ambiguity to that term which reflects the ambiguity of the nature of the changes that have been made in divorce laws during the past several decades. *Revolution* in its least transformative sense is merely "[a] motion in a closed curve around a center, or a complete circuit made by a body in such a course."[43] At the other extreme is the use of the term to designate a real transformation: "[a] drastic change in a condition, method, idea."[44]

While many think of the latter definition when considering divorce reform, it is really the first definition that more accurately describes the effect of the changes in the rules regulating divorce in the United States. While formal and rhetorical changes have occurred (i.e., the wording of laws has been altered), the revolution is the type that merely brings us back to where we substantively began. Of course, the more drastic the change is perceived to be, the more justification it provides for state intervention, regulation, and control.

The No-Fault Revolution

The initial changes in divorce regulation and legislation did not threaten the status quo, are not "revolutions," and perhaps are not even "revolutionary." For example, the move to no-fault divorce hardly represented such a dramatic deviation from existing practice as to be appropriately labeled *revolutionary*. What occurred in the move to no-fault was merely a formal change in rules which were already freely manipulated and avoided. This type of reform is an example of the language of the law catching up with the process and practice of lawyers and judges. The legal community had universally tolerated (and perhaps even counseled) fraud and collusion by its clients in order to secure divorces under the fault system.

The Equality Revolution

There is also a second set of reforms which is a candidate for the label *revolutionary*. The subsidiary changes in the laws governing the economic relations between divorcing spouses and the rules and standards applied to custody determinations are often viewed as departures from previous norms and practices. These changes occurred (and, in fact, are *still* occurring) in the wake of no-fault reforms, and could be considered the second movement in the "revolution."

It is clear that these reforms are considered significant. As Jacob asserts, "[e]quality has replaced hierarchy as the guiding principle of family law."[45] These changes altered property rules to recognize a homemaker's contribution to the family economy, removed alimony as a permanent obligation of the husband, and established an equal property division or marital partnership presumption as the norm in economic areas.

As I have already indicated, feminists perceived equality-based rules as a step toward rectifying the inequities produced by no-fault legislation. But feminists argued the need for changes in the rules governing property distribution only after no-fault had been in operation and it became apparent that fault had provided an important bargaining leverage for economically dependent wives when their husbands wanted a divorce.[46] Since a wife's cooperation was no longer necessary because unilateral access to no-fault divorce was secured, some other system had to be devised to ensure that she was financially provided for after divorce. Equal division of property was proposed because it seemed to be "fair" and was consistent with the rhetorical presentation of marriage as a partnership.

Further, of particular significance in the equality revolution in family law was the replacement of the "maternal preference"[47] in custody determinations with the idealized notion of shared parenting expressed in the preference for joint custody, discussed more fully in part 2 of this book. Equality has become the symbolically significant norm against which the validity and legitimacy of divorce rules is to be measured.

Thus, equality-based rules for making economic and custody decisions, although obviously related to other reforms, should not be considered merely part of no-fault divorce legislation. In contrast to the move to no-fault, the imposition of an equality model in divorce has generated far more profound effects and a great deal more controversy, with these new rules still under heated debate in many states.

The equality-based changes in family law should be placed in a larger context. They were conceived of as complements to the more public and perhaps therefore more significant "revolution" that was occurring in society concerning the role of women in the marketplace. Family-law reform lagged behind and was defined by the visible and vocal attempts to recharacterize gender roles and allow women to function as viable economic actors. It is a product of the political forces that defined the Equal Rights Amendment as of paramount importance in the national agenda and cannot be considered as separate from that larger reform objective.

Divorce reform must be placed in the context of the larger equality revolution that was occurring in the more public arenas of society. Divorce reform was molded in that image and was responsive to the symbolic and rhetorical ethic being fashioned in the public sphere. Suggested divorce reforms imposed a standard of formal, gender-neutral equality on divorcing families and were, for the most part, pale reflections of, or afterthoughts to, the revolution in the economic sphere.

Equality as Conservancy

Contrary to the received scholarly wisdom and consistent with the views subsequently presented in this book, one could argue that the equality-based changes in family law were in fact antirevolutionary—

operating to undermine the fledgling potential for freedom that newly won economic opportunities, coupled with the ability to leave unsatisfactory marriages, presented to women. These secondary equality reforms in family law could be interpreted not as innovations but as accommodations designed to ensure that women's new economic power did not provoke substantial challenges to the basic organization and function of traditional social and family relations.

For example, the new property rules removed economic security from women by abolishing the common-law obligation of a husband to support his wife and children (even after the marriage ends). They also destroyed the legitimacy of a paternalistic urge to give the "little women and children" the family home so they could take care of themselves. In addition, a woman now receives half the house along with half the debts. Further, a woman now shares an equal obligation with regard to children and may be saddled with her "equal" share of the family (or husband's) debt, even though she is far from "equal" in job and salary prospects.

The same sort of analysis can be applied to the new custody rules. Joint custody merely replicates the essential power relationships of the traditional nuclear family in that it reinforces one basic tenet of patriarchy—male control over women and children—allowing it to continue even if in an altered postdivorce form. Thus, joint custody preserves primary male power in the face of rules that provide liberalized access to divorce.

Perhaps ironically, equality has been a piercing and potent battle cry for male reactionaries who would lead us round once again to the preservation of basic patriarchal power. Used both to attack the existing rules governing divorce and to demonstrate the need for reforms, the ideology of equality supplied the theoretical underpinnings that shaped the formal content of the ultimately reformed rules. As a legal concept, equality gave the reform rules legitimacy, while it was simultaneously employed to remove legitimacy from the "unequal" rules that were to be replaced. Because of this, the new substantive rules are viewed both as unbiased and as conferring equality before the law.[48]

Furthermore, it is highly likely that future beneficial reforms will be difficult to implement, as they too will be measured and directed by equality rhetoric. The individuals and groups that were perceived as disadvantaged under the old rules are now viewed as having been vindicated through the process of reform, and the formal bias in the system, represented by the old rules, has been removed. As such, although once perceived as disadvantaged in the context of the reform rhetoric, women in particular can no longer complain about results because the system now formally treats them neutrally and equally under the law.

The Failure of Equality

Alternative models of equality exist beyond sameness of treatment. In light of the different structural positions women and men occupy, it seems obvious that to impose sameness of treatment, particularly within the context of family laws, simply perpetuates inequality. The failure of the reformers to incorporate this realization is attributable to the capacity of the formal equality-ideal concept to obscure the very concerns which initially motivated reform. To date there has been no attempt to develop a coherent set of rules applicable at divorce which do not focus on an equality-based formulation of rules and which are not necessarily facially neutral but instead take into account women's disadvantaged position in society. Such laws would focus on equality of results.

If one rejects the rule-equality model's capacity and power to address the myriad problems diverse families face at divorce, one must confront the fact that there are many people, particularly women and children, whose circumstances have not been addressed by equality reforms and who will not benefit from them. This perspective on contemporary divorce reforms leads us to the conclusion that it is the circular, not the transformative, definition that should be applied to the no-fault "revolution" and its secondary reforms.

Overall, these reform efforts illustrate the limitations of law as an instrument of reform and the problems associated with the use of legal concepts and rhetoric in an attempt to change social practices or rectify wrongs. The rhetoric of equality can do no more than reconstruct the spirit of the times. Furthermore, since equality is a legal concept that has been developed within a specific disciplinary context with its own rigid limitations and boundaries derived from centuries of use, it is not surprising if the intentions of reform are confused and confounded by the legalistic meaning and content of the term. Equality has a legal history, and for this reason it has a powerful potential to initiate change when utilized in the rhetoric of law reform. Its very history, however, means that the outcome of any reform will be shaped, limited, and directed by the extra-reform aspects of equality rhetoric. The concept of equality is a significant rhetorical device with strong symbolic content which may be appropriated for reform purposes but which will often take on a life of its own and be emphasized to the exclusion of the concerns that prompted the reforms in the first place.

THREE

Equality Discourse and Economic Decisions Made at Divorce

[The] law's promise of equality for men and women . . . [will] shed the anachronistic assumptions about women's roles and women's capacities . . . [and will] free women from the so-called protections they had enjoyed—protections that in reality served to make them second class citizens, and perpetuate their dependence on their husbands.

L. Weitzman*

INTRODUCTION

This chapter assesses reform legislation dealing with the economic aspects of divorce. Reform was largely the product of feminists' efforts to impose a rule-equality or same-treatment model on property distribution decisions in order to rectify perceived inequities perpetuated against women under prior law. While the economic position of women in our society provides the basis for persuasive arguments that, in general, "unequal" treatment in fashioning rules to govern the economic aspects of divorce is essential in assuring equitable results for most women, liberal legal feminists rejected this model in favor of sameness of treatment.[1] To understand why a rule-equality approach is inappropriate, we must consider three related factors: women's unequal social and economic position in society, the ways in which marriage and family decisions are affected by these and other economic and social circumstances, and the impact of divorce on women with dependent children.

Economic inequalities persist in our society in spite of decades of attempted reforms.[2] The rules governing economics at divorce perpetuate and contribute to this persistence of inequality. In the first instance, women are disadvantaged in the market. They earn less than their male counter-

---

*L. WEITZMAN, THE DIVORCE REVOLUTION: THE UNINTENDED SOCIAL AND ECONOMIC CONSEQUENCES FOR WOMEN AND CHILDREN IN AMERICA 357 (1985) (commenting on the passage of equal property division at divorce in California).

parts and, even if freed from the pink-collar ghetto, do not advance as quickly and as far as men. In addition, cultural images and socially constructed expectations compel women to assume unequal responsibilities within the family.[3] Choices during marriage as to who assumes primary care of children, for example, often result in wives' shouldering disproportionate burdens.[4] Furthermore, at divorce women typically assume an unequal, more burdensome share of the postdivorce responsibilities for nurture and care of children.[5] This is true even in cases of "joint custody," where mothers typically do the bulk of the day-to-day care.[6] The fables we have created around "modern" fatherhood and our newly coined and much-applied legal label, *joint custody* obscure the fact that unequal maternal sacrifices are assumed, even mandated, by social and cultural factors in addition to the history of a particular family.[7]

Statistical data consistently indicate that women are systematically paid considerably less than men with similar qualifications.[8] While some gains have been made, notably in wage rates, these gains have for the most part been made by women in white-collar or professional occupations.[9] At the time feminists began to seek changes in the property distribution rules, evidence showed that women were clustered at the lowest wage rates.[10] In addition, data available to them at that time established that women's wages increased much more slowly with age than men's wages.[11] For example, researchers at the University of Michigan who studied data gathered from 1968 to 1974 found that "[a] forty-year old man earns \$.70 an hour more than a similar man ten years younger. A forty-year old woman earns only about \$.18 more per hour than a woman who is thirty."[12] The same study reported that the pattern of sex discrimination differed from that of race discrimination; women faced discriminatory differentials not only among different occupations but also within occupations. Other statistics from the same era indicated that the "economic payoff of education for wives and female heads [of families] is 55% of the corresponding payoff for male heads of households."[13]

In assessing the economic reforms in divorce law more than two decades after they began to occur, it is significant to note that there is no evidence that the situation has gotten much better for the majority of women. In fact, there are some indications that it has gotten, or will get, worse. Middle-class and professional women trade their leisure in order to both work full-time and care for children. Victor Fuchs, in looking at the lack of progress for women over the past several decades, reached these conclusions:

My most important empirical finding is that the gap between women and men in economic well-being was no smaller in 1986 than in 1960. . . . The women/men ratio of money income almost doubled, but women had less leisure while men had more, an increase in the population of adults not married made more women dependent on their own income, and women's share of financial responsibility for child care rose. A striking exception is the experience of young, white, unmarried, well-educated women who made large gains relative to their male counterparts. . . . Most of these women are childless; those who are mothers frequently live under great pressure. . .

[An additional] conclusion is that women's weaker economic position results primarily from conflicts between career and family. Conflicts that are stronger for women than for men. More specifically, many different kinds of evidence suggest an average woman feel a stronger desire for children than men do and a greater concern for their welfare after they are born. This desire and this concern creates an economic disadvantage for women which is strongest at ages 25 to 45, but the effects remain throughout life. (Emphasis in original) [14]

Furthermore, recent statistics indicate that the "new poor" are single-parent families headed by women, many placed there as a result of divorce. Even the women who are single parents but not classified as poor because they have marketable skills may still experience a substantial decline in their standard of living after divorce. [15]

Societal Factors Affecting Our Perceptions of Marriage and Divorce

Attacks during this century on the legitimacy of the patriarchal family have gradually eroded the historic notion that the husband is responsible for the financial well-being of his family. The decline of this perception of patriarchal obligation has been accompanied by the transformation of the rules governing the economic aspects of divorce. [16] An earlier, status-based model of marriage, under which a husband's obligations to support his wife and children at least theoretically survived divorce and could be discharged through alimony or property division, has been replaced by an egalitarian or equality model. [17] We now view the economic obligations associated with marriage and divorce as shared responsibilities.

The way that we as a society perceive marriage and the relationship between husband and wife profoundly affects the way that we select, develop, and apply rules governing property distribution at divorce. I assert that this societal perception is most significant and shapes the way that all actors involved in actual divorce proceedings—judges, lawyers, the spouses, as well as legislators—consider the fairness and advisability of various distribution factors. The general social consensus about the nature of marriage and what it entails is the background which frames arguments over the appropriateness of specific rules regulating dissolution.

In this area, controversy has spurred many changes. One source of the controversy about property distribution rules is, I believe, the existence of two competing and, perhaps incompatible and unrealistic, political visions of contemporary marriage. The first is the more modern view that marriage as an institution has been transformed so as to be consistent with formalistic notions of equality between the sexes.[18] The second is the more traditional policy stance that the family is the appropriate, perhaps solitary, institution to resolve problems of dependency or need that inevitably arise in the context of families.[19]

The choice and application of various distribution rules by legislators, attorneys and judges, whether in the context of the legislative process, in formal adjudication, or in negotiation, are influenced by these societal factors. These legal actors must develop and apply rules in a legal system in which the longstanding recognition of dependency and need on the part of mothers and children within families is increasingly offset by the desire for symbolically compelling presentations of gender equality and independence.[20]

Marriage is no longer realistically presented as a lifelong commitment with well-defined gender-based roles establishing an interdependency that is easily comprehended and reflected in supportive legal rules. Things are more complex today—roles are less defined, and marriage as an institution is in a state of flux. Unfortunately, the laws governing property distribution and other economic aspects of divorce have often become the crude instruments by which we attempt both to implement equality and to address dependency and need. When the law is expected to do incompatible or contradictory things simultaneously, it is no wonder that confusion results.

THE DISTRIBUTION PROCESS

Although the distribution of property is only one of the economic decisions made at divorce, it has a unique procedural posture. It is a final decision, not subject to future modification should circumstances change. This means there are no potential future opportunities to correct errors. Because it is final, it appears more significant. A distribution decision may present an emotional experience for spouses different from decisions about other economic aspects of divorce. Families are more than legalized sexual relations or the repositories for products of those relations. They represent the convergence of a complex set of emotional and material needs which are inevitably frustrated in the divorce process. The distribution decision may psychologically represent to the spouses the final accounting of their contributions to the marriage—a concrete measure of their relative worth. With child support, by contrast, the emotional as well as legal justification is based on the appropriateness of continued obligations of support in the context of an ongoing, even if altered, postdivorce relationship. With children, future support obligations are based on need and premised on the assertion that divorce does not sever the responsibilities or the rights associated with parenthood.

Regarding maintenance (nee, alimony), in recent years the existence of a prior marital relationship has come to be considered insufficient justification for a continuing obligation. New theories or premises have been offered to justify the award of something labeled *maintenance* in some cases, but these new rationales suggest a different type of maintenance from the common-law expectation that a husband was obligated to support his wife even after termination of their marriage. Maintenance today is designed as a gender-neutral, temporary, and remedial measure that further blurs the line between property distribution and support. Maintenance has started to look more and more like property distribution in that, if awarded, it is likely to be limited and based on modern perspectives of contribution to either the marriage or the career of the other spouse, or awarded in lieu of property.

Property Distribution Rules

While property distribution may in fact reflect concern about a spouse's future needs, such concern is increasingly considered inappropriate as the image of marriage becomes more that of partnership than of dependency. Need may be implicit in some of the factors utilized for division, but typically the stated rules explicitly reflect notions of *entitlement* based on earnings or, more recently, on marital contributions whether economic or homemaking.[21]

Factors Relevant to Property Distribution at Divorce

Currently, a variety of specific distribution factors are typically noted in common law, state statutes, or court opinions in states with general statutory directives. These factors include:

1. The length of the marriage;
2. The property brought to the marriage by each party;
3. The "contribution" of each party to the marriage, often with the explicit admonition that appropriate economic value is to be given to contributions of homemaking and child-care services;
4. The contribution by one party to the education, training, or increased earning power of the other;
5. Whether one of the parties has substantial assets not subject to division by the court;
6. The age and physical and emotional health of the parties;
7. The earning capacity of each party, including educational background, training, employment skills, work experience, and length of absence from the job market;
8. Custodial responsibilities for children;
9. The time and expense necessary to acquire sufficient education or training to enable a party to become self-supporting at a standard of living reasonably comparable to that enjoyed during the marriage.

Increasingly, some consideration is given to the desirability of awarding the family home, or the right to live there for a reasonable period, to the party having custody of any children. In addition, other economic circumstances may be considered. These include vested or unvested pension benefits, future interests, the tax consequences to each party, and the amount and duration of an order granting maintenance payments.

If a written agreement was made by the parties before or during the marriage concerning any arrangement for property distribution, such agreements are often presumed binding upon the court unless inequitable. Some statutory systems that enumerate various factors explicitly end with a general catch-all for judicial discretion that allows consideration of such other factors as the court may in each individual case determine to be relevant.

Classification of Distribution Factors

There are at least four potential conceptual categories into which one could place the various factors considered in property distributions: title, fault, need, and contribution. These conceptual categories represent rationales or justifications for allocation decisions and may be ordered according to when they first were utilized. This sequencing has been used to suggest that there has been a progression from the simple, common-law emphasis on title to the more complex understanding of the function and purpose of the distribution system as reflecting the valuing of both monetary and nonmonetary contributions to the marriage.

While there has been a movement away from the strict common-law system based on title to the modern notion of a partnership based on equally valued though different-in-kind contributions to the marriage, I believe there is a serious problem with characterizing the movement from title to partnership and contribution as "progress." Progress implies that we have either outgrown the basis for the old concepts or that our initial perceptions were in error and now must be revised. A progression thesis might, therefore, characterize fault and need as "transitional" concepts—inelegant patches that allowed judges to do justice under a strict title system prior to the enlightened presentation of marriage as partnership.[22]

I am not convinced, however, that the circumstances that generated arguments for a distribution system focused on needs that no longer exist. Further, I am concerned that the material circumstances of divorcing women and children are being detrimentally ignored by supplanting a focus on needs with a focus on contribution as the primary distributive concept. The ascendancy of contribution may present a nice, neat instance of conceptual progress to legal academics and law reformers, but for many divorcing spouses, as well as for the practicing professionals to whom they turn for advice, adverse material circumstances and the needs they generate have not been left behind.

While title considerations do not seem to be determinative in modern distribution schemes, need and, to a lesser extent, fault are still viable alternatives to contribution as conceptual frameworks for the creation and implementation of various specific distribution factors.[23] When fault and need were first introduced into consideration, they were welcomed as helping to ameliorate the hardships of the title system. But, in contemporary divorce practice, both have increasingly come under attack because they carry negative symbolic connotations. In the context of "no-fault" divorce reform, for example, continued reference to fault as an explicit allocation category would obviously be problematic.

Further, the concept of *need* presents even more complex conceptual difficulties. As a relevant consideration, however, need is not a consideration as easily moved beyond and left behind as fault. Historically, the courts could respond to the existence of dependency, since marriage was viewed as a status relationship. The husband and father was obligated to provide support for the needs of his wife and children, and this obligation did not necessarily cease with divorce and could be extended beyond divorce through awards of alimony, through property division provisions, or through both. However, modern attacks on the legitimacy of the patriarchal family have had an unplanned legal impact: the erosion of the traditional notion that the husband is predominantly and perpetually responsible for the financial well-being of all members of the family. Attempts to cast family structure in more egalitarian terms have assisted in transforming our approach to the rules governing the economic aspects of divorce. The earlier status-based model of marriage has been replaced by an individualistic or equality model under which obligations to spouses ideally end with the marriage, and any ongoing economic obligation that is recognized as appropriate, such as child support or payment of existing marital debts, is considered a shared and equal responsibility.

Limitations on Distribution Discourse

Divorce is typically discussed in terms of the nuclear family. Outsiders to this unit, even though they may be family in a broader anthropological sense, are excluded. Moreover, it is significant that most legal writers discussing the economic allocation questions in divorce emphasize primarily the *adults* in the nuclear family. This tendency to limit the discussion of rights and objectives to those of the spouses reflects an important social dimension and is consistent with the contemporary partnership model of marriage. There are no "junior partners" (children) legally recognized with enforceable rights to share in partnership assets.

Except in extreme cases, the state will not be a significant source of support for the spouse who subsequently assumes responsibility for child-rearing. Unless the family is very poor, the resources for the care of children are extracted from the individual parent or parents. This individualistic approach, coupled with the undeniable fact that more resources are necessary when an adult has to care for children in addition to herself, means that the allocation of private resources at divorce has a profound economic and social impact because it affects the future ability of a custodial parent to care adequately for her children.

I assume that private decisions about child custody at divorce and actual assumed responsibility for children after divorce will typically be gender-related for generations to come.[24] As a result, the wife, the parent statistically more likely to be at a disadvantage in the market, will more likely also be the parent who must adjust career activities to accommodate childrearing. This adjustment will result in potentially immeasurable costs to her career and personal development.

Finally, I assume that alimony awards will continue to be extremely rare and that child-support awards will continue to be systematically low and/or only sporadically enforced.[25] Thus, given the predominant view of the children's future economic well-being as a private or family function, and given that enforcement of support orders might be a problem, a custodial parent cannot comfortably rely on future contributions from her ex-spouse in providing for the children, nor can she rely on any other source of support outside her own efforts.

Dependency has not disappeared, however. I believe that marriage often conceals or masks the poverty of women in this country and that divorce removes this mask. The care of children produces dependency, not only for the children, but also for the primary caretaker. The needs that this dependency generates must be met either by society as a whole or by individuals with legally significant connections to children. Moreover, it must be recognized that this dependency does not end when the child reaches eighteen or any other magic age. Children's needs may change with the passage of time, but the caretaker has assumed ongoing responsibilities with present as well as future economic consequences, such as a reduced amount of money in a social security or pension fund or an increased susceptibility to requests for "loans" once the children are fully grown and supposedly "independent."

The laws governing the economic aspects of divorce should be grounded in the realization that some family relationships tend to last. This is particularly true of the primary caretaking parent and her children. The obligations that such a parent may feel are not legal but moral or emotional ones. A parent who desires to assist a newly "adult" child may not be required to do so by law, but that does not mean that the law should be insensitive to (or unsupportive of) the parent's sensibilities when assessing the most socially useful allocation of property at divorce.[26]

DISTRIBUTION DISCOURSE

Assessment of the various specific distribution factors listed above reveals that four may be categorized under the concept of *contribution* while the other five fit more neatly within the concept of *need*. The fact that within any system the factors are often combined and exist simultaneously reflects the tension between the two incompatible contemporary images of marriage: the modern egalitarian partnership and the older, status-based, dependency model. These represent polar ends on the spectrum of the way society views marriage and the position of women within it, as well as the major transformation that has occurred in this regard.

The partnership image gives rise to the idea of contribution—each person contributes a different but valuable set of benefits to the good of the whole, and the whole should be divided to reflect these contributions if it is dissolved. Under this view, need has no role to play in a true partnership of equals. In fact, contribution rhetoric is often placed in opposition to another vision of marriage—that of dependency. The dependency image, in contrast to contribution, anticipates that a woman has been "victimized" in marriage. She is viewed as having sacrificed career goals and ambitions for the marriage. At divorce she is dependent, and that dependency will continue. She therefore has economic needs that should be recognized and compensated. In this context need is cast as a negative, something demeaning and to be overcome. Dependency and need are dramatized as products of women's victimization by men and marriage and are not rhetorically associated with the dependency and needs of children.

In our contemporary society, the concept of need must necessarily create some ambivalence for those who accept equality as the social and legal ideal. The predominance of the equality model evident in much of the commentary and law reform efforts illustrates that there is a strong preference for the legal presentation of women as equal partners within marriage and as independent, equal economic actors outside of it.

Liberal feminist legal reformers, for example, have adhered for the most part to the ideal of egalitarian marriage in addressing the economic questions in divorce.[27] In some states, the equality norm is formally embodied in provisions which establish an initial presumption that all property of the spouses is to be equally divided upon divorce. This rule-equality presumption is consistent with the organizing concept of marriage as an equal partnership. While need is not forgotten, the partnership model is urged because of its symbolic significance in reflecting the preferred or correct vision of women and also, secondarily, because it addresses need. Through ideological fiat, the dependent woman is considered to be benefited in being brought "up" to partnership status and made an "equal."

That factors based on both the dependency and partnership models of marriage exist simultaneously within any distribution system does not suggest that the application of these factors will necessarily reflect an explicit, principled balancing process. Rather, it seems that within the context of any distribution task, there may be unavoidable concessions to dependency within a preferred framework that focuses on contribution and equality.

If one rejects the comprehensiveness of either or both of the conflict-ing images of marriage that the stereotypes of woman as equal and woman as dependent represent, one must confront the reality that many women whose mixed circumstances may require remedial rules are neglected. The stereotypes of dependency and partnership are polar opposites. Thus no single, typical result can be fairly reconciled with the goal of doing justice to both. A woman who operates in both the mar-riage and the market as an "equal" might be better off under the old common-law system, where she keeps her separate property, and her ex-husband is liable only for child support. The true dependent, by con-trast, might by her very circumstances have been able to claim all of the property and still be found in need of continued support for herself. In either case, it would seem that what is desirable in the way of reform is the creation of a range of acceptable economic outcomes which could accommodate a variety of differences among women in various circum-stances. The focus on the stereotypes of dependency and equality and the futile attempt to reconcile them tend to narrow rather than expand the definition of acceptable results.

Equality and the Contribution Concept

The ideal of equality between spouses is at the center of our cur-rent views of marriage and therefore exerts a powerful and symbolic in-fluence on our process of fashioning rules to govern distribution of marital assets. Marriage is considered a union, a partnership of equals. This view mandates that, if the partnership ends, the accumulated assets should be divided in a manner consistent with the model under which they were acquired. The norm or standard against which rules that reg-ulate the economic aspects of dissolution are measured will be that of equality.

This approach of using equality as the organizational concept in as-sessing appropriate rules for property division creates dilemmas. In its simplest form, equality demands sameness of treatment, and differentia-tion in any sphere may be considered a concession of inferiority or "unequalness."[28]

The ramifications of symbolic adherence to equality may be signifi-cant. Contribution is an equalizing concept, while need demands an ac-knowledgment and evaluation of differences. As such, a commitment to equality initially encourages its proponents to minimize or deny differ-ences between the individuals for whose demands they have become proponents and the individuals they perceive to be in superior positions. Thus, the reformers could conclude that the rule-equality model satisfied their desire for fair treatment of women at divorce, but only by minimizing, rhetorically and conceptually, any differences between the needs of men and women after divorce occurs. Given the contrary statistical evidence on the issue of need, of which the reformers must have been aware, one must question how they could fail to make need the central theme of the reform.

Further, the idea that contribution in the form of household duties should be recognized did not resolve all the potential problems. In fact, the concept of contribution, while conforming to reformers' concern for the extreme circumstances of the stereotypical victimized housewife, may have permitted them to ignore some of the harder questions because it facilitated the perception that equal treatment was the ideal solution. For example, what was to be the standard for division in cases where a spouse made dual contributions by both working and caring for the home and children?

The point is that full-time housewives are an economically elite group—just as women who have careers in which they can earn enough to pay other women to care for their houses and children while they pursue their own interests are privileged. Many women cannot choose to stay at home and do domestic work full-time. They must work at low-paying, often unfulfilling jobs to earn money for meeting family needs and, in addition, must perform the tasks of raising children and maintaining a home.

Under the rhetoric of contribution, these women should be compensated for making a double contribution to the marriage, for fulfilling both market and family duties. Because the victimized housewife was the focus of reform, however, contribution was a concept employed only to reach the result of equality. Its implications were not thought through and coherently applied to circumstances such as these. Thus, unfortunately, these women will probably have to settle for an equal division. In addition, even if the image of the victimized housewife presented the easiest case for understanding the need for reform, it does not explain why the solution to her problems was seen as the imposition of the rule-equality model based on her contribution to the marriage— why her projected circumstances, her future needs, did not demand more than an equal division.

It may be that the reformers did have access to more complete information and therefore should have understood that sameness of treatment would not be appropriate for all women, but chose the symbolically compatible rule-equality model as their organizing concept because their sights were focused on the broader equality concerns of the feminist movement.[29] Any arguments that did not explicitly incorporate the rule-equality concept would undermine that goal.

It also may be that the imagery of women as victims had too powerful an influence on the reformers. The women who successfully initiated the reform movement by using the horror stories may themselves have felt locked in by the stories once the reform momentum was generated. This may have led them to exaggerate the divorced housewife's lack of property claims and to ignore the patterns by which the courts indeed protected these women.

Some evidence suggests that liberal feminist reformers put the equality model at the center of their organizing efforts for reasons that may be characterized as symbolic. In dividing a finite bundle of goods between two contenders, equality means that each receives one-half. On a symbolic level, this measure expresses more than just a method of division. It assumes that each individual's rights or entitlements are equal as well.

The reformers believed that equal property rights would put women in a better economic position after divorce than they would have been in under prior law. More generally, they believed that the representation of marriage as a partnership, with which the idea of equal property rights was so closely associated, would reduce sex-role stereotypes in marriage and would allow each partner to decide on the type and timing of the contributions he or she would make to the family unit. Thus, equal property rights were linked to a broader concept of equal value and freedom of choice in marriage roles.

Equality as an organizing concept is also evident in other divorce-law provisions. Just as the decisions concerning divisions of assets are to be made with a presumption of equality between the spouses, so are those concerning marital "liabilities." Economic responsibility for children is to be shared, with both parents responsible for the children's future support.

Future support for the spouses is to be primarily their individual responsibilities, unless certain well-defined circumstances indicating need justify one spouse receiving some temporary, limited support from the other to re-educate or rehabilitate herself for the job market. The equality conceptualization of marriage inherently places tremendous significance and primary focus on the symbolic nature of the "partnership" relationship between men and women, with the concept of contribution supplying the distribution standard.[30]

IMPLICATIONS OF REFORM

The dominance of equality means it will also provide the preferred method of valuing contributions and thus will further obviate the need for anything resembling detailed fact-finding or consideration of individualized circumstances regarding the actual amount of contribution. Because divorce is an economic adjustment between partners, with the ideal solution being an equal division of the assets and liabilities amassed as a result of their equally-valued contribution, the use of contribution eliminates the need for individualized inquiry. Based on a fictitious past, on some socially derived, idealized notion of all spouses' actions and conduct during marriage, contribution operates at the expense of inquiry into possible future needs.

As already noted, the partnership model is not an absolute one, and specific factors are often available which can be employed to allow deviation from the equality ideal. Various individual circumstances may exist that could indicate the necessity of making an unequal allocation of assets and/or liabilities at divorce to handle future needs. Theoretically, even in the face of an initial equal-division presumption, the existence of need-based factors provides the potential for deviation from the distribution norm of equality.

Unfortunately, in the statutory schemes and case law, the need factors are neither sufficiently developed nor sufficiently clear to offset the partnership model with its easily grasped contribution factors. While it is true that other statutory provisions dealing with child support and maintenance are designed in part to alleviate need, these provisions present practical problems which make them ineffective in many instances.

Some of these problems were created by the reform movement because the equality ideal was also extended to responsibilities. Women now share equal responsibility with their ex-husbands for the economic well-being of the children, a result which on its face is desirable and fair. However, as with property division, equality in shouldering child-support obligations may mean equally splitting the monetary costs, not contributing according to ability nor valuing nonmonetary contributions. There is an unreality about the use of equality in such circumstances. It does not allow us to focus clearly on predictable future circumstances which will have profound implications for single-parent families.[31] Thus, even without a specific mandate that the court presume that property is to be divided equally, judges and lawyers will tend to adopt this standard because of the social and professional conditioning that presents modern marriage as an equal partnership.

Alteration of the partnership model is likely to be possible only if the spouse arguing for such a deviation can meet the burden of establishing that her circumstances (needs) are clearly exceptional. The wholesale acceptance of the partnership model means, however, that the burdens of production, proof, and persuasion will be placed upon the one who argues that the rule-equality concept is inadequate given her specific circumstances.

Furthermore, even if a wife could initially meet the burden of demonstrating that her needs should outweigh the equal-contribution assumptions, her husband could argue the presence or absence of other factors in an attempt to counter the assertion that deviation is appropriate. Because the factors are not weighted or ranked, one factor or set of factors may be balanced against another in the decision-making process. As a result, unless one spouse can assert that she occupies all, or most, of the categories (an unlikely scenario since they are inherently incompatible), her spouse may use the remaining factors to push the allocation toward the rule-equality norm.

The difficulty of attempting to deviate from the equality presumption is further complicated by the fact that, in using and developing the factors, decision-makers have themselves failed to distinguish those grouped under the concept of contribution from those supported by need. Although they are really referencing different models and different sets of concerns, contribution arguments may be used to offset an appeal for unequal division based on need.

For example, a woman may argue that since her education or employment skills and the presence of small children make it unlikely that she can become self-supporting at a standard of living reasonably comparable to that enjoyed during the marriage, she needs more than 50 percent of the property.[32] Her husband need not dispute these assertions but only argue that the marriage has lasted only a few years, implying that she has not assisted in the accumulation of assets or that he has aided her by assuming financial and domestic responsibilities while she went to school or work, and these equally unweighted contribution factors may be applied in his favor to negate her need-based arguments. Since he is able to argue that some of the provisions apply to him, these are likely to cancel out her arguments, and the norm of equal division will probably prevail.

It should be recognized that the arguments are presented on different conceptual bases. She is arguing *need,* while he is responding with *contribution,* which does not meet or defeat the thrust of her assertions.[33] To the extent that contribution is defined by the equality or partnership model, only the greatly disadvantaged—the polar model of dependency—will have a chance at deviation.

In addition, since the factors are not weighted or ranked, even when employed they will be only partially effective in negating the preference for the rule-equality model. Since equality is established as the norm, justification becomes more difficult for more than nominal deviations from an equal division of assets.[34] Therefore, even in cases where deviation is considered appropriate, the combination of the failure to weigh the factors and the expressed preference for equal division is likely to lessen the distance from the equality ideal and, consequently, the incentive for attempting deviation at all.

THE DISCARDED DISCOURSE

As noted earlier, at the time of divorce reform, there were two concepts in addition to fault that permitted judges to ignore title in dividing property equitably. Using the concept of need, for example, a judge could award the bulk of the marital property to a dependent wife who would not be able to support herself adequately after divorce. Using the concept of contribution, a judge could award the wife a share of her husband's property based on the notion that her services in the home had assisted him in accumulating the property.

Only the contribution concept, however, was compatible with the reformers' overriding commitment to equality. To fit need within the context of equality, as they defined and employed the term, would have been impossible. Need is a concept that might be said to characterize women as unequal. To admit that women might have more need for the accumulated assets than their husbands may have been understood as conceding that they were not as capable of caring for themselves.

Contribution, by contrast, could be rehabilitated within the equality model by assuming that a non-wage-earning spouse supplied a sufficient amount of effort and labor to the marriage to establish her "right" to property and other assets acquired by her wage-earning spouse. Title, therefore, the traditional common-law basis for determining allocation of assets at divorce, could and should be disregarded, because she was an actual contributor to their acquisition.

The logical ramifications of symbolic adherence to equality may be significant. A commitment to equality initially encourages its proponents to minimize or deny differences between the individuals they perceive to be in superior positions and those who are in socially subordinate positions. Contribution is an equalizing concept, while need demands an acknowledgment and evaluation of differences.

Overreliance on symbolic concerns may create several difficulties, however. The contribution concept may impede the development of instrumental rules that directly address practical problems. For example, arguing that housework and child care are equal to monetary contributions and are therefore entitled to equal recognition when property is divided can be viewed as one way of dealing with need in the overall context of the equality concept. The need concept is disguised but not abandoned. This is only satisfactory, however, if the conceptual limitation on the contribution notion (one-half, or an equal share) results in decisions which satisfy need in an overwhelming majority of cases. If it cannot, the equality solution is inadequate for the problem of need. In fact, need cannot be alleviated by equal divisions so long as other factors between men and women remain unequal.

The concept of need is often the unstated argument that underlies all the arguments in the area of property division. Because it is disguised, though, the solutions which are proposed necessarily fail to deal effectively with the problem of need. To emerge from a divorce in a position that even begins to put them on an economic par with their ex-husbands, many women need to receive more in property division than the strict equality concept applied to a narrower and more traditionally appropriate definition of marital property will allow. The triumph of the rule-equality concept in this area has been by the sacrifice of equity.

Since sharing responsibility is often translated into assuming equal responsibility, the result is unrealistic, even cruel, given the practical situation of many women.[35] The problem is not that the idea of sharing financial responsibility between husband and wife is inherently unreasonable or unfair, but rather that sharing expectations must be tempered by reference to evidence indicating that equality in the financial circumstances of men and women does not exist. *Shared* responsibility, therefore, should not be equated with *equal* responsibility.[36]

Simplistic, rule-equality changes in divorce laws premised on an unrealized egalitarian marriage ideal will tend to further impoverish women and their children. Under such laws, divorced women are to assume sole economic responsibility for themselves and joint economic responsibility for their children. Theoretically, this requirement is fair because divorced women will assume this responsibility under the same terms and conditions as their ex-spouses. Equal treatment in divorce, however, can only be fair if spouses have access to equal resources and have equivalent needs. Realistically, many women do not have such economic advantages. In addition, they continue to care for children.

F O U R

Embracing Equality: A Case Study

Many leaders of the women's movement dream of a society in which there would be equality in the labor market and in the home: all careers would be open to women, and men would do half the housework and childcare. This scenario is still far from realization and its chances are not great even over the next one or two generations . . .

Judging from recent trends, some men will undoubtedly take on a larger share of domestic responsibility in the future, but some will just as undoubtedly reject family life entirely. For a society to achieve "egalitarian stability," three conditions must prevail: (1) women must earn as much or nearly as much as men; (2) Men must do as much or nearly as much housework and childcare as women; and (3) the fertility rate must be high enough to sustain the population in the long run. The evidence . . . shows why it is unlikely that the combination of these three conditions will be met.

Victor Fuchs*

INTRODUCTION

This chapter details the reform movement in Wisconsin concerning the economic aspects of divorce. It addresses the questions raised earlier as to why concepts of affirmative action, which are widely accepted by feminists in the context of market discussions and strategy, were not explicitly used in the context of divorce law. It is also intended to illustrate the way in which an overriding commitment to an abstract ideal such as equality may divert the course and content of legislative reform.

The pool of women interviewed, and the correspondence, documents, and other information collected in researching this chapter, do not exhaust the available data. I do not assert that these particular women's beliefs and motives are the only ones that might lead someone to

*VICTOR FUCHS, WOMEN'S QUEST FOR ECONOMIC EQUALITY 144 (1988)

53

espouse rule-equality reform. I believe, however, that my interviews and investigations have revealed beliefs and motivations not atypical of liberal, legally oriented feminist reformers. Wisconsin has a tradition as a state of generating or encouraging reforms in the family-law area. This has been true not only in divorce but also in the creation of the Uniform Marital Property Act[1] and in reforms in the welfare and poverty areas, such as those proposed by the Institute for Poverty at the University of Wisconsin.[2]

Those actors in the reform movement who appeared to have been most influential at the initial organizational state or in maneuvering the reform though the political process were identified and interviewed. I have also used the accounts or texts of the speeches, publications, and presentations the reformers made during the reform process, and whatever correspondence I could acquire as sources of information on how they perceived the reform, on their objectives and goals, and on the methods of discourse they employed to gather support for their cause.

The women interviewed included the Chair of the Wisconsin Governor's Commission on the Status of Women, who was also the Department Chair of the University of Wisconsin's Extension Program on Women Education Resources. The Executive Secretary of the Commission, who was the commission's first full-time salaried employee, was also interviewed. This woman acted as a liaison with community groups and organized various networking activities regarding this and other reforms. One other member of the commission was interviewed because she was identified as an early active participant and had also served as Chair of a Wisconsin Bar Committee, which vigorously supported the reform. Also included is information from interviews with the legislator who sponsored the reform legislation in the State Assembly, with the drafter of that legislation, and with the Wisconsin League of Women Voters' legislative liaison, who was active in lobbying for the reform. To preserve the confidential nature of the interviews, no further identification of the sources will be given.

The Wisconsin Governor's Commission on the Status of Women was established in the early 1960s and was modeled after a national commission established several years earlier. The Commission's mandate was to review and advise the governor and the legislature on issues having a direct impact on women.

Background of the Wisconsin Reform

In 1975 the Wisconsin assembly passed a bill that would have added a no-fault ground to existing law.[3] The senate narrowly defeated the bill.[4] The defeat was not solely attributable, however, to the lobbying of the religious or conservative elements of the population who wanted to prevent divorces except for cause. By 1975, community opinion, at least as reflected by the majority of the legislature, favored no-fault divorce, but a new concern was developing. Three senators in favor of no-fault divorce voted against the bill because it did not provide sufficient economic protection for divorced spouses and their children. In 1977, a bill eliminating fault grounds and making irrevocable differences the sole basis for divorce was successful because it provided these economic protections.[5]

Although the critics of the unsuccessful 1975 no-fault bill in Wisconsin had a variety of reasons for opposing the legislation, some critics, who otherwise supported the concept of no-fault divorce, argued that economic protections should be included in any no-fault divorce reform.[6] There were essentially two components to this argument. First, they argued, no-fault divorce tended to decrease the bargaining power of the economically dependent spouse. A wife typically had leverage under a fault system because a husband seeking divorce needed the wife's cooperation to go through the motions of showing fault in court. The innocent spouse could withhold cooperation until a satisfactory settlement was offered.[7] Thus, the argument proceeded, property divisions were usually agreed to out of court; in practice, the fault portions of the statute, rather than those concerning property division, primarily ensured equitable bargaining.[8]

Second, they argued for economic protections based on the perception that the contemporary property division law was unfair and would prevent sympathetic courts from responding to the plight of the economically disadvantaged spouse. Even though the existing statute directed courts to divide property "equitably," the critics feared it gave courts too much discretion, which would be used to disadvantage women. They were also concerned because the statute did not explicitly require courts to recognize the homemakers' economic contributions to marriages.

These critics described a scenario where, unable to bargain for property by withholding cooperation, economically dependent spouses would either have to turn to the courts in hopes of a fair settlement, or would be coerced into accepting settlements based on a court's likely response. These critics supported their arguments with examples of outrageous judicial decisions in which a wife was given no credit in the property division for decades of housework, childrearing, and other contributions as compared with her wage-earning husband.[9]

The economic provisions in the 1977 legislation addressed both aspects of the reformers' objections. Judges were required to consider homemaking and child-care contributions to marriages. In addition, the law narrowed the range of judicial discretion by creating a fifty-fifty presumption for property divisions.[10]

As this brief description of the legislative history of the 1977 reform indicates, several economic issues emerged when it was proposed that fault be removed as the basis of divorce. Fault had served to some extent as a basis for making allocation decisions at divorce. Even though the Wisconsin Supreme Court had admonished the trial courts that economics were not to be used to punish spouses at fault,[11] a determination of wrongdoing historically had some significance in determining the equities of property division.[12]

The Reformers

The group of women who initiated economic reform as a part of Wisconsin's no-fault bill was fairly small. They had been politically active in prior legislative efforts and were members of organizations that had achieved legitimacy in regard to feminist issues. They were able to use the existing political apparatus to disseminate their ideas concerning needed divorce reforms. The Governor's Commission on the Status of Women had established a network of individuals and organizations to which it could turn for support. One of the key members of the Commission described the network:

> There always has been [involvement] through the university, through the governor's commission, through organizations. As a university office we have provided program material and organizational help to women's organizations over the years including League of Women Voters, American Association of University Women, YWCA's, the old line groups as well as the new things like the Women's Political Caucus and N.O.W., . . . we have had top offices in all of those organizations and have helped them to get off the ground and have served as informal secretariat in the early formation stages of a whole lot of organizations. So there was sympathy and cooperation and collaboration. In 1973 our Commission and this [University of Wisconsin-Extension] office organized a coalition of 13 organizations that endorsed and supported the state ERA, and we began to work collaboratively to get to all of our various constituencies. . . . That coalition stayed together [and] whenever we had another important issue we knew [we] could convent at least these 13 organizations and so . . .

when the divorce reform began to move, our Commission put out
brochures. . . . We had built-in outlets for this kind of stuff . . .
and then one of the real sources of success of the Wisconsin Commission was that we always had officially named representation
from the state agencies which impinged on these decisions, so that
we had a built-in liaison with Public Instruction, the Bureau of
Personnel, Health and Social Services, Department of Industry,
Labor and Human Relations, and the Legislature.

In addition, women politicians and legislators were actively involved
with these reformers. Another of the reformers noted:

[t]he Women's Political Caucus was created and started around
the same time. It was in the early [1970s] and it included most
anybody who was interested or knowledgeable about the Commission's affairs, and I went along to all the meetings and was running women for office and [some women legislators] were very
well aware of their ties and had very close ties with the Women's
Political Caucus so that the whole thing sort of fed into itself.

One legislator who was valuable to the reformers was married to a
member of the commission.[13]

I consider the key reformers to be those women who first identified
divorce reform as a feminist issue and who later were directly involved
in the formulation of political solutions. These women had some common characteristics. They had both political and social connections
with each other before their banding together over the question of divorce. In addition to the contacts that came from the Wisconsin Governor's Commission on the Status of Women, they had joined in previous
work on feminist issues in Wisconsin, such as the legislation for equal
pay and equal credit opportunity, and the "Omnibus Bill," which had
eliminated gender references in all but a few sections of the statutes.[14]

One reformer described the group's former interaction thus:

[T]here was sort of a mini-brain trust involved in trying to make
these decisions and decide what we ought to be doing with our
legislation.

The key reformers also appeared to have shared some significant socioeconomic characteristics, and these may have influenced their approach to the issue of divorce reform.[15] All expressed strong identification with women's issues and the women's movement, and most
identified themselves as feminists. They were aware that charges of elitism were leveled at the movement during the early 1970s, and most indicated during their interviews that they felt these criticisms had been

unfair. Most of the reformers were residents of Dane County, generally considered to be the most liberal area of Wisconsin. They were all well-educated women and most were working in professional capacities; several were attorneys. At the same time, they had established stable, traditional family relationships; most were married and had children. Although several reformers recounted stories of friends' or neighbors' divorces during their interviews, most of these women had no direct experience with divorce either in their personal lives or in their professional capacities as attorneys. Some may have had ambivalent responses to women who chose to become full-time housewives and mothers and forsake careers, perhaps because of their own ability to combine career and family successfully. One reformer, for example, responded as follows to the concept of alimony or maintenance:

> I mean it is sort of just basic feminist thinking, and that is, just
> because you are a woman, if you were divorced at 45, are you then
> so helpless that you have a right to be supported until you die at
> age 70 by the person whom you were married to? It just seemed
> very inequitable that somebody should be able to sit and twiddle
> their [*sic*] thumbs.[16]

The social characteristics of the reformers and their identification with the feminist movement were significant for their approach to reform. The reformers were familiar with much of the contemporary feminist literature that had directed attention to the unequal or paternalistic treatment women have historically suffered in this society and to the ways in which the law sanctioned this treatment.[17] Other characteristics, particularly those relating to the occupations and previous political experience of the reformers, may help to explain the course of action they took once they perceived that divorce was a feminist issue.

These Wisconsin feminist reformers turned to legal institutions with their demands for change. They sought to control judges' decisions, which they viewed as biased against women, and looked to legislative reform as a means for constructing a more just society. The Wisconsin reformers were comfortable with this approach because it fit within the context of their other experiences and because they had expertise in dealing with the system.

The Political History of Reform

The political process that led to divorce reform in Wisconsin can be divided into two discrete but related stages. The first stage involved the Wisconsin reformers' identification of divorce reform as a feminist issue separate from general reforms relating to marriage and the family. This in turn influenced the way they subsequently gathered an interest group around the issue. It was at this stage that the concepts and objects of the reform discourse, which subsequently defined the problems to be addressed by legislation, were first developed and articulated by the reformers. Thus, this stage was critical to the ultimate structure and content of the final legislation.

The second stage of the reform occurred when the reformers assumed responsibility for disseminating information during the reform process. Because of their early identification and articulation of the problems and the need for reform, the reformers provided a recognized, legitimate source of guidance as their ideas evolved into legislation. Consistent with this role, they subsequently performed an important task by contributing to and evaluating the specific provisions of the proposed legislation as it was drafted.

Identification of Divorce as a Feminist Issue

A significant historical event in the Wisconsin movement occurred when divorce first became clearly identified as an independent and separate women's issue, susceptible to a feminist solution. Although today we are accustomed to the classification of divorce as a separate feminist issue, its connection to and relationship with other issues of feminist concern have not always been so apparent.[18]

During the late 1960s and early 1970s, the issue of divorce reform was approached from a more generalized, liberal perspective, and the proposed reforms centered on the removal of the various fault bases for granting divorces. Thus, the reformers' early "educational" efforts were directed toward a wide spectrum of marital relations issues, while later efforts centered on separate issues, of which divorce was one. In the later phases of the reform, a more legalistic model for judging marriages and divorces was also evident.

The reformers' early approach to the family was optimistic and perhaps naive:

> Feminists today are looking at marriage in a way that has not been done before, at least on such a wide scale. . . . [This] current thinking through of the nature of the marital relationship and of the relationship of a man and a woman is important.

The mention of divorce was in the context of no-fault:

> [T]he uniform marriage and divorce law, which has been written in model form, . . . [recommends] . . . that divorce be a no-fault

procedure; that it be a more compassionate, more egalitarian process where not so much damage occurs.

The ongoing marriage of the future was also idealized:

> The most important thing that the feminist-humanist movement is doing, insofar as marriage is concerned, is to stress the importance of *women* developing in the marriage relationship in the way that in the past seemed important for *men* to develop. Feminists think that the role of a woman should not be one of passivity and of helping only; that her identity is not to be found solely in helping her husband and in raising her children; that she has a right to choice, to [an] identity of her own within this marital relationship; and that marriage and love, real love, is something between two equals. It is an ideal that we are moving toward, but it is difficult to achieve because of the past, which clings to us in all kinds of ways.[19]

A few years later, the same sort of educational effort by the same group resulted in a different focus. It was more legalistic, based on the concept of community-property rights and objectives:

> There are really three underlying assumptions [to community property]. The first and the most basic proposition is that the family is seen as an economic unit. It is headed by two legally separate individuals who have mutuality of interests and a present vested right in all property acquired through their joint labor during the marriage. . . . In the community property system you have two heads of household. The husband and wife are seen as distinct entities and as two legally equal entities.
>
> The second assumption is that all labor is equally valued. The work done by a housewife is considered to be equally as important to the family welfare as the work done by a breadwinner. . . . [I]n a community property system, all labor is valued equally and is seen as equally necessary to maintain the family according to the lifestyle chosen by the husband and wife.
>
> And third, a corollary of this second point, is that the husband and wife have equal economic status because they make equal contributions to the relationship. . . . The husband's salary belongs half to him and half to his wife. Similarly, the wife's salary belongs half to her and half to her husband, and all of this becomes the community assets. . . . [T]he basic underlying principle is that anything earned by either spouse during the duration of the marriage belongs equally to the two of them.[20]

Background of the Reform. For the Wisconsin reformers, the event that seems to have precipitated the characterization of divorce as a separate feminist problem in need of immediate attention was a regional conference of the various states' commissions on the status of women held in Michigan during the fall of 1974. Several members of the Wisconsin Commission attended the conference, where women attorneys instructed them on experiences with no-fault divorce reform in other states. They were told that women tended to emerge from no-fault divorces with little or no property, with custody of the children, and with bleak economic futures. The conference's message was that before the enactment of no-fault in these states, women could use threats of contesting the divorce to bargain with their husbands for economic settlements, and for better terms than were available under the existing property division and support laws. The two women who attended the conference concluded that no-fault should not be enacted without specific changes in other laws governing property division, alimony, and support.[21]

Upon their return to Madison, the two women hastily called a meeting of people who they believed would share their concerns. Much to the surprise of the legislators whom they had earlier urged to sponsor no-fault reform, key members of the Governor's Commission on the Status of Women were persuaded to withdraw their support for the pending no-fault bill unless it was accompanied by extensive provisions to protect women during divorce. The head of the Governor's Commission recalled the response of the major sponsor of no-fault:

> He had been persuaded by some of us before we got really going
> on our own divorce law to endorse the notion of no-fault divorce
> and it took kind of a lot of learning on his part to come to the
> point where he thought a no-fault would be good. . . . So . . .
> when [the poor no-fault sponsor] wanted to have a no-fault law
> just plain without any economic guarantees of any kind and we
> said, "No, you can't do it now, . . . " he thought we were all stab-
> bing him in the back because we were the ones who had persuaded
> him and we're saying, "Nope, that's out of date now."

The no-fault sponsors initially refused to consider adding the provisions, evidently believing that their bill would pass that session and that interjecting the feminist concerns into the legislative process would only complicate matters.

Fortunately for the feminist reformers, other groups in Wisconsin had historically opposed no-fault divorce. Representatives of the Catholic church, for example, believed no-fault legislation would encourage divorce. Others felt it would make divorce too easy and would therefore threaten the family.[22] With these opponents of no-fault already exerting influence on some legislators, the withdrawal of feminist support had a significant impact: it took away the small margin the no-fault backers had in the legislature. The defeat of the bill in the senate was viewed by many as the result of their feminist opposition.[23]

In terms of encouraging a separate divorce reform that included economic protections for women, the defeat of no-fault was a political boon. The feminists developed a legislative plan and had an alternative bill ready for introduction the next session. They also used their existing contacts to gain support for their approach to divorce reform. By defeating the no-fault bill that did not include economic protections in 1975, the feminist reformers had shown their political strength. More importantly, they had captured the issue of divorce reform for themselves. They became a constituency with which to reckon for those who wanted no-fault. The senators they influenced would not vote for no-fault until the bill was accompanied by acceptable economic protections.[24]

The development of the feminist reformers' Concepts and objectives

The reformers were committed to certain liberal feminist principles as they approached their task of suggesting appropriate economic rules.[25] An important example was their commitment to gender neutrality, already expressed in earlier legislation that removed gender designations from many of the statutes. Such a commitment would not permit sex to be used as an explicit conceptual framework for the reform, even though the feminists initially undertook the reform because they viewed the existing law as potentially harmful to women.[26]

The reformers had a gender-specific situation firmly in mind as the prototypical case illustrating the need for economic protections. For example, in a brochure labeled *Divorce Reform Legislation,* the Governor's Commission asserted that

> [a]ny reform of Wisconsin divorce law must ensure that the rights of homemakers and children are given just recognition. Divorce settlements should be made and enforced equitably, taking into account the contributions of both spouses.
>
> Traditionally, the law has recognized only money contributions. Equity demands that the law reflect reality: that homemakers contributed to their marriages greatly but differently than their spouses.

The Victim Identified—The Focus on Equality

The way divorce first came to be considered a feminist concern may have been particularly significant for the reformers' subsequent gathering and processing of information. At the Michigan conference, the reformers had heard stories about nonworking women with children who had few marketable skills. This represented the first step in generating images exemplifying the problem.

Structurally, the focus on the housewife was also combined with the reformers' belief that these women were being victimized by the existing law, which typically awarded them one-third or fewer of the assets at divorce. This belief led to the conclusion that it was desirable to treat men and women the same with respect to regulating the economic questions of divorce. The rationale behind the argument was found in the concept of contribution. Injustice, the reformers argued, could be prevented by imposing the equal-division presumption suggested by the reform.[27] This solution was fair because it treated marriage as a partnership between equals who made equal, even if different, contributions. This presumption was also consistent with the ideal of gender neutrality, which removes any suggestion that men or women as groups should be *prima facie* treated differently. Further, it was consistent with assisting housewives, as it was believed that this group would otherwise receive much less than an equal share.

The image of the victimized housewife soon took the form of "horror stories," which symbolized and defined for the feminists the reform that was needed. These horror stories had as central characters a deserving but victimized wife, a villainous and selfish husband, and a legal system which closed not only the eyes but the ears of justice in the name of property rights, leaving the wife and children destitute and abandoned.[28] These women were particularly deserving of sympathy because they had fulfilled the role society had imposed upon them, that of dutiful wife and mother. They were, for this reason, victimized by their husbands' harsh treatment and their own inability to earn an income and care for themselves.

The reformers, when interviewed, acknowledged that their horror stories were collected in a variety of ways. Some came to their attention as they pursued activities that brought them into contact with the community. The first such activity that brought these stories to the attention of one of the reformers was the Michigan conference. She recalled:

> I think I became more theoretically aware of the problem when there was a Midwest regional meeting of Commissions on the Status of Women. I recall we went to Michigan, and they had someone there from a state out further west, and they had two women attorneys, [who] were in . . . divorce practice and they really told

some hair-raising stories. . . . They told about Florida, [which] had enacted a so called no-fault divorce, and they called it a wife stuffing bill because it allowed husbands to trade in their wives . . . and there would be no payment, no nothing, and this might be someone they had been married to for twenty-five years. And they quoted some Florida judges saying, well now you have equal rights, and women can go out and get jobs and so the marriage is ended, now goodbye. In other words, ignoring completely the different position that the women were in who had been home-makers compared to their ex-husbands.[29]

Some women attending activities of the Governor's Commission on the Status of Women presented the reformers with horror stories. As one reformer recalled:

The Commission sponsored some conferences on the homemaker in 1974 which were real eye-openers for an awful lot of profes-sional women who considered themselves feminists. And we had been in the past primarily concerned about issues relating to em-ployment, to education; the inequities which were most obvious to us, and by us I guess I mean all feminist rabble rousers of the late sixties and early seventies, were in the academic world, in the employment world. That was where we were trying to break in and those were the inequities that we saw the most clearly.

Other horror stories were explicitly sought out by combing family law casebooks or newspapers. One reformer recalled that

[t]here were stories in the newspapers of so-and-so, well-to-do attorney whose ex-wife was now on AFDC [Aid for Families with Dependent Children]. There were stories from every walk of life through every possible sort of way—I mean through the newspa-pers, through private people telling us, through organizations.

Because the horror stories focused on only one group of women, however, they stereotyped very early in the reform the kinds of disad-vantages the reformers believed would disadvantage all women in a di-vorce without economic protections.[30]

The concern for housewives and mothers was understandable. When they received funding for the first time in 1972, the members of the Wisconsin Governors' Commission on the Status of Women were told that they then had to broaden their focus from the problems of profes-sional women to those more representative of all women. The head of the Governor's Commission on the Status of Women recalled:

Some of us had a conversation with one of the Governor's assistants, who said, "Now that you have a budget and we have discontinued the Council on Home and Family [an earlier group], you had better be doing something visible on the subject of home and family." A lot of right-wingers had accused us of being only interested in employed women. That was a period when the women's movement was getting the same reaction. But it was not true in either case. People who were feeling insecure or put down because they were full-time homemakers had some of this perception in any case, and that was one of the things that got us started on planning this 1974 Home and Family conference that had so many wonderful repercussions. Of course, we tailored it to fit our point of view, but we titled it so as to include everybody and not scare off anyone.

The Commission members also wanted to disprove charges of elitism which had been leveled at the commission and the women's movement in general. As another reformer noted:

[t]he Commission's conferences on the homemaker frankly were started out mainly as public relations and not with the idea that anybody was really going to learn a whole lot. The feminist movement had been criticized because it was only for career people. It was only for white, middle-class women who had a career orientation. It was not for people who wanted to be wives and mothers. And a lot of us felt that that was unfair and untrue. I mean at that point I was going to law school, I was also married and having a baby, and doing all that kind of stuff and I didn't feel that I was really one-sided in the way I looked at things, nor that my friends were. But it was the perception of the feminist movement and so for political reasons, for public relations reasons, it looked like it made sense to do something dramatic and something that would pick up a lot of press and something we would say in some very real, tangible way; we want to hear from homemakers. Homemakers are women too, which none of us ever had any dispute about, but somehow the message wasn't getting through.

All this resulted in various programs addressed directly to housewives, who were viewed by the reformers as both a representative and a non-elite group of women. Divorce reform offered an opportunity to assist such women further.

This attempt to avoid elitism helps to explain why housewives were typified as the unvindicated heroines of the horror stories and why their problems came to represent the need for reform to such an extent that they alone became the focus of the reform movement. References to victimized housewives as though they alone presented problems of divorce are found in the documents produced by the feminists and in the manuscripts of the speeches they gave:

> The Commission on the Status of Women cannot support any proposal for the revision of Wisconsin divorce law which does not assure that the rights of homemakers and children are given just recognition. . . .
> We recognize that in most marriages the role of the woman has been that of a homemaker, and that she has been ill prepared, or not at all, to pursue worthwhile and meaningful employment. Only about a half of married women work outside the home, and few of them are in technical or professional careers. Most working married women are in comparatively low-pay jobs offering little upward or geographic mobility.
> These are the economic facts of life for most homemakers. For them, divorce is a crushing economic burden.[31]

In testifying on the desirability of economic reform before the Assembly Judiciary Committee on 19 September 1975, a reformer who was a member of the Governor's Commission made it clear that housewives were the focus of the proposed reforms:

> The Governor has charged this Commission with the task of investigating the Status of Women. A group of women about whose status we are much concerned is the housewife or homemaker. She works, but she is not employed. Her work has value, but she receives no pay. And very much, in this society, you are what you earn. For the housewife, this leads to a great many economic problems, most of which we don't even realize as long as our marriages are going smoothly. . . .
> What disturbs us is the evidence we have received from women in other states where no-fault has been adopted that housewives are being treated very shabbily by their courts. Therefore, we believe, that in adopting no-fault we must take care to see that housewives do not get a worse deal than they already get. Obviously, this bill makes no distinction between homemakers and women who work for pay. Yet the problems this bill is intended to meet are largely problems faced by housewives and homemakers.

There is little doubt that the reformers believed that their reforms would substantially improve the position of this group of women.[32] However, the housewife horror stories alone presented an unbalanced picture. There was no explicit consideration of information on the circumstances of other groups of women, such as nonprofessional working mothers, women who supported their husbands and children during the marriage, or women who were in their second marriage and maintaining obligations and assets from the first.[33] More complete information would have allowed the reformers or their constituents to judge the overall fairness of the existing divorce procedure or to assess the range of possible reforms. They appear, however, to have made no systematic search outside of the housewife-victim paradigm for additional information that would have allowed them to evaluate a variety of factual situations before determining appropriate solutions. When such information was presented to the reformers in the form of criticism of their equality ideal, it appears to have been either ignored or discounted. It may be that the general ideology of the reformers and their predisposition toward a rule-equality model for addressing societal problems influenced the way in which they sought out and interpreted information on divorce.

Focusing on the need for just treatment of housewives facilitated the focus on equality for two reasons. First, the valuation of individual non-monetary or housewife-type contributions would have been very difficult to calculate. Practical considerations forced the general conclusion that husbands' and wives' contributions were in all significant ways the same, thus mandating equality in treatment. Second, the lack of recognition of a non-wage-earning spouse's legal rights in property secured by her husband's earnings historically had been the subject of feminist concern. The resolutions of the questions of whether a wife had a right to her husband's property and, if she did, the extent of such a right, had important symbolic meaning to the feminists because they touched upon basic assumptions about the value of "women's work" in the domestic sphere.[34]

The reformers approached these questions in the context of the feminist assertions that the value of domestic work is equal to that of work performed in the marketplace. Framing the discussion in terms of rights based on an assumed equal-but-different contribution to the marriage was to conclude that the property should be divided equally upon divorce. A statement by U.S. Congresswoman Martha Griffiths summed up the symbolic meaning of such a conclusion:

> The rights of homemakers under support laws, property laws, divorce laws, and inheritance laws are the concrete evidence of the value society places on the homemaker's role. If women's work is not valued in the home, it has a low value outside the home. If our daughters (and sons) cannot expect that their work in the home will be recognized as *of equal value and deserving equal dignity* with that of the spouse who works outside the home, the institution of

> the family and our society will suffer. The laws in most States are
> not grounded in this evaluation of the homemaker's role.[35]

The reformers could conclude that the rule-equality model satisfied their desire for fair treatment of women at divorce, however, only by minimizing, rhetorically and conceptually, any differences between the needs of men and women after divorce occurred. Given the statistical evidence to the contrary on the issue of need, of which they must have been aware, one must question how they could fail to make need the central theme of reform. The reformers were well aware that support orders had failed to adequately take care of need. Ms. Griffiths' testimony before the United States House of Representatives stressed both the inadequacy of initial awards of child support and the failure to enforce the large number of awards that were in arrears.[36] In addition, a 1955 Wisconsin study indicated that 62 percent of parents under order for child support failed to comply the first year after the court order; 42 percent had not made a single payment.[37] Furthermore, in 1979 Karen Seal argued that given inequality in the market, feminists in California could have predicted that equal division would have an adverse impact on women. She concluded that the "belief in equality is so fundamental, however, that arguing for more than equal division of assets or income for women could be interpreted as discrimination against men."[38] The idea that contribution in the form of household duties should be recognized did not resolve all the potential problems. In fact, the concept of contribution, which conformed to their concern for the extreme circumstances of the stereotypical victimized housewife, may have permitted the reformers to ignore some of the harder questions because it facilitated the perception that equality was the ideal solution. For example, what was to be the standard for division in cases where a spouse made "dual contributions" by both working and caring for the home and children?

It may be that the reformers, having access to more complete information, understood that sameness of treatment would not be appropriate for all women, but chose the symbolically compatible rule-equality model as their organizing concept because their sights were focused on the broader equality concerns of the feminist movement.[39]

Any arguments that did not explicitly incorporate the rule-equality concept would undermine that goal.[40] It also may be that the imagery of women as victims had an overly powerful influence on the reformers. The women who successfully initiated the reform movement using the horror stories may themselves have felt locked in by the stories once the reform momentum was generated. This may have led them to exaggerate the divorced housewife's lack of property claims and to ignore the patterns by which the courts indeed protected these women.[41]

An often-cited case was a 1953 Nebraska decision where a court refused to require a miserly husband to provide plumbing, heating and better clothing for his wife. This case, while it did *not* involve a divorce, represented to the feminist reformers to what extent the law could go and how tenuous the woman's right to be supported in some kind of reasonable manner really was. One typical representation of this case was as follows:

> The McGuires lived in a shack outside a town that did not have running water or central heating; they drove a pickup truck that was twenty-some years old and about to fall apart.
> Mr. McGuire generously bought Mrs. McGuire one new dress a year; any other clothing she had was given to her by her daughters. Mr. McGuire had the telephone disconnected because Mrs. McGuire made long-distance calls to her children. The guy was just an incredible miser. So Mrs. McGuire went to court and said that she had been living with him for forty years and would like a car with a heater, central heating in the house, indoor plumbing, and a new winter coat. . . .
> Mr. McGuire, who was apparently a miser in everything except legal fees, . . . and the Supreme Court of Nebraska said, in effect, Mrs. McGuire, if it's so bad you wouldn't have stuck with him for forty years. Now go home and stop complaining. So the court decided that Mr. McGuire was providing the necessaries, since there was a roof over Mrs. McGuire's head, she did have something to put on her body, and she did have food to eat, besides that, he paid medical bills.[42]

The effect of the horror stories on the reformers' own presentation of information to others can be seen by comparing a 1975 and a 1977 exposition of the rules governing property division in a publication entitled *Wisconsin Women and the Law,* published by the Governor's Commission on the Status of Women. The 1975 version read:

> There is no clear legal standard in determining how the assets and debts acquired during a marriage are to be divided. *While some cases justify a split of one-third to the wife and two-thirds to the husband, the opposite sometimes occurs. A 50–50 division is common.* Many factors must be considered, including services performed and income generated, the ability to assume debts, and the prospective income levels of the parties in the future.[43]

This description conforms fairly well to that suggested by the cases described earlier in this chapter.[44] By 1977, the description as well as the tone had changed:

> The court considers all relevant factors in determining how the assets and debts acquired during a marriage are to be divided. While there is no clear standard establishing the proportion of the resources that goes to each party, *a split of one-third to the wife and two-thirds to the husband is common.*[45]

By 1977 the reformers also were openly advocating an answer to the perceived inequities:

> *It should be noted that under a community property system . . . each spouse would presumably be entitled to one-half of the marital assets at divorce*—a presumption that could be modified by the factors in each individual case. *This situation, where the homemaker has a legal claim to one-half of the property, treats a nonwage earner more favorably than does current Wisconsin law where the homemaker must depend on good will or extraordinary circumstances to receive more than one-third.*[46]

The stereotypical housewife horror story encouraged the reformers to argue that legal institutions were systematically biased against women in resolving the economic incidents of divorce. This perception may have been accurate in terms of the cases the feminists compiled to support their arguments. Whether it was accurate from a historical perspective is questionable. Furthermore, it is even less clear that it was accurate in terms of all, or even most, contemporary divorce cases in Wisconsin. In fact, as the excerpts from the earlier version of *Wisconsin Women and the Law* and cases decided prior to 1979 indicate, it is at least arguable that the prereform system allowed judges the discretion to divide property fairly and worked in favor of many women because of prevailing feelings of paternalism.[47] While eliminating paternalism as a legal and social principle might have been a desirable goal in the abstract, some information available at the time of the reform at least suggested that paternalism sometimes resulted in decisions favorable to women, particularly housewives.

Several attorneys, for example, explicitly suggested to the reformers that paternalism operated to ameliorate some of the practical hardships many women would feel under a more uniform (nonpaternalistic) rule, which would assume an equality that does not exist in a sexist society. The husband of one of the reformers, an attorney who had handled a large number of divorces, indicated that he was doing much better for his women clients in property division than the proposed equal division. He expressed concern that many of his female clients would not do as well under a statute adopting an equal-division model.[48] Attorneys in other parts of the state made similar comments. The implications of the equality model for alimony awards were also the subject of some concern for attorneys. For example, a Milwaukee attorney wrote to the key legislator in regard to the proposed reform:

> As a general comment, and we feel much like a Cassandra in so
> stating, but each of the recent changes in family law have [*sic*]
> made it increasingly difficult to secure equity for women before
> the courts. This is especially true with respect to women involved
> in marriages of long duration and where the children are growing
> up or have grown up.
>   Each step in the statutory changes [has] left these vocationally
> ill-equipped women further and further out in the cold. We have a
> deep foreboding that your well-intentioned provision for voca-
> tional rehabilitation will be utilized by the court for women in
> their 40s and 50s as a basis for small payments, for retraining, and
> alleviating many errant husbands, who have become interested in
> younger women, from paying alimony.[49]

There were other perceived difficulties also. For example, another attorney wrote:

> I am particularly anxious about the implementation of [the prop-
> erty division provisions]. As written I find it not definite enough. I
> favor a clause stating that assets solely held prior to marriage not
> be included in figures used for the 50–50 split. I have in mind
> women or men with assets from a first marriage making a poor
> second choice of spouse and possibly being wiped out.[50]

These suggestions had little or no impact on the direction of the reform movement.

Perhaps the fixation on the equality solution channeled the reformers' attention, or perhaps the limited information upon which they relied compelled the solution. In either case, the horror stories had served an important function. They may have been generated as an organizing tool but, because they were so vivid and compelling, they came to substitute for a more generalized articulation of the problems for women in divorce. Very early, the victimized women, labeled *displaced homemakers,* became the exclusive measure against which the reformers judged which reforms would embody the ideals of fairness or justice from their feminist perspective. This development closed off consideration of various types of non-homemaker problems when the reformers reached the stage of formulating actual legal solutions to the problems they had identified. In addition, because the reformers distorted the issue even in regard to the historic legal treatment of the homemakers themselves, the reform was directed toward the substantively unproductive rule-equality model, epitomized by the partnership metaphor, which despite its symbolic appeal is unresponsive to possible future needs.[51]

The ideal of leaving property division to the discretion of trial judges and trusting them to reach an equitable result was unacceptable to the reformers.[52] The fact that judges were mostly male and the belief in the prevalence of patterns represented by the horror stories proved that judges could not as a group be trusted to protect wives and children. Since the reformers did not trust judges to reach fair results, the reform rules had to limit judges' discretion. Rules flexible enough to permit women to be awarded more than half the property at divorce could also be used to achieve the same result for men. The clear directive represented by the presumption of equal division in the statute would seriously curtail the judges' discretion, they believed.

The reformers reached this particular conclusion about the undesirability of a system that leaves much to trial judges' discretion very early, but it was contrary to some of the advice they subsequently received. It was also criticized in a thoughtful letter from a member of the Commission on Uniform Laws, which had drafted the Uniform Marriage and Divorce Act. That Act had embodied the notion of "equitable distribution," giving discretion to trial judges, who were to consider a list of specifically enumerated factors in reaching a just result. John McCabe, the Legislative Director of Commissioners on Uniform State Laws, analyzed the draft of the Wisconsin legislation and noted the "clear analogy [of marriage] to a business partnership which is in the process of dissolution." McCabe expressed his reservations about the partnership ideal of marriage, and pointed out the criticism of the equal division idea in California:[53]

> Most married couples have one major asset, if any, the family house. A common property division under the common law allows the wife to keep the house, especially if there are children, with the husband maintaining the mortgage payments. In California now, there are apparently a significant number of cases in which the home has been sold, because it is the major asset, to meet the equal division mandate.[54]

Even more fundamentally, the letter observed:

Marriage is more than a business partnership. . . . A marriage can also be analogized to a conspiracy, but that does not mean such notions should be used to judge it. The marital relationship is a not-for-profit social partnership. It exists to provide shelter and support for its members. It is an educational institution and a health care organization. When it must be dissolved for some exigent reason, the court should attempt, insofar as possible, to make the property distribution the basis for sustaining the parties after dissolution. The strict partnership idea simply does not accomplish that. . . .[55]

In the letter, McCabe contrasted the equality-model approach of the proposed Wisconsin legislation with that of the equity or result-equality model taken by the Uniform Marriage and Divorce Act:

Contributions are important, but the continuing needs of the parties are even more important. The court, in the Uniform Act, considers the status of the parties by a number of factors, and the "needs of each of the parties." Need as a factor in distribution is of particular importance to a party who has not contributed actual income to the unity of the marriage. Need may provide a basis for that person of more equitable distribution, notwithstanding efforts to value that contribution. The Uniform Act simply takes a broader view of marriage and divorce, and that cannot fail to fit the parties' interest better.[56]

The reformers would have been unable to characterize such a critic as someone opposed to the notion of just reform for women in divorce. Nonetheless, the reformers were committed to the notions that judicial discretion had to be curtailed and the displaced homemaker had to be made an equal, and this commitment affected the way they received advice from any source.

Communications and Acceptance of the Reformer's Images

In the initial stages of the reform process, the feminist reformers took steps to involve a few members of the legislature, persuading them of the need for and feasibility of legislative actions. Specifically, they selected one woman representative, and she became a part of the process from the beginning. She sponsored the reform and later acted as the bridge between the reformers and others involved in politics.

As the reform process gained momentum in the political arena, other groups began to have an independent impact on the process. Generally, however, the reformers' images continued to dominate at this stage of the process; no serious challenges were made to their perception of the reality of divorce, the victim model, or their ideal, the equality model.[57] In part, this was a tribute to the involvement and skill of the legislator sponsoring the reform. Her function shifted from that of an interest-group member intimately concerned with generating an ideal to that of a politician concerned with the best and most politically feasible method of translating that ideal into legislation. In fact, few political compromises were necessary.[58]

Contemporary newspaper accounts of the reform movement concentrated heavily on the arguments for and against the removal of fault.[59] Little was mentioned about the extensive economic reforms that would accompany the bill, were it to pass.

In fact, to some extent the reformers managed to co-opt opponents of no-fault. Their legislator was careful to send drafts of her proposed revisions to these opponents and attempted to convince them that if no-fault was inevitable, it would be more palatable with these protections.[60] The process of communication and solicitation of advice was repeated by the legislator with other groups that might have presented opposition. A group representing divorced men was soothed by specific provisions modifying the notion of long-term alimony, and by child-custody provisions that, being gender-neutral, might give men a better chance for custody in the future. The support of the Wisconsin State Bar was facilitated to a great extent because one of the reformers was chair of the Bar committee that assumed major responsibility for assessing and commenting on the reform. Court personnel had been pulled into the process as advisors very early, and correspondence soliciting their support and advice continued throughout the process. For the court administrators and judges, there was also the promise of clear, easily implemented rules that would make cases quicker and easier to process.

Thus the reformers and their legislator gathered support for the reform without ever compromising the equality ideal or losing sight of the victimized homemaker and the need to curtail the discretion of judges. They tailored their explanations of the virtues of their proposal to the groups being persuaded, but kept their basic symbolic structure intact.[61]

A pamphlet on *Divorce Reform,* published in 1976, illustrates the Commission's focus on the contribution concept:

> The court should presume property is to be divided equally, but should be permitted to alter this distribution after consideration of such factors as the *contribution* of each party to the marriage, giving value to *contributions* in homemaking and child care services;

contribution toward the education, training or increased earning power of the other. (Emphasis added.)

The initial proposed reform bill had this statement of intent:

> It is the intent of the legislature that the spouse who has been handicapped socially or economically by his or her *contribution* to a marriage shall be compensated for such *contributions* at the termination of the marriage, insofar as possible. (Emphasis added.)

The idea that contribution is symbolically more compatible with feminist objectives than need was not limited to the Wisconsin reformers. As one commentator from Newfoundland observed in 1977: "[J]oint contribution to the family assets is a sounder basis [for the reallocation of property on divorce] than the negative approach of [the wife's] inability to contribute directly through her own earnings."[62] Contribution was seen as a positive rather than a negative approach to the issue of women's economic dependency. One difficulty with this focus is that it may force women into molds which are patterned on those developed by and for men.[63]

The logical ramifications of symbolic adherence to equality may be significant. A commitment to equality encourages its proponents to minimize or deny differences between the individuals for whose demands they have become proponents and the individuals they perceive to be in superior positions. As the Wisconsin reform shows, however, overreliance on symbolic concerns can also create difficulties for women with more than symbolic concerns.

PART TWO

Equality Rhetoric and Child Custody Decision Making

FIVE

Child Custody: Equality as the Aftermath of Economic Reforms

More women are entering the labor force rather than devoting themselves to full-time child care roles, and the trend toward more role sharing and egalitarianism in marriage will probably result in increased demands for equality in divorce. . . . As women gain liberation from traditional roles, they will define themselves less as mothers and will have fewer needs for the role to be primary in their lives.

C. Ahrons*

INTRODUCTION

This section analyzes contemporary child-custody policy and the changes in traditional law that have occurred during the past few decades. In the chapters that follow, I detail the ways in which custody reforms—like those in the area of property—have also been fashioned according to the ideal of equality to the disadvantage of women and children. The result of the application of the equality model in this area is that even though divorce is now easier to obtain, its occasion provides the justification for ongoing, extensive state supervision of the custody determination and of the typical postdivorce family unit, comprised of mothers and their children.

Equality rhetoric has been most influential in the custody area, as we shall see in the chapters that follow. Of principle interest is how the same-treatment model has been adopted and implemented with a vengeance in the context of family law, as compared to more general laws.[1] For example, custody rules were a doctrinal area in which women had an explicit preference in the form of the tender-years presumption that gave them custody of young children unless they were found unfit. As equality and the concurrent concept of gender neutrality have been incorporated into custody decision making, such old, tested, gendered rules that permitted predictable, inexpensive decisions to be made with-

---

*C. Ahrons, *Joint Custody Arrangements in the Postdivorce Family*, J. DIVORCE, Spring 1980, 189, at 203

out protracted litigation have been set aside. As a result, one problem
confronting the new, formally degendered, family-law system is the
need to create new, gender-neutral factors or processes to handle decision making in individual cases. The result has been increased state regulation of the postdivorce family.

Custody reforms occurred against the backdrop of significant social
and legal developments. These developments have been characterized
by the establishment of, and response to, the women's movement in the
United States. As already detailed in chapter 2, during the 1970s there
were successful attempts in most states to make laws gender-neutral.
Such campaigns were particularly significant in the family-law area,
where gendered rules had been the norm. Feminists concerned with law
reform considered the push for degendered rules a symbolic imperative
even when they recognized that such reforms might actually result in removing an arguable advantage for women, as in the case of maternal
preference rules for deciding custody cases. For example, in the Wisconsin divorce reform effort discussed more fully in chapter 4, one of the
Wisconsin reformers expressed understanding of the "risks" associated
with the rule-equality model they advocated as follows:

> [We acknowledge] that things would and have gotten more diffi-
> cult as both parents have the expectation that they would or
> should get the child. . . . Under a system where you assume that
> one sex is going to get the children, then some people don't even
> try and hope. And so we knew that we were stirring up some pos-
> sible problems.

The process of communication and solicitation of advice from
groups that might have presented opposition was an explicit part of the
Wisconsin reform. Divorced men and their representatives, in particular, were wooed by the reformers with child-custody provisions that,
being gender-neutral, gave men a better chance for custody in the future. One legislator had these comments on gathering support:

> [M]en lawyers, in particular, representing male clients [were] in-
> terested in the custody issue. . . . We didn't do as much as they
> wanted, but we did a number of things to please them. . . . [I]t
> included the provision, which some people weren't happy with,
> about when you're leaving the state [with children]—notification
> [or consent of the court and/or noncustodial parent is required.] I
> thought that was very wise. . . . I don't think that's a group that
> could have beaten us, but it was good in terms of dealing primarily
> with a male-dominated legislature . . . to say we've dealt with this

group; we've dealt with that group. But our basic basis of support
was not just the women's movement, we had a very good support
from a lot of people in . . . counseling and mental health and some
religious groups, so they were part of our coalition.

In addition to convincing liberal feminists that they should embrace
gender-neutral roles, the women's movement's push for equality in the
family and workplace generated various backlashes. For example,
amidst rhetoric that labeled delinquent fathers as "deadbeats," state and
federal governments enacted stringent state and federal provisions for
the collection of past-due child support. Reforms in the child-support
enforcement area spurred the formation of fathers' rights groups, which
appropriated and successfully employed the feminist rhetoric of equality and gender neutrality to force reforms in the family-law area, such as
mandatory joint custody.[2]

Moreover, the rhetoric and, incidentally, the career interests of various
professional groups involved in the divorce process further reflected the
position that the traditional rules were biased in favor of women. These
groups thus also fueled the successes of the fathers' rights adherents. For
example, "helping professionals" used the images of excluded (but worthy
and caring) "dads" to fashion a professional standard of "shared parenting"
after divorce, a new custody norm to be implemented by way of the mediation skills of these same professionals.[3] To these professionals, joint custody is not only "fair"; it is also the most therapeutic result:

> There is no doubt that joint custody yields two psychological par-
> ents, and that the children do not suffer the profound sense of loss
> characteristic of so many children of divorce. The children main-
> tained strong attachments to both parents. Perhaps the security of
> an ongoing relationship with *two* psychological parents helps to
> provide the means to cope successfully with the uprooting effects
> of switching households.[4]

In this area, as in the reforms of the economic aspects of divorce,
symbolic ideals have obscured more instrumental concerns, but the process of incorporating equality ideas has been more complex. The need
for an authoritative articulation of alternative standards exists and sets
the stage for political and ideological battles that bring within the fray
various groups of professionals, both legal and nonlegal, who claim to
have as their motivation the desire to protect the child. To place custody
reforms in context, a discussion of traditional law and an overview of
changing contemporary doctrine are useful.

Early Custody Rules

Prior to the turn of the nineteenth century, early American custody law followed English precedent, which gave fathers absolute control of their children. Although mothers were entitled to respect, the right to child custody upon divorce was located in the father under the *pater familias* doctrine.[5] In essence, under the formal rules, fathers had an absolute right to their children, "owning" them as if they held title, and having a corresponding duty to support—to pay for—them. Despite some exceptions which were developed in extraordinary cases, the doctrine operated in a relatively simple and straightforward manner. Judicial decision making was limited to determining if a particular set of circumstances was one of the exceptional cases which required deviation from the stated standard of paternal custody and control.

The notion of paternal possession was successfully challenged during the latter part of the nineteenth century, both through feminist agitation, which stressed the role that mothers played in children's day-to-day upbringing,[6] and through the "enlightened" rhetoric characteristic of turn-of-the-century welfare state do-gooders.[7] Children were said to be endowed with a right to the best custodial situation, independent of their fathers' property interest in them. This reformist discourse viewed children not so much as individual property to be divided between parents, but as a form of social investment in which custody produced concomitant social duties on the part of each parent, the performance of which the state could supervise.[8]

The legal expression of this view came in the adoption of the standard of the "best interest of the child" as the governing substantive principle in custody adjudications. Instead of granting fathers an automatic right to custody, the courts were directed to select the best custodial placement for the child. This test created problems for the legal system, however. Determining what was in a child's best interest involved assessing a multitude of factors. In contrast to the more absolute test accorded by the father's-right rule, this new test required judges to make case-by-case substantive judgments and comparisons, and therefore was indeterminate. In order to deal with the indeterminancy of this new standard, as well as to ease the burdens of judgment and to avoid the need for difficult predictions about future effects, many jurisdictions rapidly developed "rules of thumb,"[9] principally the tender-years doctrine, to allow easy implementation of the best-interest rule.[10]

Formally, the tender-years doctrine was a legal presumption that directed the placement of children younger than seven—children of "tender years"—with their mothers, unless their mothers were "unfit" to provide care. Essentially, this presumption gave content to the term *best interest of the child* by assigning "ownership" to the mother. This ownership was not absolute, however, as courts awarded fathers "visitation," often for extended periods during school vacations, and placed other limitations on custodial mothers' control over their children. A related but less common presumption favored placement of older children with the parent of the same sex.[11]

The movement away from the father's absolute right to custody to the less absolute guidelines of the best-interest test and its accompanying tender-years presumption can be viewed as a shift in principles governing the distribution of property interests in children by way of the state's asserting its own proprietary interest in them as future citizens. It can also be understood as the state's recognition that good mothers had "paid for" or "earned" their children through continuous and systematic care of them. This latter view incorporated the notion of children as a "reward" for mothers' socially productive labor in raising future citizens.[12]

These new rules reflected middle-class norms of the late nineteenth and early twentieth centuries and represented the setting apart of women from the world of work and the market. Assigning women care of younger children in the home was consistent with the notion that women needed to be sheltered and protected so that they could fulfill their destiny and reproduce and nurture the species. Both the social and legal systems recreated Motherhood in a manner which enhanced women's position concerning their children both in marriage and at divorce, provided they did not violate patriarchal norms such as fidelity, temperance, and so on.[13]

Thus, both the system that gave fathers absolute rights over their children and the reform of that system, which led to the formulation of the best-interest test, were consistent with the dominant paternalistic rhetoric of the time. Individual men had to relinquish some control over the private or domestic sphere, in that they did not retain an absolute right to their child's custody, but the structures were still patriarchal. Women remained in the private sphere, and codes of conduct could be enforced through a custody doctrine that denied deviant mothers custody of their children. While the wave of domestic feminist ideology initially challenged patriarchy, it was absorbed and adapted so as to remove the potentially radical aspects of its opposition.[14]

The Impact of No-Fault Divorce on Custody Decision Making

For decades custody was considered to be a relatively settled area of law and not a focus of much debate. Fault governed the availability of divorce and, by and large, custody questions were resolved by designating the innocent spouse at divorce and using the parallel doctrines of the best interest of the child and/or tender years.[15] After the movement to no-fault divorce, however, resolution of custody questions no longer automatically followed the determination of who was the innocent spouse.

In the context of a society that still recognized and accepted the gendered nature of the division of family responsibilities, the best-interest test, even without a companion fault determination, was nonetheless equated with mother-custody. Judges, therefore, continued to apply the tender-years doctrine as a way to give content to the concept of best interest. While this in part continued to reflect vestiges of the fault system in that a woman could be denied custody if found unfit, the tender-years doctrine as applied also accorded a preference for the performance of primary caretaking tasks in children's development, valuing the care and nurture of child-rearing. Moreover, since it was only an evidentiary presumption, the tender-years doctrine could be justified by nothing more than reference to commonly held beliefs about who most likely performed primary child care.

THE FOUNDATIONS OF MODERN CUSTODY POLICY

Various factors combined to produce changes in traditional custody policy. Three significant developments led to the construction of modern custody policy, which favors such equality-based resolutions as joint custody or shared parenting, a construction of policy under which both parents are considered equally capable and are equally empowered regarding care of their children. Even when formal joint custody is not the legislative or court-mandated solution, doctrines that dictate the award of custody to "the most generous parent" (that is, the one most likely to share the child) reflect the basic principle that parents are, and should be, equal.

In the subsequent chapters in this section; I analyze these three developments in some detail. At this point, however, it would be helpful simply to articulate the three events and relate them to each other, because in combination, they have shaped our thinking about contemporary custody policy. These three events occurred in overlapping phases.

The first step in forming a foundation for contemporary custody rules was the conceptual separation of the child from the family unit as the object and source of legal concern. This is manifested in the creation of the concept of *child advocacy*; where an outsider to the family is deemed necessary at divorce to perform a representative function so as to ensure that the child's interests are protected. The second development involves the process of producing information, or knowledge labeled as *neutral* and *definitive*, which is deemed relevant to custody decisions in the new, degendered legal climate. Social scientists have filled the void left by the removal of gendered custody rules such as the tender-years doctrine, and the information they produce has been used (and misused) to try to give the best-interest test its contemporary content. The final phase of the equality reforms in this area is found in the imposition of the shared parenting concept by the practitioners of family decision making—social workers, mediators, court personnel, and others in the helping professions, who are the implementors of equality in the context of custody decisions. This final stage, in which the real practitioners of equality are nonlegal professionals, is also an acceptance of the oft-repeated assertion that legal institutions have failed to perform adequately in the custody area.

The Failures of Legal Institutions and the Concept of Advocacy

The two legal institutions that have been instrumental in developing the idea of children's interests at divorce are state courts and state legislatures. These institutions make legal decisions in different ways and with different constraints, all of which have an impact on the institutions' respective abilities to address custody issues in a coherent manner. Courts, for example, are traditionally considered inappropriate for the formulation of major policy directives because they are institutions that resolve disputes between individuals. As a result, courts define and resolve custody questions in individual cases by focusing on the rights or obligations of the individual family members. The current best-interest test encourages such a focus.

The best-interest test necessitates a comparison of parents' qualities and a determination as to which of them could be the preferable custodian. The test is so fact- and circumstance-specific that it defies any articulation of universal standards. No wonder the courts have welcomed the idea of independent, professional advocates to assist them in decision making under the best-interest test. With gendered decision making no longer permissible and no other societal norm emerging to replace the maternal preference, courts have searched for efficient ways to make individual custody decisions. The referral (or deferral) of the issue to a professional, particularly when that professional is also considered unbiased, allows the adversarial nature of the proceeding to operate while assigning a designated neutral actor the task of ensuring that the child's interest is not sacrificed to the parents' anger. Child advocacy is a procedural solution which allows courts complacently to conclude that the child's interest is in fact brought to light and protected.[16]

In contrast to courts, legislatures are capable of performing as broad policy-making bodies. However, these bodies are susceptible to political pressures and to the creation of simplistic, universally imposed, idealized norms. This susceptibility has been demonstrated throughout the entire spectrum of divorce reform, from marital property rules to the establishment of a preference for joint custody. Legislatures have been particularly responsive in the divorce area to the equality rhetoric of the fathers'-rights groups. As argued earlier, equality as a model for decision-making has symbolic as well as political appeal.

Complicating the problems inherent in viewing legislatures or courts as rational policy- and decision-making institutions is the fact that doctrinal family law during the past several decades has rejected the idea that the family has "rights" associated with it as a unit, or as an "entity." The thrust of law concerning the family currently reflects an adherence to the notion that the family is nothing more than a collection of individuals, each with specific individuated and potentially conflicting rights. Therefore, the real unit of modern concern for family law and policy and for the legal institutions that implement them is the individual. Laws focus on single issues isolated from other circumstances in order to "help" specific family members. In fact, family law has begun to reflect an assumption that the family may be harmful to an individual's (economic, emotional, and physical) health.

To minimize the evils inherent in divorce, the law now focuses on and identifies the rights of the individuals. When the individual is a child, the law mandates "protective" state intervention. Children as one set of individuals with separate and potentially conflicting rights and interests in relation to their parents need an "advocate," and the state is the logical supplier of persons to fulfill that role. This view of children and their need for state protection has made it difficult to offer acceptable substitutes for the best-interest-of-the-child test. The very phrase suggests the protective goal.

The Continued Viability of the Best-Interest Rhetoric

Even in the context of joint-custody rhetoric, the substantive test has tended to remain the best interest of the child. The best-interest rhetoric has tremendous symbolic appeal, focusing as it does on the child. In addition, attacks on the test are easily deflected within the context of the current paradigm that views families as mere collections of individuals whose interests are often in conflict. Attempts to change the test to make it more predictable are met with charges that parents' interests are being substituted for those of children.

Continued adherence to the best-interest test has serious consequences, however. It has necessitated a continuous search for alternatives to the court as the legal decision-maker in custody cases. As is detailed in chapter 9, judges are uncomfortable with the lack of specificity in the test and increasingly resort to the "helping professions" as assessors of what constitutes the best interest of a child. The resort to nonjudicial decision-makers as advocates for children in order to apply the best-interest standard masks the severe problems with the substantive test. It does not solve them and, in fact, allows the best-interest test to remain functional long after it should have been discarded.

In addition, the test fosters the rhetorical strategy of asserting that one is concerned only with the best interest of children in advancing one's own solution to the custody problem. The focus on *best interest* means there is a struggle over giving this term content, an ongoing war in which never-ending battles are won and lost as fads or trends in the social sciences and professional literature evolve and change. Furthermore, *best interest* is also susceptible to the winds of political and ideological change. This is clearly illustrated when we consider what has happened to the best-interest test under the mandates of equality and gender neutrality.

Setting the Stage for Legal and Political Change

As the incidence of divorce increased in the early 1970s, fathers'-rights groups successfully challenged the tender-years doctrine and criticized child-custody decision making for manifesting what they perceived to be a "pro-mother" bias.[17] At the same time that fathers began to reassert ownership interests, mainstream feminists attacked gender-specific legal tests as inherently discriminatory.[18] The fathers'-rights movement picked up on the idea of gender neutrality and turned it to the father's advantage in the custody area.[19] These two forces—male backlash and the liberal legal feminist equality rhetoric it appropriated—set the stage for more recent challenges to the traditional method and manner of custody decision making.[20]

The contemporary trend toward joint custody could be characterized as holding that it is the biological nexus or relationship between both parents and the child that buys or earns control over the child. In this view, neither parent has a superior claim to custody based on his or her gender or on the investment in day-to-day care for the child; rather, each parent appropriates an equal interest.[21] Joint and equal interest, embodied most clearly in the modern custody norm, was a virtually inevitable result of the successful attacks on the old rules, because no viable gender-neutral alternative to the tender-years doctrine existed. This modern trend illustrates a move backward toward the more explicit treatment of children as property embodied in the *pater familias* doctrine—only this time the property is to be divided equally.

With the removal of the old rules of thumb, custody decision-making became much more complex. No permissible, easily applied guidelines remain under the best-interest test, and questions exist as to which rules should govern. Without the old gender presumption, the legal system is asked to do too much. Judges and attorneys feel ill-equipped to make determinations about what placement will be in the best interests of children. This discomfort has set off a search for more determinate rules.

The Politics of Reform: Popular Attacks on the Maternal Custody Norm

Increasingly, fathers'-rights groups have focused on the fact that mothers continue to receive custody in the vast majority of cases. These men's groups arose as a forum for expressing backlash to some of the successes of the feminist movement.[22] Many of these groups initially organized around the issue of child support. The problem of nonpaying fathers had begun to be publicized, and the groups attempted to counter the image of the "deadbeat dad" with their own political interpretation of the situation. Custody soon became an issue for the fathers' groups, as they justified widespread nonpayment of child support with the images of beleaguered fathers who were only reacting to a court system which always gave mothers custody and treated them as nothing more than "walking wallets."[23]

One tactic employed by these groups was to attack the concept of motherhood as being something distinct, separate, and somehow superior to the generic term "parenthood."[24] In doing so, they picked up on earlier feminist rhetoric, often confusing the issue with their own interpretations and assertions that the feminist focus on gender neutrality required that all considerations of "typically motherly" characteristics be eliminated from judicial consideration.

The fathers'-rights groups based such novel custody arrangements as joint custody on their interpretation of the child's best interest, here translated into a "right" to have equal access to both parents. Equality was evident, as well, in their assertions that the father has a right to have equal control of decisions affecting the child after divorce. Calling themselves names such as the "National Congress for Men" and "Fathers United for Equal Rights," these groups articulated a range of issues in which they perceived that the law was giving preferential treatment to women. Child support and custody were important targets, probably because they were the only areas in which it could even be argued that women had any significant, demonstrable advantage.

These groups consciously picked up, exploited, and were assisted by the simultaneous attacks by liberal feminists and certain professionals on the popular concept of motherhood. Popularized notions of feminism had urged the undermining of prior existing stereotypes, urging that in the interest of a society that values equality they be discarded as irrelevant. By denying the uniqueness of the mothering relationship, however, the liberal feminist rhetoric could be used against women, since nurturing characteristics seen as maternal contributions could be neutralized by being balanced off against other less gender-specific "skills."[25] Assistance by professionals in this regard had also furthered the assault on motherhood, questioning the common understanding of what is desirable for children, what constitutes good parenting, and which parent is better able to provide it.

SOCIAL WORKERS AND DIVORCE

One of the most profound implications of the revised vision of family law has been the move to remove divorce cases from the courts, or at least from direct legal supervision. In the custody area the "natural" alternative to the courts and lawyers has been considered to be social workers or other members of the helping professions. Under traditional legal rules, the helping professions were confined to a supplemental role in the family court system: agency social workers functioned as counselors or custody investigators.[26] With the current changes in traditional custody decision-making ideology, however, social workers are moving from a supplemental role to the role of substitute decision-maker, displacing guardians *ad litem* and, ultimately, replacing judges as the final arbiters of child custody.[27]

Prior to the enactment of no-fault laws, divorce was seen as a legal event accomplished through adversarial procedures—one spouse, the "innocent" party, instituted a civil suit petitioning for divorce and sought to prove grounds on which divorce could be granted. Social workers therefore had a limited role in the divorce process under fault-based divorce systems.

No-fault[28] legislation worked several significant changes in divorce law that greatly expanded the role of the social worker in divorce cases.[29] Liberalized laws dramatically refocused the inquiry away from the question of whether divorce should be allowed to questions about the impact of divorce on the family and society. The mental health professions became more interested in divorce as a psychosocial event—an emotional crisis.[30] As such, social workers argued that divorce should be treated with appropriate therapeutic intervention and should even be turned into a potentially growth-promoting experience.[31]

The removal of fault did not, however, end the controversy between spouses. Conflict between spouses often was simply displaced, with child-custody questions providing one focus. Whereas prior law tended to place children with the party who was not "at fault" for the divorce, the no-fault "irreconcilable differences" determination could not serve as a standard for deciding custody issues.[32] Successful challenges to gender-specific standards like the tender-years presumption further increased uncertainty in the area of child-custody decision making. The best-interest-of-the-child standard without the legal presumption of maternal custody, as well as the emergence of concepts like the "psychological parent,"[33] mandated the involvement of mental health professionals in custody decision making.[34] Current custody reform efforts are in part the product of the mental health profession's success in labeling divorce an emotional crisis, particularly for children.

The intersection of interests and rhetoric that occurred when professional and political actors espoused children's and father's rights, coupled with the movement away from gender-based family laws, have left custody decision making uncertain. While "best interest" historically was understood to mean "mother custody," this association is no longer accepted. The term *best interest,* now without content or meaning, produced a search for new, gender-neutral factors and decision-makers for custody determinations.

Conclusion

Today, the legal situation is such that a man who pursues a custody case has a better than equal chance of gaining custody.[35] Many states have passed, or are considering passing, joint-custody statutes which formally grant fathers equal control over their children, regardless of who provides the day-to-day care and nurturing. What may have started out as a system which, focusing on the child's need for care, gave women a preference solely because they had usually been the child's primary caretaker, is evolving into a system which, by devaluing the content or necessity of such care, gives men more than an equal chance to gain the custody of their children after the divorce if they choose to have it, because biologically equal parents are considered equal in all regards. Nonnurturing factors assume importance which often favor men. For example, men are normally in a financially better position to provide for children without the necessity of child-support transfers or the costs of starting a new job that burden many women.

The power and persuasiveness of the attack on gendered decision-making in the custody area have had a more profound impact than merely making the legislatures' or judges' tasks more difficult. This fetish with gender neutrality has had important implications both for the articulation of what substantively constitutes the best interest of the child and for what safeguards are considered necessary to achieve it. In fact, it seems that the force of the gender-neutral logic has extended beyond attacking explicitly gendered rules to attacking those that operate to produce results which tend to favor one gender over the other. For example, rules that focus on the performance of nurturing or caretaking tasks as the basis for preferencing parents have been attacked, not because they are explicitly gender-biased, but because in operation they will act to favor women, who traditionally perform such tasks. Nurturing as a decisional *value,* even though it is not inherently gendered and is potentially a choice for both men and women, is thus devalued. This expanded version of neutrality favors fathers by labeling as gendered the things women stereotypically tend to do for children, tasks which are grouped under the term *nurture.* The search is not only for language but for *factors* that are gender-neutral. Neutrality in the context of an active and operating gendered system of lived social roles is antimaternal and is hardly gender-neutral in its impact.

This unfortunate and misguided result can be seen in the position of Judith Areen, an influential family-law casebook author, who, in the teacher's manual which accompanies her *Family Law Cases and Materials, Second Edition,* concluded:

> On balance I find the primary caretaker approach [. . .] objectionable because it does not look first to the needs of the children, and because it is at the same time unnecessarily hostile to men because more gender neutral reforms (i.e., economic reforms) could be

adopted to offset inequities in bargaining power. . . . I believe a
more appropriate way to offset financial disadvantage is by direct
modification of statutes governing child support, alimony and
division of property, not by a presumption that is not gender neutral in impact.[36]

Professor Areen thus dismisses caretaking, elevates the concern
for fathers, and naively minimizes the harmful economic consequences
of a divorce system which refuses to acknowledge disadvantages to custodial parents.

In addition, this expanded concept of neutrality operates to set the
stage for increased state control over custody decisions. Experts, from
the legal as well as the helping professions, are considered necessary to
construct and implement new, degendered standards and procedures
under the best-interest test. The rationale for this increased intervention
is, of course, the presence of children. Thus, children are used politically
as the imprimatur for the development of processes and rules which
conceptually alienate children from their parents and place their futures
in the control of state-designated experts. In the case of child advocacy,
many states' legislatures now require separate representation for children when custody is contested, and a few have proposed that such advocacy be provided whenever a divorce involves children, even if there
is *no* contest over custody.

Additionally, any new substantive standard must emerge under the
best-interest rubric. The most popular equality-based custody reform is
joint custody, with various groups stressing the "right" of the child as
well as the egalitarian nature of this custody form. Joint custody is desirable, according to these groups, not only because it is equal and fair,
but because it safeguards children from the "loss" of one parent through
the designation of a sole custodian. The symbolic appeal of these arguments, incorporating equality concepts and a focus on children, made
them a particularly powerful political device for groups advocating an
increased recognition of fathers in custody determinations.

Similarly, the question arising as to who is the best decision-maker in
custody cases has generated uncertainty. The changing rules have weak-
ened the legal profession's monopoly over custody decision making and
have made it easier for social workers to assert increasing power and perhaps eventually to dispossess lawyers. Those in the helping professions
have made inroads into this domain with the cooperation and, in some instances, the encouragement of lawyers and judges who feel inadequate to
determine what is in the best interest of the child in custody cases.[37]

Accepting the difficulty of applying a best-interest test without the now prohibited rules of thumb (which were disputably gender-based) should not mean that the test should be discarded or interpreted out of existence, nor that judges and lawyers should be excluded from the process. The changes that have occurred have political and moral implications that should be subject to more public debate and scrutiny than are possible within the confines of the discourse and practice of the helping professions. Law is a public and a political discourse, and that is one of its major advantages. The question of what should replace it cannot be ignored.

For example, shouldn't it be the cause of some concern that as a result of the assault on the best-interest test, the biological relationship between parent and child is being placed in a superior position to other affiliating circumstances that might be the basis for decision making?[38] The extreme expression of this biologically defined right in the custody area is that of joint custody, where neither parent's rights are viewed as superior, regardless of the source of the nurturing and care that has been provided. When discussing joint custody, some recent commentators have elevated biology to the analytical equivalent of destiny—a tie that provides an absolute right in regard to children.[39]

Consistent with the feminist commitment to gender neutrality, parenthood (like personhood) has become the preferred designation because it encompasses both male and female without the idealized distinctions associated with the terms *father* and *mother*. The desire to have all rules gender-neutral represented an important symbolic component of the battle to demonstrate that there were in fact no relevant differences between the sexes and thus no basis for treating them unequally in law. It was also anticipated by certain feminists that the rise of these egalitarian expectations in language would have concrete effects on the behavior of people in marriage and divorce situations.[40]

Consistent with the goal of gender neutrality, any preference based on motherhood (or gendered in any way) was to be eliminated.[41] This had to be accomplished for important symbolic reasons, no matter how accurately a gendered rule seemed to conform to either intuitive or empirical evidence as to which parent actually was most likely to invest time and effort into child care in a systematic and continuous manner.[42] The well-documented imbalance in caretaking functions (women performing the overwhelming majority of tasks) was not considered appropriate for making a formal distinction in the form of either a custody preference or a presumption.[43]

In fact, the removal of the rules of thumb in custody decision-making has created a crisis.[44] In effect, the ability to decide custody cases in any consistent or efficient manner has been technically removed from judges. The old rules have become labeled as impermissible sexist manifestations of a paternalistic system which should be purged in the interests of equality and justice. But, in fact, these old rules were more than simpleminded sexist manifestations.[45] They also paralleled fairly well the situation that existed in most families with regard to which parent assumed primary care for the children.

S I X

The Individualization of the Family: Child Advocacy

[Children] may have a profound interest in the preservation of the marriage and be substantially and irreparably harmed by the granting of a divorce. Such a right to intervene or status as a necessary party [for children] would not imply that divorce could not be granted where there were children, for in every lawsuit some represented parties lose. It would mean that where the grounds for divorce permit or encourage courts to consider the presence of children in deciding, for example, whether sufficiently "cruel treatment" exists to justify a divorce, that children through their counsel would be permitted to articulate their interests. Public policy does not favor divorce, so there can be no general objection to permitting the entrance of a party who may decrease the probability that it will take place.

A. Kleinfeld*

INTRODUCTION

This chapter analyzes the development of the concept of *child advocacy* in divorce cases. Characterizing children as innocent victims in need of protection is typical of professional reformers' rhetoric in this age of no-fault divorce.[1] Much of the rhetoric supporting the need for independent advocacy calls into question central aspects of legal ideology. Further, there is a strong underlying antidivorce aspect to this rhetoric and the reforms it supports, as demonstrated by the quotation at the beginning of this chapter.[2] Kleinfeld saw child advocates as a divorce deterrent, and his statement is an example of the underlying antidivorce aspect of these reforms.

Child advocacy can have many dimensions and can take different forms. It is part of the larger political and ideological struggle over control of the divorce and postdivorce processes. This chapter considers one aspect of custody decision making that occurs within the context of

*A. Kleinfeld, *The Balance of Power among Infants, Their Parents and the State*, 4 FAM. L.Q. 319, 333 (1970) (footnote omitted).

the advocacy debate, the construction and articulation of a need for independent, legal representation for children in divorce proceedings. Such advocates are frequently called *guardians ad litem* and are usually attorneys required to be part of the process in contested custody cases in many states. In recent years there have been suggestions that legal representation should be mandated for children whenever divorce occurs, whether or not custody is contested.

The institutionalization and professionalization of the concept of child advocacy have operated to facilitate and justify increased state regulation of custody decisions at divorce, a trend that in contemporary divorce practice has given men greater control over their children's and thus their ex-wives' lives.[3] This has occurred because the premise underlying child advocacy is that the child is a separate, independent holder of rights, a potential victim of divorce whose rights must be advocated by someone outside of the family unit. The child's interests are considered as independent from, perhaps even in conflict with, those of his or her parents. More specifically, any gains made through earlier reforms, in which presumptions such as the tender-years doctrine gave legal support to the institution of modern motherhood, have been eroded. The development of the institution of guardian *ad litem* revealed ideological changes in society's perception of the child's place in the family. The conceptual isolation of the child from the family as a unit was further compounded by the rejection of a special mother-child bond, a rejection that occurred as a by-product of the move to gender-neutral family law. Giving definition and content to the child's "best interest" has now become yet another battleground to which the equality war between adults has been extended.

In addition to offering an occasion for defining the meaning of equality as between the divorcing adults, proposals for reforms in the custody area also reflect competing perceptions of large segments of the legal and nonlegal professional communities about the functioning of families and individuals within families, about the implications of divorce, and about the appropriate role of the legal system in the creation and imposition of social norms.[4]

The Advocacy Arguments

Concern for the child's need for legal representation and its implications in custody debates are best understood when considered in the larger context of the rhetoric used to assert the need for child advocacy as a general concept. The control over decisions concerning the custody of children has increasingly been viewed as appropriately removed from parents and placed within the public or political sphere. Such state involvement and control from a legal perspective may occur at the macro level, as in the wholesale imposition of doctrinal norms such as a presumption of joint custody, or at the micro level, as in state control over and confinement of individual custody disputes by mandating the use of mediation or court-controlled experts.

A shift in legal perception concerning the locus of legitimate custody decision-making is evident in the transformed ways in which the issue is discussed and understood. Proponents justify state involvement by referring to an asserted need for independent advocacy for children, who are compellingly characterized as the innocent victims of divorce. This theme is strongly presented in the very influential work of Wallerstein & Kelly:

> Psychologically, an individual's rage against an ex-spouse, often expressed in litigation in which the child is the pawn, can apparently remain undiminished by the passage of time or by distance. The fight for a child may serve profound psychological needs in a parent, including the warding off of severe depression and other forms of pathological disorganization.[5]

Increasingly, the mere presence of children at divorce, whether there is conflict over their custody or not, is viewed as *mandating* state involvement and control of the decision-making process in order to ensure that the decisions made are in the best interest of the child.[6]

Children are viewed as creating the need for state control since they cannot be their own advocates. In fact, children are viewed as separate, individualized focal points to such an extent that state intervention is mandated. Because of their perceived separateness and vulnerability, children now require legal protection against their parents. Thus freed, children, or more accurately, the idealized concept of children, presents not only a problem but an opportunity for intervention by the legal system and the professional actors who cluster around it. Unencumbered by the presumption that mothers, unless unfit, should care for children, or that parents in general protect their children's interests, the perceived need for a child advocate beckons seductively on a policy level.

At the same time, it both symbolically and practically bestows significant influence and power on such advocates within the system. Since under the present conceptualization of children's position at divorce their parents cannot be trusted to act in their interests, advocacy becomes the state's responsibility. Moreover, the child-advocate position is structured in such a way that by definition it is placed beyond criticism. It is understood to be the morally and, therefore, the politically superior position, being the only one which is sanctified as officially advocating for the divorce-victimized child.

Coincidentally, this conceptualization of children's needs in divorce creates fierce competition among groups who publicly assert that they seek the improvement of the position of children within the legal system.[7] Asserting that one's professional (or political) position advances the best interest of the child has become the rhetorical price of entry into the debate over custody policy. One way to describe the politics of custody in the United States in the past several decades is to note that virtually everyone who addresses the issues involved begins by asserting that his or her position is *the* one which incorporates and represents the interests of children. Such assertions mean little. The "best-interest-of-the-child" rhetoric obscures what is in large part a struggle among professional groups, special-interest groups (particularly fathers'-rights advocates), and legal actors who control both the substantive standards as well as the process and practice of child-custody decision making.

The very fact that so many different groups use the same best-interest standard to advocate such different conclusions about what ideal reforms would look like indicates that there are profound problems with the very articulation of the test. What, for example, is the child's interest to be represented? How is it determined? By whom? Using what methods? Most recently, those in the mental health professions have successfully made substantial inroads into legal decision making in this area, becoming accepted as experts in individual cases and as interpreters of social science information on the basis of which to advocate broad legislative standards for custody decisions, such as mandatory joint custody.[8]

The Need for Legal Advocacy

The legal profession initially created and fashioned the ideal of child advocacy. The profession presented child advocacy as the integration of legal and social science skills.[9] The potent idea of a legal advocate for children in divorce actions can be traced back to a series of articles, which constituted a campaign, by judges in the United States who sought to provide protection for children from the adversary model.[10] In part, the creation of the advocacy role was a result of family court personnel's and judges' early recognition that the best-interest test was not functioning well in the traditional adversarial court context.[11]

The creation of something like the child-advocate position was an inevitable product of the general unease generated by the widespread acceptance of no-fault divorce and by the breakdown of the best-interest test, which was considered to be unworkable when the old, gendered rules of thumb, such as maternal preference, were attacked as unacceptable. The emphasis on gender neutrality, which occurred as a result of liberal, legal feminist agitation during the 1960s, called into question the desirability and the legality of the presumption that children belonged with their mothers unless they were unfit. Gendered considerations, at least explicitly stated as a way to make custody decisions, began to fade from favor.

As gender and fault disappeared from the divorce process, however, it became apparent that the best-interest test had worked in large part because these other references served to resolve most cases. Increasingly, degendered and free from fault, the best-interest-of-the-child test was viewed as unworkable by the judges and attorneys who had to employ it.[12] Thus, the search began for other sources to guide decision making. Since custody decision making always takes place within the context of a legal proceeding, it is no wonder that the first step in the evolution of child advocacy was taken in the area of providing independent legal counsel for the child at divorce.

The Creation of the Child-Client

When one takes a serious historical look at the academic literature that underlies the notion of an advocate for children in divorce cases, one is struck by the fact that neither the arguments for nor the arguments against the institution have changed much over the past several decades. Essentially, the assertion is made that children need representation, that they are victimized by divorce, and that the traditional adversary process does not protect them and may even further victimize them. Little conceptual development has occurred beyond this assertion, however. No consensus has emerged about the functions that a child advocate should fulfill or even who should serve as the advocate. Thus, child advocacy is an ideal that continues to be ill defined. Nonetheless, because of the political context of current family law reform, it is an increasingly powerful ideal, even if idiosyncratically implemented in the form of a variety of so-called child-centered reforms which are ineffectively criticized or controlled.

I think it is essential to examine two central assumptions underlying the concept of independent child advocacy. The first assumption is that the child should be considered as separate from the parent. The second is that it is possible to independently define children's interests when these interests are conceptually separated and set apart from those of their parents. The first assumption is the foundation of advocacy in all its forms, but the second has particular significance for the notion of legal representation. I ultimately conclude that the implementation of the institution of an independent child legal advocate as a necessary and desirable goal in the divorce process operates to empower certain professionals, and greatly increases the power of fathers in the process, while doing little to benefit children.

QUESTIONS ABOUT THE CURRENT PARADIGM

There are two critical problems with the idea of child advocacy that I want to explore. The first problem is with the creation and acceptance of the child as an independent client separable from his or her parent and in need of advocacy services at divorce. Even were the need for such advocacy clear, however, there is a second problem concerning the process of articulating and defining the child's best interest. The very fact that the client is also a child raises questions about the feasibility of accomplishing this difficult task.

The Focus of Advocacy

For purposes of this discussion, the significance of the continued use of the best-interest test, post-maternal-preference and post-fault, is found in its theoretical separation of the child from the family. When the maternal preference was viable, the child was conceptually aligned with the mother, and (absent compelling evidence) it was presumed that she acted in her child's interest. The designation of the "innocent" (not at fault) spouse could be viewed as functioning in the same way—as an allocation device. Removing these "easy" indicators necessitated a focus on the child alone, as an independent individual with interests that might differ from those of both of his or her parents. It is this development that clearly created the need for a child advocate distinct from those who represent the parents or family.

The child is now viewed as a free-floating entity and as the focus of the custody proceeding. As in all assertions of "rights" in the United States, with its constitutional tradition, the language used in advancing arguments for child advocacy is symbolically powerful and compelling. This is particularly true because the term *child* is highly sentimentalized in our culture. For example, in an early Family Court "Bill of Rights for Children in Divorce Actions," the first right listed is that of the child "to be treated as an interested and affected person and not as a pawn, possession or chattel of either or both parents." The justification for child advocacy is set forth in the form of a right attached to the child: "the right to recognition that children involved in a divorce are always disadvantaged parties and that the law must take affirmative steps to protect their welfare, including the appointment of a guardian *ad litem* to protect their interests."[13] Note that this Bill of Rights emphasizes children's need for, and right to, protection from their parents. This protection is to be implemented through a legal advocate. It argues that the right of the child to advocacy is one to which the state must respond. Intervention is not only desirable but inevitable. The entire argument is built upon the unquestioned assertion that children are being used as "pawns" or are viewed as "property" by their parents.[14]

Implications of the Paradigm

There are two questions we should ask. The first is whether or not it is accurate or helps discussion of the issues to cast children as victims of divorce. The second question to consider is, Even if children are victimized by divorce, does this necessitate the establishment of separate, independent legal advocacy?

The first question gives rise to additional ones. For example, if it is true that parents during the divorce process are typically so self-absorbed as to use their children as pawns, isn't it appropriate to require child advocates in all divorces where there are children? After all, pawns are not only sacrificed in games that end up in court, but are equally at risk in negotiated or noncontested cases.

Further, and more importantly, if it is true that a large number of parents can comfortably be presumed to have the tendency to sacrifice their children's well-being in this way, isn't the real conclusion we should reach that there are many people out there who are unfit parents, unable to separate out their own needs and act in their children's best interest? Could they ever be trusted to do so? Can a parent who views his or her children as property or treats them as pawns be expected to convert and be nonexploitive with the granting of a divorce decree and a custody award?

The second question about the ability of child advocacy to remedy victimization also raises additional considerations focused on what ideological or political purpose such advocacy actually serves. The typical characterization of the problem places great faith in professionals and assumes that, at best, parents involved in the vast majority of custody cases become temporarily incapable of acting in both their own and their children's interests. I am not sure we should be satisfied by unadorned assertions of wanton parental self-absorption and blatant sacrifice of children's interest, no matter the degree of professional assurance or the force with which such assertions are made.

The net result of the uncritical acceptance of the child-as-victim construct is state-sponsored substitution of informal, nonlegal, professional decision making for that of parents or that of the courts. The significant input into the custody decision-making process is no longer from parents but from professionals, inaccurately designated as "neutral" or "disinterested" and legitimated by the notion that they alone are capable of acting in the best interest of the children. For example, on the role of behavioral scientists in custody disputes, one commentator has stated:

> [A]n analysis of the criteria inherent to the recently enacted [custody] statutes reveal [*sic*] a strong reliance upon factors that can best be evaluated by behavioral science. Among other factors, assessments must be made of the parent's intelligence, morality, knowledge of child development, personality, child-rearing attitudes, emotional ties with the child, and a host of other factors that are of a social and/or psychological nature.
>
> The behavioral scientist has essentially been given a societal mandate for involvement and must be prepared to function appropriately in child custody determinations.[15]

Furthermore, the locus for the decision making is no longer the judge but these same professionals. I am far from convinced that this development benefits children and have serious doubts as to whether it is even desirable. There is a belief among professionals associated with custody disputes that representation is the only way to protect the child(ren) of a divorce: "The most important single safeguard which could be utilized to assure the psychological best interest of the child, in a custody action, would be to provide counsel to represent him."[16]

The acceptance of children as victims, which is evidenced by the rhetoric surrounding discussions of divorce and is manifest in the interpretation of the best-interest test, is the ideological basis upon which the arguments for increased state involvement implemented through extrajudicial actors have been constructed. A battery of experts who are presumed to act in the best interest of children are added to the process. As a result, both the questions and the solutions concerning any individual child are developed *independent of parental decisions or initiative*.

The description and characterization of the problems facing the child, the important judgments which must be made, and the solutions which are suggested are all in the hands of the professionals. The rationale for this is that the divorcing parents can no longer be trusted to act on behalf of their children. Child-advocacy proponents believe that if a child's future cannot be entrusted to his or her parents, then a child advocate is essential. To these proponents, the fact that the parents are enmeshed in an adversarial contest is sufficient to deem them incapable of acting in their children's best interest. They are assumed to be concerned only with their own self-serving ends. As Rosenberg, Kleinman & Brantley stated:

> In addition to the universal and unconscious distortions and misunderstandings of relationships by each individual, in custody evaluations everyone is consciously distorting and misinterpreting. The situation precludes total honesty. Each parent is trying to present him- or herself as the best, the other as the worst, and will often censor or distort information to achieve that goal.[17]

Construction of the Child-Client's "Best Interest"

Related to the observation that the terms of the substantive legal test for custody have created a climate in which we easily accept the necessity of child advocacy is the question of how a child's best interest is to be ascertained. When the child is perceived as separate or independent—a client in need of separate counsel—there must be some way in which to assess what the content or goal of the representation should be. How does the child's advocate in the divorce proceeding determine what is in the child's best interest and act to advocate that interest?

If the advocate is a member of the helping professions, the assumption is that he or she possesses the skills to make the best-interest determination. Normally, however, these professionals are not advocates within the context of particular cases but are viewed as expert, neutral witnesses. Thus, professional assessments are considered evidence to assist in the determination of best interest, yet another actor is necessary to perform the advocacy role in the adversary context—to represent the child. In most instances this advocate is a lawyer.

The presence of an attorney as the child advocate creates problems that transcend (while they also complicate) those associated with the involvement of mental health professionals who perform custody evaluations. This is particularly true because of role confusion between these professions,[18] coupled with uncertainty as to who and what is represented.

The Function of the Legal Advocate

Even if one accepts the idea of a need for independent child advocacy, a critical problem is connected to the perceived need for legal representation, or an adversarial "champion."[19] Once we establish a need, we must consider the problem of the appropriate function of the independent child's advocate.[20] This creates a dilemma because the role of the advocate is dependent upon the acceptance of and belief in the characterization or creation of the child-client as the potential victim of his or her parents. If this is a true characterization, then the parents cannot be trusted to provide objective or neutral information about the child and his or her interests. All information from them is suspect. The parents going through a divorce are portrayed as using their child(ren) for purely instrumental reasons in the divorce proceedings:

> It is tempting to believe that in a case where two parents are contesting the right to custody of a child, each one is arguing for the child's best interests as he or she perceives them. Unfortunately, the motivations behind the custody demands of the parents are often ambivalent. Mothers may seek custody of children though antipathetic to them, in order to exert influence over their former spouses who seek visitation arrangements. Fathers may seek custody as a bargaining tool to lower the mother's child support and alimony demands, or may fail to seek custody, despite their fitness, because of the realization that mothers obtain custody in most cases. Finally, many parents seek custody as a vindication of their innocence in the break-up rather than to provide the best home for the child.[21]

Thus, ascertaining the child's interests involves the advocate in constructing the child's best interest—that which is to be represented or advocated in the divorce proceeding. The significant question is, How is this interest created independently of parental input?

Since the modern conceptualization of the process has already eliminated parents as sources of this best-interest determination, and the desire for gender neutrality has made social and informal empirical observations about mothers and nurturing suspect, we are left with three potential sources of determination. First, and easiest to dispose of quickly, is the suggestion that we look to the child to ascertain what solution should be advocated. The legal advocate could ask the child which parent he or she prefers and then simply advocate whatever result the child indicates. This is roughly how an attorney would act in representing a competent adult client. However, many children are unable, or unwilling, to express a preference between competing potential custodial parents. Further, some research indicates that it may even be harmful for older, competent children to choose between parents at divorce. Thus, the children's-choice approach is not considered a viable option, at least for children under the age of fourteen or fifteen.[22]

The vast majority of legal child advocates do not adhere to such a narrow view of their responsibility. They do not conceptualize the role of the child advocate as that of an advocate for the child *per se* but as that of an advocate for the child's best interest. This is a distinction of considerable importance. Instead of merely representing the child's preference, such an approach demands that the child's legal advocate undertake the task of assessing or evaluating what is in the child's best interest independently of, though it may consider them, the child's wishes as to his or her custody.

The Advocate and Ascertaining Best Interest

How, then, can the legal advocate make an evaluation of what is in a child's best interest? In practical terms, the requirement of independent advocacy means that there are two nonparental contenders for the role of primary determiner of the best interest of the child at divorce. There is a need not only for the advocacy but also for the construction or creation of what is urged as being in the child's interest. The societal signals which would indicate that in most instances this would lead to a maternal preference are to be excluded by the demands of gender neutrality. Structurally, we are thus presented with a choice between two types of professionals who hover around the divorce process: the legal advocate on the one hand and the helping professional on the other.

The legal professional may make the decision, acting first both as an investigator and collector of information, and thereafter as an informed expert who has examined the evidence and reached a conclusion as to what is in the best interest of the child. This choice creates the necessity for the legal advocate to investigate, to collect information from both experts and nonexperts about the child and family, and to make a judgment about what should be the appropriate placement.[23] Thus, the legal advocate acts as an investigator and as an expert within the legal process; in this regard, the role of advocate is one with substantive dimension.

In these circumstances, not only has a client been created for the legal advocate, but the characteristics of that client necessitate that one primary function of the legal advocate is to construct the client's interest in a manner which, to a large extent, is independent of the client's direction. In this instance, where the legal advocate is making an independent assessment of the quality of evidence accumulated, he or she is no better equipped than a judge to make such an assessment and would seem, for that reason alone, to be unnecessary to the process.

In other circumstances, the legal advocate's role may be more limited, and the various mental health professionals who have increasingly become more significant in the divorce context will explicitly serve as the arbiters of the child's best interest. In this process, the legal advocate often acts as nothing more than the advocate of the expert helping professional's opinion as to what is in the child's best interest. Thus, in effect, the mental health professional becomes the substituted client, one who speaks for the constructed child-client, and is the vehicle through which the child's best interest is realized.

As is detailed in the subsequent chapters, experts' conclusions in this area have increasingly centered on imposing the ideal of shared parenting after divorce. In a gender-neutral world seen to require the devaluation of nurturing, these experts have undertaken the task of bringing fathers back into the postdivorce picture. This has resulted in the creation of professional norms which give custody to the "most generous parent," or the parent most willing to share the child with the other parent.[24] A desire for sole custody has been labeled "pathological"[25] and is to be discouraged or punished by legal rules which mandate postdivorce cooperation and sharing. The child advocate is part of a larger process whereby professional norms such as these are incorporated and made operative within the context of the legal system, with the child advocate representing the professional ideal.

Function of the Independent Advocate in Practical Terms

There is an important additional problem with the concept of a legal advocate as a child's independent advocate. It is not clear why one needs a legal advocate to interpret and assess expert and other information and reach a conclusion as to the best interest. Isn't this what a judge would do? What does an attorney for the child add in this process? Historically, considerably fewer critics than fans of advocates for children have existed; however, one early critic noted the following regrading the issue of the worth of a legal advocate:

> The present use of guardians or attorneys ad litem often fails to
> prevent decisions unfair to the persons they represent, and conse-
> quently their use debases the quality of the bar. When an attorney

is paid for doing nothing, he is perpetrating a fraud on someone. . . .
Encouraging new young lawyers to take money under false pretenses
by the perpetuation of the present guardian ad litem practice certainly
does nothing to advance high ethical standards in the bar. . . . Lawyers should not be permitted to benefit from a system which jeopar-
dizes the rights of the weaker members of society.[26]

In some instances, perhaps, some witnesses not called by a parent
might be produced, or an expert employed who was not consulted by
either parent nor scheduled by court personnel. One wonders how often such a positive contribution by the legal advocate occurs, however,
and whether the information placed before the judge in such cases is
typically dispositive or merely cumulative.

Furthermore, there are real dangers with accepting the child advocacy model. When the legal advocate represents the helping professional's opinion as to the child's best interest, the presence of an attorney
designated as the child's advocate may give added undue weight to professional advice that should be only one factor in fashioning a judge's
opinion. This may result in the social worker or psychologist function-
ally being the ultimate custody decision-maker when the child's attorney uses the helping professional's recommendations to establish what
is in the child's best interest.

A primary issue in the current construction of the various roles in
custody decision making should be a consideration of whether the legal
advocate can be independent of the mental health professional. A powerful combination emerges when social worker and child's attorney
agree, for whatever reason. In addition, the judge's role may be compromised, since the presence of the child's legal advocate may provide
the judge with an easy way out through reliance on an additional refer-
ent, another "neutral" actor who is cast as representing only the child's
interest, allowing the illusion that his or her conclusions can be safely
trusted. Furthermore, the legal advocate, as the advocate of best interest, will inevitably be in the position of merely parroting idealized notions of what is in all children's best interest according to the current
theories of mental health professionals.

POLITICAL IMPLICATIONS OF THE ACCEPTANCE OF THE IDEA
OF CHILD ADVOCACY

As stated earlier, the crux of the problem is that the evolving best-
interest standard without its historic referents is so amorphous, undi-
rected, incomprehensible, and indeterminate as to be meaningless with-

out a substantial "extra-judicial implementation team." The only response to a degendered, no-fault divorce system, short of scrapping the best-interest-of-the-child test, is the creation of alternative decision-makers and the referral of all substantive decisions to them. There are problems with this no matter which professional is the source of the best-interest determination. However, as discussed earlier, the problems for a legal advocate are extreme.

The legal advocate functions to give the illusion of neutrality to the decision-making process. This illusion allows the system to limp along without serious reassessment of the political and practical roles played by mental health professionals and others who seek to define the best interest of children through processes and standards which enhance the position and power of their own professions. Custody decision making and the rules that govern it involve more than just making individual decisions regarding placement of children. Submerged in the rules and processes are political and ideological conflicts between "mothers" (or nurturing and caretaking values) and "fathers" (or independence and financial security values); between the legal profession (or advocacy and adversariness as values) and the helping professions (or treatment and therapy as values); between the moralists (who would burden the divorce system so as to impede or discourage divorce and to punish those who seek to divorce) and the secularists (who would seek to implement rules that ensured no one lost too much in deciding to leave a marriage). The illusion and pretense of objectivity and neutrality, of which the legal advocate is but one part, serve the interests of those empowered by the status quo and the bias in professional opinion-making.

SEVEN

The Use of the Social Sciences in Custody Policy-Making

> Women have no attributes that so especially suit them for childrearing that they merit a preference in custody disputes simply because of their gender.
>
> D. Chambers*

INTRODUCTION

In this chapter, I consider the process of reforming the custody policy that has occurred in the past decade, in which the appropriateness of certain longstanding legal rules for making custody determinations was challenged, and new factors based on social science insights were suggested to legal policymakers. I am not concerned with the uses of social science information in individual cases, though I realize that this aspect of custody decision making is also affected by shifting professional discourses, since the testimony of expert witnesses in cases reflects the broader professional judgments of their disciplines.[1] I am concerned, however, with the initial step in the process of incorporating social science information into legal decision-making, a step that precedes the acceptance of expert testimony in an individual case. This step is the acceptance or recognition by policymakers of a shift or change in the recognized professional "norm." Such shifts eventually may lead to the abandonment of an old ideal and the creation of a new one in professional literature and rhetoric. In an era and an area where social science information is considered highly relevant, if not essential to law reform efforts, such a change in professional paradigms is likely to be conveyed and incorporated into the legal discourse and policy-making.

In the area of custody, changes in legal policy seem to have been derived from the changing cultural and professional images of what constitutes a "good mother" and/or a "good father." The emerging legal rules in this area are therefore, to a great extent, the result of a complex

---

*D. Chambers, *Rethinking the Substantive Rules for Custody Disputes in Divorce,* 83 MICH. L. REV. 477, 527 (1984).

process whereby the cultural and professional discourses concerning custody converged and merged in the creation of a new, legally recognized ideal of parenthood after divorce. There was enough integration of these two areas that the identification of the appropriate legal rules to govern the award of rights and the assignment of obligations connected with postdivorce parenthood seemed "naturally" to flow from the new images that had been created and accepted. In this process of creating a new image or ideal, a crucial step was the absorption of social science and professional discourses into the policy recommendations of legal experts working in the area of children's issues, particularly custody. Therefore, it is important to understand how law professors and other legal-policy proponents translate, summarize and use social science literature, not as expert witnesses espousing custody rule-making and policy, but as rule-makers.[2]

Although the process through which social science data are absorbed and transformed into legal policy arguments is only one example of how laws might be changed, it is my belief that, in our modern legal culture, this is a particularly important method and one that has not been adequately criticized. It is my assertion that much of social science literature, which is designated as objective, neutral, and scientific, may in fact be inherently political and/or ideological, though this is shielded and obscured by the scientific mantle in which it is wrapped.[3]

Rules governing custody awards at divorce based on social science data are typically framed in broad terms and are often designed to limit the discretion of judges, or at least to guide that discretion, so that legislatively designated factors are determinative in the bulk of individual custody decisions. While there may be some positive aspects of this trend toward using such data in the formulation of broad policy rules, the integration of law and social science may create problems. The social science data are susceptible to misuse in a variety of ways. For example, legal policymakers who are unfamiliar with social science material may use it to make generalizations based on small, select, and unrepresentative samples, or undue weight may be given to limited research findings. In addition, legal authors may be unable (or unwilling) to acknowledge methodological problems in the social science studies upon which their legal policy arguments are built.

Some legal policymakers have turned to social science research on children of divorce in efforts to fill the void created by the removal of rules which preferred mothers over fathers. In the gender-neutral confines dictated by the concern for implementing equality, social science research is seen as providing an objective basis for the formulation of specific general rules and/or factors which embody a new ideal for individualized determinations in custody cases.

The newly created ideal of egalitarian marriage is far from reality for many (if not most) divorcing parents, however. Typically, child care is a burden unequally distributed during the course of marriage. Criticism of this gap between ideal and real presentations of child-care patterns is blunted by reference to social science research which, for the most part, has been consistent with a shift in custody rules that would give nonprimary (secondary, usually male) parents more postdivorce control over their children.[4]

While I do not condemn the use of social science information in general, it seems important to be aware that there are major ideological divisions within our society as to what should constitute the legal rights associated with the labels *mother* or *father* after divorce, positions that have important political ramifications. Such beliefs may influence the ways in which the studies are used by lawyers and policymakers.[5]

PROFESSIONAL ASSISTANCE: THE ATTACK ON THE MATERNAL-CUSTODY NORM

Attempts to redefine the best-interest test using social science data so as to rehabilitate it for use in a world free of gender bias should generate concern. Such attempts have prompted a search for "objective" information to rely on in making distinctions which are necessary if one is to choose between parents. Some legal policymakers turn to the social sciences because they are uncomfortable with what their intuition tells them—that it is mothers who care for children in this society. These policymakers may not accept this conclusion and the implications it would have. Acceptance of such a conclusion would lead to rules which would be incompatible with their goal of eliminating gender-specific rules (and the "larger" goal of freeing women from social stereotypes associated with their biology). They may believe it is possible to establish idealized rules that would actually foster more participation by fathers, both in and out of marriage, in the upbringing and care of their children.

Within the context of changing custody policy, one of two notions is articulated. The first assumes that gender-neutral rules simply mirror reality in that there are no differences between mothers and fathers in their ability to parent. Under this view, proposed changes in custody policy that recognize fathers as equally competent parents are the reflection or legal recognition of changed sex roles. The premise is that they merely elevate father to the status of mother's equal, since her position was previously held superior while his was unacknowledged.[6]

Some may mistrust unscientifically collected historical facts and be seeking some objective indication that social engineering through law is possible. This view assumes that gender-neutral rules are necessary to promote the symbolic ideal of equality between the sexes. Encouraging men to assume more responsibility for home- and child-care tasks fosters various instrumental concerns: most globally, the potential for women to increase their market participation, thus decreasing their economic dependence on men; and, within the context of divorce, relief for the "overburdened" custodial mother, as well as an increased financial commitment by fathers to payment of child-support obligations, owing to the stronger parent/child emotional bond.[7]

Social science is seen as a panacea by many legal policymakers, as the source of neutral rules which will lead to an objective and fair norm or set of norms to facilitate custody decision making. Less laudable, however, are those who would use (or misuse) social science data in an effort to further their single-minded goal of bettering the position of fathers in custody cases. From their perspective, the resilience of the maternal-custody norm has been a major problem in custody decision making. Enactment of gender-neutral rules has not appreciably altered behavior—mothers continue to obtain custody. While I assert that this is a proper result, supported by the real-life choices and preferences of a vast number of people, others are unhappy with the tenacity of this pattern. For them, many of them are either joint- or paternal-custody proponents, social science data can serve as an important tool to erode and negate the maternal-custody preference through the documentation that it is no better than, and perhaps inferior to, paternal custody. Social science literature provides a necessary component of their rhetoric. It gives them the language and ideas to promote their attack on maternal custody and to "neutralize" its holding power on the judiciary.

The use of social science literature in the area of custody has shifted the parameters of the legal debate. Within this context, social science data may be used to aid in the consideration of new rules, or it may be misused. Scholarly legal writing that does not overtly and clearly express an understanding of the problems with the use of such literature does little more than provide a facade of neutrality. Much of the legal writing in this area has been consistent with ideologically and politically compelled attacks on the maternal-custody norm without being critical of the social science methods that support such attacks, and/or without being self-critical or revealing the legal policymaker's own bias.

USES AND MISUSES OF SOCIAL SCIENCE DATA IN CUSTODY POLICY
Bias in the Production of Social Science Literature

Legal policymakers should be particularly careful in using social science data. Social science data is not a substitute for (though it may be a supplement to) traditional legal and political methods of ascertaining the appropriateness of legal rules. Even if one is trained in sociology, psychology, political science, or some other discipline, it is easy to overlook some important studies unless one has diligently kept up with the literature. In addition, secondary use of the results of social science studies is a process full of pitfalls. Some legal authors who use social science data present them as though they reflect and represent a coherent world of rationality, of truths and of values. Further, they may uncritically accept research findings as having universal validity.[8]

Beyond these preliminary concerns is the controversy among social scientists and philosophers of science about empirical or positivist research.[9] This debate has significance for those legal theorists who would too readily use social science data as "facts" to bolster their legal policy statements. Lawyers and policymakers, of course, understand the importance of the establishment of "facts" to justify and support legal results. Too often, however, social science conclusions may be used to encourage the formulation of legal rules without careful and critical examination.[10] The social science data may be substituted for a critical inquiry into the assumptions and policy choices underlying a proposed rule change. The legal policymaker utilizing social science information may misuse it or use it to urge results with which the policymaker is ideologically comfortable, even though other plausible interpretations may be derived from the data. In addition, if the social scientist's own inherent biases are undisclosed in his or her research, any legal-policy conclusions based on such research should be critically questioned.

While the scope of this chapter does not permit a detailed discussion of the various schools of criticism of social science methodology, I hope to provide a few of the ideas which are central to each in regard to the issue of the role of values or normative assessments in social science research.[11]

The Problems

The use of social science data in legal policy-making should be viewed as potentially problematic because too often the conclusions of the social science researcher are viewed as neutral facts, divorced from the researcher's own bias. Critics of social science or positivist research claim that it has been invoked to reinforce dominant, but problematic, beliefs, as well as used to maintain the ideology of the status quo.

Modern criticism has noted the phase of inevitable bias that enters into all positivist methodology. Bias enters into the selection of the issue to be examined, the questions asked in the examination, and the compilation of the data. In addition, the critics caution us to remember that it is always possible to question the meaning of even "neutrally" established facts. Of course, lawyers are well aware that interpretation plays a major part in the conclusions drawn from the observed facts in law. This is no less true in the social sciences. As Russell has stated:

> One of the major issues with any form of research is the many different ways in which a researcher's own beliefs and values can intrude into the research process at the level of types of questions posed, and the method of interpretation of findings. It is impossible to achieve complete objectivity and it should perhaps be mandatory that people state their biases so that others may better interpret and understand their work.[12]

It is important to note that a very different definition of objectivity is being developed here. It recognizes the impossibility of the complete removal of self and therefore is an attempt to take into account the extent to which one intrudes into one's own work. Piaget offers a valuable definition:

> Objectivity consists in so fully realizing the countless intrusions of the self in every day thought and the countless illusions which result. . . . Pseudo Objectivity . . . consists in ignoring the existence of self and thence regarding one's own perspective as immediately objective and absolute.[13]

This definition means that objectivity and knowledge come to be closely linked with the researcher's own subjectivity, and it underscores the importance of the acknowledgment of what feminists have called *the personal* in one's work. This in turn implies an open recognition of why some piece of research that one has chosen to do is meaningful.[14]

Modern critics of positivism may be comfortable with the understanding that the researcher's view of the world will influence his or her methodology and conclusions, but many people are not.[15] Inherent in the elevation of positivism to the position of providing answers is a belief that values have not interfered with the framing of the questions or the presentation of the answers and that facts are discoverable, knowable, and dispositive.[16]

Modern Criticisms of Social Science

The criticism of positivist methodology comes from different directions and is varied and complex in content and form.[17] There is, however, a common theme running through these criticisms: the recognition that values are centrally and inescapably linked to the many choices that social science researchers make in designing and implementing a research task. This is viewed as true both in terms of the selection of specific facts from what must seem an infinite number to be examined and in the drawing of inferences based on those facts once they are found.[18] Feminism, phenomenology, critical theory, and linguistic theory all tackle the positivist's basic assertion that the social sciences are sciences with testable hypotheses and theories framed and assessed in a value-free manner.[19]

Some critics, for example, have begun to examine traditional social science methodology from a perspective which incorporates feminist insights and theory. They have indicated that mainstream social science, defined by such goals and/or constraints as "rationality" or "objectivity"— which they label as *male*[20] norms—impoverishes reality. This, they would argue, may result in the failure of social science literature to take account of important factors that do not and cannot fit within a rational or objective framework. If such factors were considered, they might suggest alternative explanations to the interpretation the social scientist has offered.

The elevation of rationality as a primary virtue can result in the construction of a model that depicts only a small segment of the "real world."[21] Some feminists have labeled as "male" the perceived desire to impose order in social scientists' attempt to impose a map over previously uncharted areas. This attempt is destined to be insufficient to describe the terrain in its entirety and is dangerous because those who use the resulting data are frequently unfamiliar with the process and take the partial explanation as the whole.[22]

Many feminists also believe that the scientific assumptions of rationality and quantification often deny the qualitative nature of experience. A range of experiences with different dimensions and qualities from those that are given primacy in traditional social science work may simply be ignored because they are not susceptible to quantification. If one gives legitimacy to only one form of data, it will create the illusion that there is a single reality and a single mode of looking at the world. This position, intensified by the privileging of quantitative over qualitative data within the social sciences, is one which seems untenable in experiential terms.[23] However, admitting qualitative data as a valid form of experience would generate a responsibility to come to terms with different ways of seeing the world and would create the need for constant negotiations between people with different realities as to how their different worlds are to be managed. In this regard, one can understand why policymakers who must choose an answer to a defined problem, according to means that can easily be administered through existing institutions, would find the simpler quantitative approach attractive.

Other feminist writings have stressed what is seen as male value of control, and the prevalence of this value both in society and in the profession. Perhaps science and professionalism enhance the illusion of control.[24] To regard knowledge as scientific is to make certain assumptions about an orderly, objective world, separate from the observer, which can be known through rational inquiry and a process of quantification that allows control. Benston asserts, as do others, that the goal of scientific knowledge is to control and predict.[25]

Against the backdrop of such criticisms, feminist researchers have attempted to define an alternative to traditional social science methodology. Feminist critics have asserted that research should be seen as a *collaborative* endeavor between interviewer and respondent in order to increase the internal validity of the research. The concept of collaborative research creates a very different relationship between researcher and researched from that normally associated with social science studies. It implies a mutuality of interest in the shaping, as well as the conclusions, of the study, and uses an interactive rather than hierarchical relationship in realizing the endeavor. The researcher does not rely simply on her own interpretation of what questions are valid and what answers are valuable, but is constantly engaged in checking and modifying her perspective as a shared process with her respondents.[26] Any researcher who has had to struggle with the implication of a colleague's question as to what hypothesis her research is designed to test, before she even is aware of what questions are significant to her respondent, can appreciate the significance of this type of difference in methodology.

In short, feminist theory, like the other theories critical of positivism, reminds us never to forget the value questions.[27] Critical theorists have argued that positivism tends to transform what Habermas calls *real* issues into *technical* or *professional* questions.[28] As things become classified as technical, they become susceptible to control. This control enables social scientists to focus on means/ends, or relationships among variables, and not on the moral and social consequences of the acts involved. The technical focus of positivist social science, therefore, obscures the production of meaning and value.[29]

Acceptance of social science conclusions by those not sophisticated enough to realize that the methodology cannot control all variables (or even isolate them successfully) can lead to the adoption of solutions that deny the complex and systematic interweaving of relationships. There must be some realization of the extent to which the personal awareness and motivation of the social scientist act to shape knowledge, both on an individual level and through its expression in social institutions. The point is that the data are never totally separated from the political, personal, and professional opinions of the person manipulating them. As one observer notes regarding the difficulty feminist authors have in getting their work into print in professions which are largely male-dominated, "What gets published can influence those who read *and* those who write; . . . there can be little question that the 'literature' is instrumental in establishing the issues in a discipline. It constitutes the parameters in which discussion occurs and defines the terms of the debate."[30] This observation is further complicated by the realization that the professions that produce the data are themselves, inevitably, reflections of bias.

As should be evident from this brief account of the critical literature, the self-criticism within the social science community should make attorneys and legal policymakers wary of accepting as facts the products of social science which may be essentially normative and value-laden.[31] The uncritical acceptance of the conclusions of social science may give such values a false legitimacy because they come packaged within the context of empirical observations.

Other Criticisms

On a more mundane level, the use of social science literature also may be inappropriate because it contains methodological flaws. A social scientist's conclusions or observations, for example, may be based on information that is the product of a one-interview research design, as contrasted with observations based on repeated interviews. Questionnaires are thought to be less reliable than person-to-person interviews. Information that is gathered by self-reports also may not be as reliable as information secured by other means.

Finally, it is often difficult to design and implement an adequate study with positivistic methodology. This may be particularly true in the custody area. Children are exposed to a multitude of variables during their formative years. Control by the experimenter is impossible, separation of parental and external influences infeasible, and agreement on measures of "success" unlikely.[32]

These problems are methodological in nature, though they focus on the shortcomings of the social science data itself and not on its misuses by legal commentators. Use by legal commentators adds another dimension to the problem—one that requires close examination.

CONTEMPORARY DEBATE OVER THE SUBSTANTIVE RULES FOR CUSTODY DISPUTES IN DIVORCE
Social Science Origins of the Attacks on Maternal Custody

It is possible to explain the current debate over the appropriateness of custody rules as a backlash to the perceived gains that women have made in some of the economic areas of divorce policy. It is also possible to view this debate as a spinoff of another debate among social workers and psychologists over whose professional opinions are to dominate in regard to the needs of children. Either of these approaches to the topic of the shifting norms in the custody area would provide for a different, more critical assessment of the social science literature than that which has recently been produced concerning comparisons of maternal and paternal custody and parenting skills. My approach, prompted by a refusal to accept at the onset that there is a problem, legal or social, with the fact that mothers continue to receive custody of their children in large numbers, generates a very different perspective on the studies from what is common in contemporary legal discourse.

One common problem with the use of social science data in the area of custody policy is the tendency to generalize limited data in unqualified terms to the wider population. The reinterpretation of one very widely used book, *Surviving the Breakup*, by Wallerstein and Kelly, provides an example.[33] This study explores the effect of divorce on children and the problems facing women in separation and divorce. As one of the first empirical and longitudinal studies on the effects of divorce and custody arrangements, this work has been influential and is used to support a range of suggestions for reform.

The findings of Wallerstein and Kelly have been interpreted by some commentators to cast considerable doubt on the coping capacities of women with regard to their children in the postdivorce setting. Some authors, for example, focus on the difficulties that women experience in the early stages of separation, indicating that the qualities which mothers reported they had lost were those that "many writers might associate with primary caretaking mothers and that might incline us to prefer placement with them."[34] The reported economic and emotional problems of the mothers that Wallerstein and Kelly noted have also become, in the hands of such legal policymakers, an argument for paternal involvement and for joint custody.[35] Indeed, such an argument can provide the basis for policies that prefer fathers over mothers as the more stable parents in sole custody cases. Careful examination, however, shows that, far from presenting a generalized statement that women's adjustment problems are the cause of distress to their children, Wallerstein and Kelly conclude that a wide range of factors affects any given situation.

If one looks at their work and only alludes to the difficulties women experience in the early stages of separation, one might conclude that mothers are not emotionally capable of maintaining relationships with their children after divorce. In reality, however, Wallerstein and Kelly emphasize that the passage of time is a critical factor in evaluating the way that any one family is coping. They also indicate that, by the end of the first year after the separation, a substantial number of mothers who initially had some adjustment problems were able to reestablish their ability to parent at the level of the predivorce family.[36]

A careful reading of the results also reveals that the authors found that half of the children studied experienced no deterioration in parenting in the immediate postseparation phase.[37] The profile of the average mother at the eighteen-month follow-up showed a person who, though moderately depressed, had nonetheless increased her sense of well-being and general happiness more so than had her male counterpart, and who had achieved a new level of competence.[38] Perhaps the conclusion to be drawn is that divorce and sole custody are good for women.

Compounding the Problem: Policy Uses of Social Science

Some legal authors have used Wallerstein's and Kelly's work to support the proposition that nearly all children experience severe emotional distress and grieve for their absent fathers after divorce.[39] The difficulty with this sort of generalization is that it implies that there is but a single dimension of emotional distress. Wallerstein and Kelly have noted several factors that complicate this rather simple conclusion. For example, they find that the intensity of distress was unrelated to the quality of the children's relationships to their fathers. Children who had been severely abused and/or rejected as well as those who had had a consistently warm relationship with their fathers evidenced distress. This finding, of course, could be used to support the conclusion that children do not specifically mourn the loss of their fathers (as well as the typical interpretation that they do). The clear implication is that children experience a loss, and that grief is associated with a range of factors. The intensity of distress suffered by younger girls, for example, appeared to be associated with the fear of double rejection if they were then left alone in the care of an emotionally impoverished mother. In older children the loss was not reported to be related to the quality of parental relationship: "the youngsters' distress was related to their disapproval of the divorce and to the amount of distress they were experiencing about the dissolution of the family."[40]

Against the black-and-white picture of maternal inadequacy and child distress that is often painted by those who simplify their study findings, one should consider the following quotation written by Wallerstein and Kelly to describe the effects of divorce on the children they studied at the five-year follow-up. The authors found that the outcome for these children depended on the following:

> (1) the extent to which the parents had been able to resolve and
> put aside their conflicts and angers to make use of the relief from
> the conflict [of] divorce; (2) the course of the custodial parent's
> handling of the child and the resumption or improvement of
> parenting within the home; (3) the extent to which the child did
> not feel rejected in relationship with the non-custodial . . . parent,
> and the extent to which this relationship . . . kept pace with the
> child's growth; (4) the range of personality assets and deficits
> which the child had brought to the divorce, including the child's
> history within the pre-divorce family and the capacity to make use
> of his or her resources within the present, particularly intelligence,
> and capacity for fantasy, social maturity, and ability to turn to
> peers and adults; (5) the availability to the child of a supportive
> human network; (6) the absence of continuing anger and depression in the child; and (7) the age and sex of the child.[41]

Lest these qualities be considered by the reader as absolutes and given unqualified and concrete values, the study further points out that the children who did well, while they had these qualities, had them in different combinations. In addition, it is indicated that children from the same family followed different paths for reasons that were not always clear and that "the combinations that led to deterioration were not simply the reverse of those that promoted progress."[42]

An important but often ignored aspect of the study indicates that regular contact with the noncustodial parent did not always ensure good psychological health; nor was parental well-being always reflected in the child.[43] All this suggests a much more qualified and complex picture than the one often presented by legal authors who use the Wallerstein and Kelly research. The problems of generalizing from this data are enormous, and further research is only likely to add to rather than reduce the complexity—making the elaboration of clear custody rules based on such research unlikely.

Finally, it is important to note that Wallerstein and Kelly studied children from a clinical population. Even so, the problems experienced by these children were diminishing over time, and most of the adolescents had done well or were doing better after the divorce. It may well be that there has been a consistent overestimation of the distress suffered by children at divorce because recounts of the study have tended to focus on children who were having difficulties.[44]

The difficulties noted above with use of the Wallerstein and Kelly study are hard to avoid. The tendency is to make generalizations and leave out the qualifications noted in the studies themselves. Any text that lists such qualifications soon becomes too complex and ambiguous. The qualifications do exist, however, and should not be ignored. They are important and essential information when considering changes in legal policy. Qualifications can assist policymakers in evaluating the conclusions and interpretations of the author who has used social science data.

Political Uses of Social Science

The political and policy implications of social science research are often explicitly recognized by researchers. For example, a follow-up of the families studied in *Surviving the Breakup* ten years after divorce is reported by J. Wallerstein and S. Blakeslee in *Second Chances: Men, Women, and Children a Decade after Divorce* (1989). Not surprisingly, Wallerstein concludes that divorce can and often does have a profound and lasting impact on family members, including a profoundly negative economic impact on women and children.[45] For example, in her study of middle-class couples, one in four families experienced "a severe and enduring drop in their standard of living and went on to observe a major, lasting discrepancy between economic conditions in their mothers' and fathers' homes": few children were helped by their fathers with the costs of college despite the financial resources to do so and in spite of the fact that mandated inclusion of a divorced father's income to calculate student need disqualified many children for scholarships; and, few mothers and children enjoyed a postdivorce living standard that approximated that of the fathers.[46]

The real insight contained in Wallerstein's most recent book, however, is captured in the following vignette:

> Since 1980, when I founded the Center for the Family in Transition, and in addition to my regular work, I get at least two, sometimes three, telephone calls on an average day from people asking for help in the midst of divorce. Mostly these are strangers who have read my name in a newspaper or heard of my work from a friend. Many of the calls are from parents. Just the other day a man called from Pennsylvania and said, "I'm a teacher. My wife is suing me for divorce." His voice was strained. "I understand you have written about the importance of fathers, how much their children need to still see them. Can you direct me? Can you send me something to help?"
>
> On the same day I got a call from a woman in southern California who told me that the court had ordered her to send her nursing infant to spend every other weekend with the child's father, who lives several hundred miles away. The woman, who must express and freeze extra breast milk to send along with the baby, told me that she was never married to the baby's father, only lived with him briefly, and has no idea what kind of parent he is. She asked, "What should I do?"
>
> Shocked by her story—reflecting an intrusion into the most intimate of human relationships, that between a nursing mother and her child—I could say only that there is no psychological research anywhere to support the court's decision but that I knew of no immediate way that I could help. We are staying in touch.[47]

I cannot help but be surprised that Wallerstein is "shocked," as her research can be and often is used to justify a variety of legal positions within individual case litigation and, more broadly, to support new, increasingly intrusive and regulatory policies concerning divorced families. Despite caveats about the infancy of research in this area, as Wallerstein continues to note in her various works, legal policy relating to contemporary divorced families is debated daily in states across the country with new rules emerging that will be applied in all divorces occurring with a jurisdiction.

Even more unsettling than the problems with the use of any individual item of social science research is the way policy concerns are jumbled together in cause-and-effect presentations. Consider, for example, speculation based on the emotional needs of children as it might be shaped in conjunction with other insights we have discovered about parental behavior before and after divorce. For example, much has been written about the problems associated with collecting child support even though men generally hold a higher economic status than women. In addition, it has been noted that after divorce the frequency of fathers' visitations with their children tends to decline. Thus, many children are abandoned both financially and emotionally by their fathers after divorce. Add to these factors the finding that noncustodial mothers are much more likely than noncustodial fathers to maintain ties with their children through consistent visitation, and mix with the recommendations that each parent's emotional investment in his or her children be considered "equal," and what may emerge is a policy in favor of awarding custody to fathers. Such awards, the argument would go, would solve problems associated with child-support collection. Since fathers have greater financial resources, and since both parents have "different" but "equal" emotional investments in their children, neither will suffer more than the other from not having custody. Similarly, given that women tend to maintain greater visitation frequency, there will be fewer overall losers if fathers are given custody, since children will benefit from a continued relationship with both parents. Thus, what initially might appear to be the basis for a pro-mother custody stance (because women are presumed to be more emotionally involved with their children after divorce, regardless of the custody form, than men) is easily reduced to a pro-father custody argument.

The point is that the information used by legal policymakers and the very rules they propose are given ideologized and political content in the reform process. This is obscured because proposals seem based on neutral social science observations and are presented in a manner that assumes only one conclusion is appropriate. Hidden assumptions are not revealed, such as the conclusion that financial support is as significant as (or more significant than) emotional involvement and sacrifice, which was the underlying basis for the pro-father custody interpretation just offered.

Significant assumptions are often hidden or ignored. For example, another common suggestion to guide custody determinations is that older children be placed with the parent of the same sex. A simple practical consideration which would militate against such a proposal is that, in many families, this would lead to splitting up siblings; but further, there is an assumption being made that children can learn how to be a man or a woman only from a biological parent of the same sex. An essential problem with this rule is the beliefs it represents about sex, gender identification, and child development. Should the law assume that fathers are better parents for boys and mothers for girls merely because they share a gender? Even if the assertion were susceptible to "scientific" proof, thereby defying everyday observations of sons raised by custodial mothers, there would still remain a significant issue. Do we as a society really want to perpetuate the gendered role division we now have? This particular example also illustrates profound problems with the way that custody decisions are conceptualized and discussed in much of legal literature. Contemporary legal inquiry focuses on the relationship of adult parents to their minor children in terms of the parents' rights and claims to the children and fails to approach the question from a more child-oriented position. Recent research on siblings presents evidence that siblings play important roles in each other's lives, even into early adulthood and beyond.[48]

Another rule receiving some serious treatment in legal academic journals is one that recommends placing children with the parent who has the greatest financial resources. In some articles, this serves as a "counterweight" to placement with the primary parent.[49] It should be a matter of concern that such a view is seriously considered at all, when it is abundantly clear to whose advantage such a stance would work in the custody context.

In terms of more general criticisms of the use of social science data by legal policymakers, where the legal author or policymaker already has a strong leaning toward a particular mode of custody resolution, it is relatively easy to find social science data, often research within a different context, which can be held up as illustrative and supportive of a particular rule. Those readers without a social science background or lacking the time to refer to the original research are not in a position to criticize such selections.

In addition, just as there is a bias on the part of social scientists, the selection and interpretation of social science literature presents opportunities for interjecting the values of the legal author using the data. The choice of what to report or include in a legal policy statement that relies on social science for its justification may reflect the legal author's unstated or unrealized bias. Bias distorts the processes of selection and interpretation in both the scope and the content of the social science information reported.

Related to the distortion in the selective presentation of social science studies by legal authors is the practice of burying relevant or contradictory information in footnotes. This tactic, while it avoids the more drastic academic compromise of omitting unfavorable articles, may be no less a distortion given the probability that the information will be skipped over by all but the most conscientious of readers.

Problems may also arise when legal policymakers draw inappropriate analogies on the basis of sociological data. For example, sometimes a legal author will use the results of studies of one phenomenon to explain or predict the occurrence of something quite different, as happens in the custody-policy literature when the results of studies of intact families are used to draw conclusions about divorce situations. When legal authors formulate policy, they may be tempted to use only data which support consistent and palatable conclusions, particularly if the author already has firm convictions as to what the rules should be.

Generalization is another common problem. Many of the social science articles cited in legal-policy pieces on the issues of custody decision making are in fact qualified by the researchers as reflecting, at best, the construction of a model that represents an isolated, small part of reality. Legal authors may, however, treat such research as though it actually contains unqualified facts or conclusions about the subject.

Distortion also arises in the translation of this social science data into legal principles. Even if one is scrupulous in collecting and reporting the data, there is always the problem of interpretation. Rules do not leap automatically from the pages of psychology journals; they must be suggested, then bolstered with supportive interpretations. There is a tendency to minimize, or to omit entirely, the qualifications appropriate to social science research when it becomes the focus of legal-policy discussions. Sometimes this is done even when the research itself explicitly states that its conclusions are of limited generalizability.[50] A variation of this distortion is to note the qualifications initially but to omit them in subsequent versions. This simplifies the research in such a manner as to make it buttress the author's conclusions devoid of its qualifications.

CONCLUSION

Now that there is some recognition that men and women may actually construct and occupy different social worlds, researchers should consider redirecting their attention.[51] The question would then be not whether women and men can parent, but whether there are different, complementary, or antagonistic ways they go about it given the material and social worlds they occupy. Such an inquiry would place an emphasis on motivation, degrees of intimacy with the child, and ways in which parents develop and express relationships.[52] Perceptions of self as parent and how these perceptions change within the sole-parent context would also be important areas to examine. These qualitative questions are full of nuance and do not necessarily have "correct answers." They are unlikely to provide easy rules to facilitate custody decisions, but exploration of the questions suggested would shift the focus away from research which ignores the content of parenting roles and emphasizes biological connections.

EIGHT

Constructing the Social Science Foundation for an Ideological Solution

In the context of custody disputes, the issue of special nurturing traits associated with one sex is posed most purely in cases involving newborns when neither parent has become the primary caretaker for the child and in cases involving preschool children when parents have shared in roughly equal measure the caregiving responsibilities. . . .

[W]hen fathers and mothers are observed with their own newborns before either has assumed differing caretaking roles, fathers are in general as likely to hold them closely, rock them, talk to them, and look directly at them. New fathers seem as skilled and gentle as mothers with their own children. Observers in the home at later stages, even after differing roles have been assumed, have found that although fathers interact with young children differently then mothers do, with more physical and less patterned, rhythmic play, there still seem to be few differences in the degree of parents' interests in their children or in their capacities to respond to their infant's signals. . . . [T]he issue is not whether 'father's touch' is identical to 'mother's touch' but whether 'father's touch,' whatever it is like, is likely to lead to a less desirable quality of life or less desirable outcome for the child in either the short or long term.

D. Chambers*

INTRODUCTION

A major shift has occurred in the way that important segments of the professional population (both legal and nonlegal) view and articulate what constitutes good parenting. To some extent this has been accompanied by a reexamination of the idealized notion of "Mother." Some legal commentators have used this shift in the professional and social science literature as an opportunity to offer suggestions for

---

*D. Chambers, *Rethinking the Substantive Rules for Custody Disputes in Divorce*, 83 MICH. L. REV. 477, 519–20, 522 (citations omitted).

changes on the basis of this literature. These changes, if implemented, would substantially reallocate bargaining power in favor of "Father" in the divorce process, particularly in regard to custody decisions.

Previous ideology exalted the position of mothers and the nurturing that they provided, and this was reflected in earlier social science literature. More recent studies, however, have focused on the role of the secondary caretaker (or father) in regard to the children's well-being.[1] These studies, often referred to as *father-custody* literature, were influential in fashioning the initial proposals for joint custody and the construction of other important policy positions focusing on fathers' rights. This literature has not only concentrated on the ways that fathers may be missed by their children after divorce, but has also attacked many of the positive cultural assumptions associated with motherhood. For example, one consequence of this new focus on a noneconomically centered place for "Father" within the postdivorce family has been the denigration of the (stereotypical) nurturing tasks performed by "Mother."[2] As a result, the nurturing ideal is being read out of custody policy or minimized in favor of more biologically centered goals which recognize both parents' rights to control of the children after divorce.

This explains in part why attempts to impose equality in the custody decision making process have not taken the direction of assessing whether men have adopted a "mothering" or caretaking attitude toward their children and have therefore "earned" equal rights to consideration as the parent who will provide for the best interest of the child. Rather, their focus has been to question the entire traditional conceptualization of best interest as a recognition of the importance of the child's needs, particularly by minimizing the desirability of stereotypical motherly characteristics such as nurturing and caring.

Stereotypical masculine characteristics, those of "independence" or "assertiveness," presumed to be learned from fathers, especially for male children, have emerged as new countervalues to the "interdependence" and "nurturing" traditionally associated with motherly behavior. Father is viewed as someone to place between mother and child, a buffer for the stifling and crippling effects of maternal love and obsession. These trends reflect the underlying disagreement over what characteristics are desirable in children as well as what is valued in adults. This battle has significant gender as well as social implications that are hidden from view in most of the legalistic debates and policy arguments, but that manifest themselves there as well as in the assumptions made in the selection, use, and translation of social science data for legal uses. In addition to the gendered implications of selected values, it appears that men may be judged as parents by a different, much less demanding standard than are women. Combining work and child care is admirable when men do it, but neglect when women must balance both responsibilities.[3]

Father-custody studies which provided the foundation for father-centered reforms such as joint custody during the early 1980s are of relatively recent origin. They seem to have been initially prompted by the publicity surrounding the 1973 publication of *Beyond the Best Interests of the Child*, a book which recommended that the "psychological parent" retain complete control over the child's exposure to the secondary parent.[4] This suggestion was widely characterized as excluding fathers from postdivorce contact with their children. Essentially, giving primary caretakers or psychological parents control over their children's lives, including the amount of contact they had with the other biological parent, was asserted to be the same as ensuring no contact at all. Mothers were not trusted to be "generous," even reasonable, in regard to permitting visitation if given such power. The father-custody studies appearing subsequent to this book tended to be the basis for favorable comment on paternal capabilities in child care and for arguments for fathers' mandated access to their children after divorce.[5] These studies were significant contributions to the development of the equality model in custody decision making, and they provided the justification for state policies designed to provide "fairness" to fathers at divorce.

DISCOVERING DAD IN THE SOCIAL SCIENCES

The image most frequently constructed in the father-custody studies was that of the competent man moving smoothly into a series of different roles with relative ease. The observations upon which such conclusions were based, however, seemed to represent only minimal parenting skills—skills that certainly would be considered inadequate if we were talking about mothers rather than fathers. For example, notice the difference when a paragraph from the Chang and Deinard father-custody study is amended to refer to mothers rather than fathers:

> [The single mother] is a highly educated, capable, self-confident person whose marriage has broken up because of [her husband's] change in lifestyle or increasing incompatibility. [She] seeks custody of [her] children because of [her] love for them and [her] confidence in [her] ability to perform [maternal] parenting functions, inasmuch as [she] had been fairly involved in caring and

> rearing [her] children prior to the disruption of the marriage.
> Many of these [mothers] have completed the adjustment process
> quite well. . . . [P]rofessionals (involved in the determination of
> custody) should take into consideration this and other reports of
> seemingly positive and successful adjustment of custodial
> [mothers].[6]

Congratulating and suggesting rewards for a mother for showing love for her children and involvement in their care would seem ridiculous, while fathers doing much less than a typical mother were thus deemed worthy of praise and their efforts deemed to be due "consideration."

In contrast to rewarding mothers for care and involvement, the tone and direction of some of the father-custody studies appear to view the pathological potential of divorce as located in mothers' behaviors while regarding men as supermen and heroes.[7] Such perceptions are internalized. Luepnitz, writing in 1982, for example, reported that 56 percent of the sole-custodial fathers thought that their social status had improved as a result of being the sole-custodial parent, while 94 percent of the sole-custodial mothers thought that their status had declined. One outcome of the women's movement has been to create a social climate in which people not only begin to believe that men might be more involved with their children than in the past, but also give them considerable kudos for doing so, while single mothers remain stigmatized.[8]

The Studies in General

Father-custody studies were particularly important to substantiate the assertion that men were more than adequate parents and, in some cases, were to be preferred over women. If one were to approach the issue purely as a "dedicated" social scientist, the methodological problems with these studies alone would raise serious questions about any definitive conclusions. All the father-custody studies shared some major difficulties, including the lack of randomness of samples and the mixing of samples to include widowers as well as divorcees. In addition, all the research was conducted after a significant time (sometimes years) had elapsed since the father had taken custody. Fathers were, therefore, interviewed long after the period typically reported to be the most difficult in terms of adjustment for mothers.[9] Furthermore, the father-custody study samples were typically small. In addition, the researchers usually did not interview both the children and the parent; thus, there was seldom an effort to substantiate or question the assertions made by the fathers as to their children's progress. Only occasionally did the studies point out the limitations of sample size and the randomness and generalizability of data, and those that did were the earlier studies conducted and written in a less polarized climate.[10] Interestingly, these studies expressly cautioned against generalizing from their findings.[11]

All of the major studies relied on self-reporting and on information gained by a single interview. In addition, several of these studies relied on questionnaires—a fact which obviously limited the amount, depth, and accuracy of the information obtained. In contrast to the rather narrow approach taken in the father-custody studies, some commentators, in writing about family research, have pointed to the need for an array of research tools. For example, child-development researchers have expressed doubts as to the adequacy of self-report questionnaires as a means for obtaining accurate information. These commentators have pointed out that there is no evidence that parents actually relate to children as they report on questionnaires or in interviews. In fact, there may be little similarity between parental self-report and actual parental behavior. Brody & Endsley, for example, believe that in order to be significant an assessment must be based on the interaction between family members, so that a researcher is able to see "the natural ecology in which adults and children provide each other with continual feedback."[12] They conclude that research is only as good as the data from which it is generated. The absence of this feedback component in self-report indices was partially responsible for the lack of correspondence between self-reports of child-rearing behavior and actual child-rearing behavior.

The depth of information gained through the single-interview process often utilized in the father-custody studies may also have been inadequate. Over the last decade, the value of conducting several interviews with the same respondents has been widely recognized.[13] Multiple interviews enable the researchers to achieve a different content and quality of information when they—the interviewers—seek to get beyond a cursory description of events and attempt to elicit or understand a respondent's meanings.[14]

Beyond purely methodological critiques, there are additional problems with these studies. For example, the view given of the fathers in much of the research is unidimensional. It lacks sufficient data not only about the children but also about the ex-spouse, so that the very negative statements and conclusions about the absent and silent wife go unchallenged.[15] Giving a one-sided version of events leads the reader to believe that there is but one definition—the father's—of the past and present marital and family situations. No criteria are given in this father-custody literature to help the reader evaluate the father custodian's claims to be the "better parent." Nor is there any description of what factors the father considered when formulating and applying his definition of what constituted adequate parenting. It is interesting, in this context, to note that at least one study has indicated that parental perceptions of children's distress at divorce depends on different factors. Fathers' perceptions of their children's distress were related to the degree of influence they felt they had retained over the children. Mothers' perceptions, however, were related to the impact the divorce had had on them, the degree and frequency of violence prior to separation, and the extent of their religious beliefs.[16]

Finally, the father-custody studies fail to take account of the different social expectations applied to men and women that affect ultimate perceptions of how responsibility is carried out. An example of this which occurs frequently is the failure of social scientists, and those who use their work, to control for the relative economic and social positions of men and women when comparing them as custodians. The men in the studies, in contrast to many ex-wives, enjoyed both high economic and social status. In not recognizing such obvious real-world disparities that affect parenting performance, the literature treats women poorly while giving men the benefit of every doubt. For example, the failure to appreciate that many women at divorce find themselves forced back into the labor market at wages that compare unfavorably with those of their ex-husbands may lead to the formulation of facially neutral rules that in fact disadvantage women. Consider in this regard the fact that some legal authors treat seriously the suggestion that the person with the greater earning power should obtain custody, justifying this through the assumption that degree of wealth equals degree of "happiness"—a concept which is not defined and does not appear to have any empirical foundation.[17] Moreover, at least one author who puts forth such a recommendation recognizes that this approach may work to disadvantage women, but he appears unsympathetic. While acknowledging women's depressed economic power, this author failed to give substantial weight to the structural origin of this phenomenon within the family. For example, he indicates that he would be sympathetic if women's lower wages were the result of systematic discrimination in the market. But if disparity in earnings results from choices made in the family with regard to who cares for children, the mother would receive no counterweighing credit against the father's superior economic position.[18]

In addition, it appears that women generally have more major realignments to make after separation than do men. In comparison to men's social and economic security, many women upon divorce have to face finding employment for the first time.[19] Many women, even when they are working at the time of divorce, will not have the status in their work to command the job flexibility and salaries that men do—both of which are useful in coping with child-care problems.

Given the inadequacies of the father-custody studies, statements by legal policymakers indicating that "[t]hese studies help us to understand the experiences of children raised by men, and the experience of children whose care is taken over by secondary caretakers," are quite misleading. The studies did not focus on the children at all. It is incomprehensible from anything other than a political viewpoint why, in spite of their recent origins and incomplete nature, these studies received the degree of attention they did.[20]

The Santrock and Warshak Father-Custody Study

In addition to methodological problems, the father-custody articles also tend to misstate the overall findings of the research. A more critical reading would not have sustained the important policy conclusions that legal authors using the studies reached. An illustration of this was the use of a father-custody study conducted by Santrock and Warshak which is frequently quoted in the father-custody literature.[21] The study used sixty children from white, middle-class families (thirty-three boys and twenty-seven girls), divided into intact, father-custody and mother-custody families. The sample was gathered through community agencies. There were no differences in social class, but there were significant differences in income among the three custody arrangements, depending on the sex of the parent: mother-custody families had the lowest incomes. To observe these families, Santrock and Warshak used a range of methods: laboratory observations, structured interviews, self-reports, and projective tasks. Santrock and Warshak, like other researchers, tended to utilize as measures those characteristics that are customary in contemporary social science methodology. So, for example, notions like "independence" were evaluated as indicators of successful or poor child development. Clearly, such notions incorporated normative assessments of what was desired for appropriate behavior.

It is perhaps impossible for a social scientist to criticize the inherently normative aspects of the behavior traits typically measured in social science endeavors and still receive the imprimatur of "acceptably academic work," but the uncritical acceptance of such norms, especially when the research is imported for use in legislative policy-making, allows "[s]cience to become an activity far removed from the sphere of . . . moral action." This in turn, "supplies . . . social engineers . . . with the legitimation of measures in accordance with the dominant value system."[22] The Santrock and Warshak study has been cited for the claim that boys in father custody do better than boys in mother custody. One legal commentator, for example, used this study to assert that boys in the study "who lived with parents of the same sex were less anxious, less demanding, and less angry; were warmer and more honest; and displayed higher levels of maturity, self-esteem, and social conformity than the children living with parents of the opposite sex."[23] He failed to note, however, that the study indicated that boys in mother-custody families had higher self-esteem and were less anxious than boys in intact families.[24] He also introduced an unwarranted distortion of Santrock's and Warshak's work by suggesting that the reason that girls living in father custody were doing worse than girls in mother custody or in intact families was because the girls had unresolved problems with the absent mother.[25]

The Santrock and Warshak study must be read carefully, however, and note should be taken of the authors' statement that a "particular void [is] the absence of information about the effects of father custody on a child's development."[26] The study set out to answer three questions: (1) How did children of divorce differ from children in intact families? (2) What differences and/or similarities existed between mother-custody and father-custody families? (3) What factors (parental styles, personality characteristics, availability of support systems) helped a child to cope with divorce? The authors predicted that intact-family children would be more competent socially, and that a child with support systems and an authoritative style of parenting would do better. Authoritative parenting was defined as parents having clear rules, allowing extensive verbal give and take, and providing a warm environment. The support system consisted of friends, neighbors, family, child-care centers, and so on.[27]

The results of the Santrock and Warshak study were interesting. The researchers first compared the relationship between fathers and sons in father-custody settings and in intact families. They also compared the relationship of mothers and daughters in mother-custody settings and in intact families. In these comparisons, the children from the intact families did not do as well as the children from the divorced families. Other comparisons by Santrock and Warshak yielded the conclusion that boys in father custody do better than boys in mother custody. Girls in father custody, however, did less well. In a comparison between mother-custody children and children from intact families, mother-custody boys showed higher self-esteem and were less anxious, although mother-custody girls were lower in self-esteem than girls in intact families.[28]

Overall, the authors indicated some astonishment at the lack of dramatic results in their study. They suggest that the results might be explained by the fact that three years after the divorce the children had adjusted. They conclude that the only difference attributable to family structure was that mother-custody children were more demanding than intact family children. It is important to stress that, contrary to some uses of their work, they did not state that boys in mother custody were faring poorly.[29] In the comparison among single-custodial families, however, the authors did state that the boys in mother custody did *less well* than those in father custody. The mother-custody boys were seen as more demanding and less mature than father-custody boys, a result that the researchers described as being consistent with child-development theories. They also noted, however, that authoritative parenting and the availability of support systems are linked with social maturity.[30] Mothers' parenting styles typically are less authoritative, and as the study indicated, mothers also have less support available.

Santrock and Warshak suggested that whatever the benefits of father custody for boys, the success of father custody may have depended in part on people other than the father. They observed that noncustodial mothers had more contact with their children than did noncustodial fathers, for example, indicating that in such cases there was more likely to be continued interaction with both parents. No attempt was made, however, to evaluate this factor in terms of the extent to which ongoing contact with the mother assisted the development of self-esteem and maturity in the boys in father custody. In addition, father custodians were found to rely much more on outside assistance in raising their children. The authors suggested that the degree of help the custodial fathers received from support networks may have resulted from either their active solicitation or the perception of relatives that they were in need of help. While these factors were not explicitly evaluated or explored, the authors did find a positive correlation between the participation of external caretakers and a child's level of maturity. They also made the rather obvious suggestion that a parent less depleted by continuous child care might have more to offer a child.

Santrock and Warshak suggested several reasons why an individual parent might have been able to get help. These reasons were purely speculations. For example, they suggested that warmer, socially mature, and conforming children are easier to leave with other adults in a care situation, thus attributing success to characteristics they identified with father custody to begin with. Alternatively, they hypothesized that parents with little support might be in that position because they themselves are lacking in warmth and socially conforming behavior, thus attributing pathological behavior to mothers.[31]

There may be other reasons why women in particular received less support from other adults than did single fathers. For example, women may not have been able to afford extensive child care; the children in father custody spent more time in paid child care than did the children in mother custody.[32] In addition, mothers may not have been seen as requiring help, nor felt able to ask for it, since mothering is seen to be within women's natural role and competence and is typically not viewed as an assisted activity. The fact that both economic factors and the significance of the differences in the wider interactive systems were insufficiently accounted for militates against too readily accepting the conclusion of the Santrock and Warshak study.

Moreover, additional problems with the interpretation of the data by the authors need to be taken into account. For example, the assumption was made that the input of sole-custody fathers was responsible for the greater degree of maturity, self-esteem, and warmth that their sons displayed. But these children spent a much larger portion of time per week in child-care situations than did the mother-custody children (twenty-four hours per week as contrasted with eleven hours per week).[33] It would have been legitimate to assume that the caregivers in these extended-care situations were usually women. Moreover, father custodians also typically had access to women family members, were they second wives or mothers, in addition to the financial resources to purchase child care for extended periods. The authors did not consider the possibility that such women may well have had a hand in promoting the well-being of these boys.

One could conclude from looking at the data that when men received custody of their children, their response was to turn the care of those children over to women who were not the children's mother but who may have been in the men's employ or related to them in some manner, though not necessarily to the children. The difference in reliance on outside help, regardless of whether or not the parents were working, was noted in the study.[34] The authors linked the use of support systems to the previously noted advantages of authoritative upbringing, but they gave no indication of how they would have assigned the extent of the influence upon a child of time spent within the support system rather than with the father. By contrast, it seemed that women spent more time caring for their children when they obtained custody, a demonstration of their willingness to consider the children's interests as at least equal to their own. This study illustrates the failure to contextualize—to put conclusions in a larger framework. Such a failure is a persistent, ideologically significant problem in such studies.

An additional problem with the Santrock and Warshak study is that it was sparse on comparative data. No indication was given of how much warmer or less dependent the father-custody boys were in comparison with the mother-custody boys, although the reader was told that the differences are statistically significant. Further, and more significant, is the fact that there were inevitable value judgments being made about the constitution of behavior. I believe that it was entirely inappropriate for the authors not to make explicit the underlying assumptions and value judgments that influenced the formulation of their questions and the way in which judgments were weighed and values assessed. To take but one example from Santrock's and Warshak's list of qualities, how was "maturity" assessed on the part of the boys studied? Was the assessment different for girls? Were there unstated assumptions about what constitutes appropriate growth and maturity in boys that would value independence and autonomy more than connectedness and community identification.?[35] In fairness, it should be noted that Santrock and Warshak did try to indicate in their studies the limitations that they saw. Their work may have been subsequently misused, simplified, and distorted by others seeking to elevate the position of fathers vis-à-vis mothers, but a careful researcher can consult the original text and easily pick up most of the criticisms listed above.

Recognition of the limitations of the methods whereby information is collected and assessed should be an important part of any serious policy consideration based on social science data. In addition, it is often equally important to look for the information that the researcher *failed* to include in the study. Social scientists may not feel the need to place their observations within the context of the larger economic, political, and cultural climates, but lawyers and legal policymakers must do so in order to be responsive to the needs of those to whom the law will apply.

GENERAL CRITICISMS OF THE STUDIES
Adjustment and Motivation

In a large number of father-custody studies, the authors seemed single-mindedly to assert the capacity of fathers to adjust and become primary caretakers after divorce. These studies of paternal adjustment, however, have used very limited measures to assess such adjustment. Moreover, the really important question of *how*, rather than *whether*, the fathers have adjusted was not asked at all.[36] Gasser & Taylor,[37] for example, offered a definition of adjustment which focused on role rearrangement and on performance of household tasks only. Other studies offered no definition of adjustment. In this regard, White and Mika point out that there has been a failure to define terms, a dependence on conclusory terms such as *adjustment*, and a focus on only a few aspects of what constituted that adjustment. Such narrow inquiries ignored stressful life events which can have a wide variety of effects.

Some of the studies did focus more on what motivated fathers seeking custody, which is a more complex way to approach the subject of paternal adjustment. Mendes, for example, analyzed fathers' motivations for seeking custody and their difficulties in adjustment after receiving custody. In examining these factors, she divided her sample into four categories of fathers: (1) aggressive seekers; (2) conciliatory seekers; (3) aggressive assenters; and (4) conciliatory assenters.[38] Aggressive seekers were defined as the men who fought for custody and for whom the children had important symbolic meaning. Conciliatory seekers were older men who sought custody while they were still living with their wives. Conciliatory assenters were the men who had acceded to requests from their wives that they accept custody, and aggressive assenters were men with no option but to accept custody of their children.[39] She found that the difference in motivations among the groups was related to parenting quality, and that the poorest relationships existed between fathers and children when the father fell into the aggressive assenting group—the group which had no option but to accept custody.

Mendes also found that gaining custody of children had different symbolic meanings for the different groups of men surveyed in the study. For example, she speculated whether the real function or value of the children to conciliatory seekers (older men who sought custody of their children while still living with their wives) was to keep them from being isolated socially. On the other hand, for the aggressive seeker (men who fought for custody for what were termed *symbolic* reasons), fatherhood represented an important aspect of self-validation. Mendes found that this group of men, in order to obtain custody, resorted to deception, threats of abduction, and the expulsion of the mother from the home.[40] Mendes indicated that part of these men's motivation lay in remembering their own traumatic childhoods. Mendes recognized that the actions resorted to by the aggressive seeking men could have been stressful for the children, and certainly the capacity of men who indulge in such actions to be sensitive parents is at least open to question.[41] Mixed motivations have been noted by other researchers. Gersick, for example, noted that "[a]mong the men who received custody, father-child relationships often took on particular intensity and multi-generational meaning." The fathers that he interviewed were anxious to reverse their own experience of a distant father. Gersick did not, however, discuss the difficulties for those attempting to reverse or substantially change the pattern of child-rearing that they had experienced as children.

Bolstering Father-Custody Studies—Crossover Studies

In addition to utilizing studies of children in divorce situations, some of the articles explicitly dealing with recommendations or conclusions considered appropriate for divorce and custody policy have used studies of intact families to substantiate their point of view. There are both methodological and conceptual problems with this research which should affect the weight it is accorded.

Consistent with the development of divorce studies focusing on fathers, there was also a movement away from mother-focused research in the intact family literature. Perhaps because fathers were viewed as having been "ignored" in earlier studies of the family, they were placed in the position of occupying the major role in contemporary family research. The study of fatherhood became "a prestigious substantive issue."[42] A focus on mother-child relationships was, for example, described as "cultural ethnocentricism" because of the extent to which its dyadic focus excluded the recognition of the interaction of other members (fathers) of the "system."[43] Unfortunately, this criticism in regard to the intact-family literature tended to lead researchers ultimately to merely substitute a father-centered dyad for the criticized mother-centered one.

The inadequacy of the dyadic point of view was generally not acknowledged in this intact-family literature even at the time it was developed. Systems theory had become more integrated into psychological thinking. A systems approach recognized the need to take account of the way that dyadic relationships are impinged upon, and modified by, the family as a wider social system. Because systems theory was essentially concerned with the interrelationship of members and their processes of interaction which are maintained over time, it viewed each member of the family system as active within it, influencing and being influenced (positively and negatively) by all other family members. In this regard, Hipgrave stated his criticism of dyadic research succinctly:

> A language of dyads can often serve to distort the psychological and sociological realities of an environment within which each individual is influencing, and being influenced by, those around him. Families . . . are united in a constant state of negotiation . . . both as individuals and as a collective entity. The tendency to reduce this ecological complexity to linear models based on particular dyads needs to be readily recognized and treated with appropriate caution.[44]

This criticism of dyadic research applies equally to the father-child dyad that is the basis of the father-custody research. It questions the appropriateness of the tendency in intact-family literature to merely measure mother-child dyads against father-child dyads, with no recognition of the systematic influence of the whole family in either its nuclear or extended form.

Social Science Criticism of the Notion of Fatherhood Studies

There was also some concern expressed about the nature of fatherhood studies within the social science community. McKee and O'Brien asked whether the preoccupation with fathers stemmed from an expression of and desire for equality in child-rearing and from the expectation that fathers would take a full role in this. For example, Hipgrave noted that in contrast to British studies, he found no American studies which indicated that fathers had given up work to care for their children. This was, and continues to be of course, a common expectation for mothers.[45] Alternatively, McKee and O'Brien posited that the elevation of fatherhood research represented a backlash against women, as men facing competition in the marketplace have moved to compete with women in the home area.[46]

Furthermore, the fatherhood studies were constrained by the lack of an adequate theoretical framework.[47] The word *fatherhood*, for example, was treated as though it possessed generally accepted connotations, in spite of the lack of understanding about the way that feelings and attitudes develop within and toward fatherhood. Richards discussed this more extensively when he noted that the growing body of research on fathers

> arises more from a well-meaning attempt to balance the earlier almost exclusive concentration on mothers than from an examination of what might be exclusive or special to fatherhood rather than motherhood or parenthood. At worst men . . . are presented as alternative mothers and much writing is concerned with demonstrating adequacy, if not desirability, as parents. Little of this kind of research rises above comparisons of the behavior of men and women with their children.[48]

In contrast to the lack of definition of *father*, Finkelstein points out that there is a depth of meaning associated with *mother*. The specific role fathers have historically occupied has been that of providers who maintain a somewhat distant relationship with their children.[49] One of the major problems in many of the studies was the assumption that fathers would react in the same ways as mothers in caring for their children. There was little systematic and careful exploration of the different ways that mothers and fathers reacted to their children in ongoing or divorced families.[50]

It may have been, and may continue to be, unrealistic to suggest that the court in any individual custody determination embark on an exploration of how particular parents understand and practice their roles, how they constrain and are constrained by each other within the family system, and who has provided the primary care for the children. Given the cost of individualized assessments, we may have no choice but to rely on carefully constructed models of each parental role. The question is how these models are to be generated. The overall quality of custody judgments will not improve through simplistic and speculative assessments of the abstract merits of one type of parenting over another.

There should be, therefore, considerable concern about the way both father-custody and intact-family research has been used in custody policy-making discussions. It should be clear that, at best, much of the research has failed to contribute anything to our understanding of the specialness of parental roles at divorce. It contains covert assumptions about and idealization of the nuclear family evident in the researchers' dyadic approach and in their failure to give value to the extended family. At worst, the research has constituted an opportunity for an ideologically grounded attempt to undermine mother custody in order to elevate the role of father with rules that may result in substantial harm to children.

COMPOUNDING THE PROBLEM—THE LEGAL CONSUMER
OF SOCIAL SCIENCE

There is a tendency in contemporary legal scholarship concerned
with custody merely to balance off the emotional investment of the
mother, as exemplified by her caretaking contribution, against the material investment of the father, as exemplified by his economic contribution. Furthermore, juxtaposing mother's caretaking with father's economic contribution obscures the dual contributions that most women
make to their families when they not only assume the majority of responsibility for child care, but work outside the home as well. In addition, as long as both parents are assumed to be emotionally invested in
their children (though such investment may be experienced in different
ways), these emotional considerations are likely to be of little value
when choosing between parents. Indeed, such logic could be construed
to support imposing joint custody. Similarly, it is difficult to see how a
guideline like this would aid in obtaining certainty within the context of
custody decision making.

Social science information is being used in the debate over custody
rules without being subjected to any really critical examination and
without being put in the context of the forces producing and urging
changes in the area. In fact, challenges to present rules have simply been
viewed as the product of changing sex roles. Although the bulk of the
literature discussed in this chapter has presented the recent scholarly
and professional focus on fathers as a "natural" evolution, some authors
have argued that this shift has not necessarily been the product of neutral, detached observation or analysis. As one observer noted:

> In my five years of professional experience in an academic pediatric
> hospital, divorced women with children occasioned little com-
> ments, other than negative. They were dealt with routinely, given
> appointments without asking about their schedules, handed in-
> structions imperiously without a thought as to how they would
> carry them out amidst the conflicting demands of work and child
> care. Yet when any father with custody of this children appeared,
> the staff went out of its way to praise his efforts and laud his hero-
> ism. They agonized over the conflicts he must face in the exigen-
> cies of caring for his child and managing his life. In both situa-
> tions, one adult had sole responsibility for parenting and work.
> What differed was the way the parent was viewed.[51]

Father-based studies are but one illustration of this pattern of unequal responses based on underlying gendered assumptions. The studies that uncritically focus on fathers are used to supplement discussions

of research that present the shortcomings of maternal sole-custody placements and that focus on children's need for fathers in intact and postdivorce families.

In particular, those concerned with formulating custody policy should be leery of these studies. Just as empirical scholarship is more than simply counting, legal policy-making involves more than the uncritical recounting of various studies indiscriminately assembled. At a minimum, it is about the political and moral implications of the policy recommendations which are based on the research conducted and the data obtained. The extent to which discussions of custody policy and rule changes are predicated upon data that incorporate a fathers'-rights perspective has often been overlooked, and the more subtle notion that we can change fathers by devaluing motherhood has not been directly confronted. Also, only limited recognition has been given to the real problems facing single-custodial mothers. What I find most disturbing in many custody studies is that they ignore custodial mothers' reality under the guise of presenting a neutral review of social science research.

I encourage the reader to understand the current custody debate within the political and social contexts in which it has developed. Only then can the effects of scholarly activity in this area be understood.

NINE

The Resort to Alternative Decision-Makers

Social workers can understand how damaging [the adversarial] process is. Many of the emotional hurts and feelings of guilt are displayed during the struggle for an economic settlement. The attorney is neither equipped nor interested in dealing with a client's emotional upheaval. He is looking for a settlement that can be taken into court for approval. . . .

The concept of mediation is implicit in the role of social worker. Not only because of their professional ethics, but also because of their training and experience, all social workers, but particularly those specializing in family therapy, are uniquely qualified to perform the task of mediation.

J. Haynes*

This chapter explores how social workers and mediators have been successful in appropriating the business of child-custody decision making. An integral part of this process has been an attack on the nature of existing rules and decision-making institutions, a phenomenon that can be viewed metaphorically as the helping professions' claiming of the custody decision making terrain through the rhetoric of reform which was developed by, among others, social scientists, fathers'-rights groups, and child advocates. The helping professionals are the consumers of those discourses. They also are the "practitioners" of equality in regard to custody. They apply the equality principles in the context of individual cases and in recommendations for process reforms. The extent to which equality concepts and values have been incorporated into and dominate the public and political language of the escalating custody debate illustrates the success of the efforts of the helping professions.

The recent trend in the legal area is to mandate mediation of custody and related postdivorce disputes.[1] This contemporary shift in custody policy is best understood in the context of the rhetoric and ideology of social workers and mediators, proponents of this trend who, as a profes-

*J. Haynes, *Divorce Mediator: A New Role,* 23 Soc. Work 5, 6 (1978).

sional group, have transformed divorce practice. In this chapter, I argue that the establishment of mandatory mediation as the preferred process and of joint custody or shared parenting as the substantive norm represents a significant divergence from previously accepted legal doctrine.[2] Yet, because these changes are presented in procedural terms, the rhetoric concerning mediation has masked, at the same time that it has facilitated, the extensive shifts in substantive results. Labeling changes as procedural makes them easier to accept but also obscures the substantive changes that are taking place.

My primary concern is with the imposition of these procedural and substantive changes as mandatory rules to govern all custody decision making at divorce. Therefore, this is not a discussion of the merits of *voluntary* joint custody or *voluntary* mediation as alternative dispute-resolution techniques. Similarly, I am not primarily concerned with debating the relative capacity or desirability of legal and nonlegal decision-makers in custody cases, although, as this chapter sets forth, I do not think the solution to the undeniable problems associated with the adversarial model is simply to turn over the decision-making task to another professional group. In fact, to do so creates another set of problems. Recognizing that the behavior of attorneys in custody cases has at times been outrageous, it is not my intention to defend legal professionals.

In addition, it is important to note that my criticism of the mediation process differs from the typical feminist or liberal critiques.[3] I do not necessarily disagree with the literature that points out that the "weaker" partner in a marriage is likely to be disadvantaged within the mediation context.[4] I am concerned, however, that this type of criticism will lead us to look to the wrong methods of "reform." If we focus on inequitable bargaining positions—the continuation of the "woman-as-victim" model—the solutions that suggest themselves are individualized ones which are located within the control of the mediators themselves. For example, in response to feminist criticisms that unequal bargaining power mars the process, the mediation profession recently has produced a mass of literature on how practicing mediators can remedy such inequality.[5]

My concern is broader. In this chapter, I reveal the shifts in substantive rules that have been the inevitable by-products of changes in the methods and manner of resolving custody disputes. These changes have consequences in all custody decision making. Therefore, the focus of my inquiry is not the power of individuals within any particular mediation context; rather, it is the lack of power that leaves custodial mothers disadvantaged in a political process that permits or encourages such changes. This type of power imbalance can only be understood at the macro level.

I assert that custodial mothers, as a group with shared problems and concerns, have not had access to the political system in any meaningful way. Their voices (at least insofar as they would call for the continuation of sole-custody arrangements) are not heard because their concerns cannot be expressed through existing and accepted discourses or rhetorical concepts. The fact that their interests cannot be expressed in acceptable language denies them access to the system that shapes and implements decisions having the most profound impact on their lives. Custodial mothers are unorganized and unrepresented. The groups that should have their concerns in mind are caught up with the dominant rhetoric, which now defines the terms of contemporary discussions about custody and effectively excludes or minimizes contrary ideologies and concepts. In addition, on an individual level, custodial mothers have lost their only potential advocates with the displacement of lawyers by social workers who are either advocates for the child or concerned with the entire family as a unit in the custody process.

In this chapter, I criticize social workers and other members of the helping professions in part because they represent themselves as neutral, nonadversarial decision-makers in contrast to attorneys, whom they characterize as both adversarial and combative. Yet social workers are not neutral; they have a professional bias in favor of a specific substantive result—shared parenting. That result benefits their profession by creating the need for mediation and counseling. The bias inherent in mediation is different from, but no less suspect than, the bias that can result from overt favoritism of one party over another. This bias and self-interest demand political consideration. From my perspective, there is no mutually acceptable, objective, professional decision-maker, and we must confront moral, political, and legal questions from which the "experts" cannot save us.

The Ideal of Shared Parenting

The helping professions' discourse has presented shared parenting as the only truly acceptable custody policy.[6] This is because they view joint custody as the only "fair" result. For example, one commentator made the following sweeping conclusion based on *four* cases:

> There is no doubt that joint custody yields two psychological parents, and that the children do not suffer the profound sense of loss characteristic of so many children of divorce. The children main-

tained strong attachments to both parents. Perhaps the security of an ongoing relationship with *two* psychological parents helps to provide the means to cope successfully with the uprooting effects of switching households.[7] (Emphasis in original)

Fairness in this context is seen as having both a practical and theoretical basis. Another commentator found that

> [m]ost supporters of joint custody contend that it significantly improves parental cooperation. The need to reach an agreement on all major child-rearing decisions, combined with equalized parental power, fosters an atmosphere of detente rather than hostility. . . .
>
> Joint custody is said to reinforce and facilitate several modern social trends. It is consistent with the movement for sexual equality and its many corrolaries, such as the right of the individual to determine his or her own lifestyle. . . . Increasingly, fathers are sharing child-rearing and nurturing responsibilities. All of the developments are perfectly conducive to joint custody arrangements in the event of divorce . . .
>
> . . . There is also evidence that joint legal custody makes default on child support payments less likely. Several practitioners believe that the involvement in family affairs due to joint custody results in fathers paying child support more readily.[8]

Ironically, although they might question the capacity of legal processes and institutions to resolve custody disputes in accordance with this ideal, they view law itself as possessing vast power to transform people's behavior. The helping professions, therefore, have little hesitation in resorting to law for the implementation of their social policies.

The merits of shared parenting as a legal and social ideal have not been critically debated in political and legal forums in any meaningful way. Although there has been limited criticism of the feasibility of the ideal, this criticism does not challenge the degree to which presumptive shared parenting actually reflects pre- or postdivorce family structures. Similarly, there has been uncritical acceptance of the empirical proposition that women and men make undifferentiated, exchangeable contributions to parenting. By focusing on the importance of the father/child relationship, the helping professions' discourse undervalues a mother's real-life role, assuming it not to be different from a father's. The extreme presentation of this view is that at times a mother's "mothering" may be characterized as pathological and harmful to children. The creation of such a stereotype has gone largely unchallenged.

The shared-parenting discourse of the helping professions found rhetorical compatibility with other family-law reform efforts that also incorporated notions of equality, partnership, and gender neutrality. The joint-custody rhetoric of the helping professions, like other discourses, assumed and advocated egalitarianism—arguing that there are no differences between women and men, and that none should be promoted through gender-specific laws. Within the context of custody theory, this perspective denied and obscured recognition of anything "special" between mothers and children, innately or in fact. On this level, arguments for joint custody were consistent with feminist discourses that called for increasing male participation in child care to free women from anachronistic roles.

In focusing on ideal sex roles and egalitarian marriage, the helping professions' literature emphasized that traditional custody policy discriminated against men by unjustifiably favoring sole maternal custody.[9] Not unlike the emerging fathers'-rights discourse, their rhetoric asserted that there was no basis for maternal preference, which was grounded in the sexist assumption that men could not nurture but women could. In real life, according to the helping professions, parents share parenting, and "parents are forever."[10]

THE TRANSFORMATION OF THE CUSTODY DEBATE

Divorce and child custody decision-making have traditionally been the preserve of legal institutions: legislatures established laws to govern "domestic relations," and judges decided cases presented by attorneys representing adverse parties. Early divorce reforms, which sought changes in legal rules, particularly the movement from a fault-based to a no-fault system, sought adjustments that would mediate the harshness of the legal system.

In part, then, the current debate about the content and form of child-custody law reflects a struggle between two professional ideologies— those of law and social work. Fundamental questions have been raised about the appropriateness of legal institutions, legal solutions, and legal processes in divorce and custody cases. Such objections have culminated in a substantial redistribution of decision-making authority from judges and lawyers to the helping professions.

Concomitantly, there has been a transformation in the discourse concerning custody policy. This can be better understood by contrasting the competing discourses of the adversarial model, populated by judges and attorneys, and the therapeutic model, populated by social workers and mediators.

Traditional divorce policy envisioned the termination of the spouses' relationship as its goal, establishing different legal relationships with differing legal consequences for the custodial and noncustodial parents.[11] In this way, the law recognized the status of sole custodian as an institution or legal category and presumed that the law should designate, recognize, and protect the relationship between custodial parent and child. At the same time, the law acknowledged the noncustodial parent's relationship with the child through the imposition of visitation rights.

Helping professionals and other proponents of joint custody asserted that the win/lose philosophy of naming a sole custodian was inappropriate, because parents had equal rights and responsibilities in relation to their children during marriage.[12] In addition, they found the notion of "visiting" one's child ideologically and emotionally offensive.[13] By contrast, the symbolic ideal of parental equality was compelling. The desirable custody policy, therefore, was postdivorce shared parenting. It was this notion of a legally mandated and constructed continuing relationship between divorced parents, so central to joint custody, that was so foreign to traditional family-law policy. In essence, the social workers' ideal of shared parenting was a rejection of the desirability of a legally acknowledged sole custodian.

As this view has become accepted, it has altered the way we articulate and conceive of custody issues. The dominant rhetoric no longer describes divorce as a process that terminates the relationship between spouses, establishing one as the custodial parent with clear responsibilities. Rather, divorce is now described as a process that, through mediation, restructures and reformulates the spouses' relationship, conferring equal or shared parental rights on both parents, although one, in practice, usually assumes the primary responsibility for care of the children. This is an important substantive shift.

The helping professions' ability to suggest and obtain such radical change in substantive policy derives in part from their ability to present the debate over divorce and custody as one involving the treatment of an emotional crisis rather than a solution to a legal problem. Custody was merely a "label"; what was really at issue was the states of mind or attitudes of the family members. In this sense, the helping professions ignored the fact of, and the justifications for, the differing legal consequences that flowed from the labels of *custodial parent* and *noncustodial parent*. These designations were also considered to be offensive to noncustodial fathers, which added weight to arguments that the terms and rules had to be changed. Terms such as *shared parenting* and *periods of physical placement* replaced *physical custody* and *visitation* as the proper way to discuss custody arrangements.[14]

The attempt to accommodate fathers' interests in a symbolically pleasing manner by changing the language with which custody policy is discussed has had political ramifications, however. Because the change in terminology may alter substantive results, it has worked to reallocate power between parents in custody cases, profoundly affecting bargaining between spouses at divorce. The change in rhetoric disadvantages functioning custodial mothers and their children, the occupants of the shadow institution of sole-custody parenting, who have not had a voice in the reform of custody laws.

The helping professions' concern with symbols overshadowed the fact that, in practice, joint-custody dispositions continue to resemble sole maternal custody and paternal visitation.[15] In fact, the social role and function of a sole-custodial parent continues unchanged.[16] Whether or not custodial mothers exist as a legal category, they exist as an institution—as a practical reality experienced by many children of divorce and their mothers. The recent rhetorical disapproval of and attempts to abolish formally the institution of the sole-custodial parent have not destroyed it, but only placed it in the shadows.

The Creation and Use of Discourse

The helping professions' discourse has two conceptually distinct components. The first component is procedural, focusing on the way in which decisions are made. This component describes the differences between the processes used by the legal and helping professions and is the most visible and prevalent part of the discourse. The second component concerns the substantive nature of decisions, and critiques the different results produced under each decision-making method. The substantive discourse is intimately related to and dependent upon the procedural discourse. It is a more obscure and subtle discourse, however, than the one that focuses on procedure, and its premises are often not exposed for examination.

Because the substantive component of the discourse is less salient, the real nature of the competition between the legal and helping professional or therapeutic models for handling divorce has not always been clear. In fact, the debate has been largely confined to the procedural realm, and it therefore is decidedly one-dimensional, with social workers exercising control over the concepts discussed. As characterized, the terms of the debate deter outright opposition by legal professionals because such criticism can be dismissed as the product of mere "turf" concerns. The focus on process has effectively prevented the emergence of a contrasting "legalistic" narrative, which would develop alternative visions of both procedural and substantive goals. This impediment to the development of a contrasting narrative is an important factor whereby a discourse becomes politically dominant as the vision that captures, incorporates, and expresses existing predominant ideological assumptions.

The Social Worker and Divorce

The first expansion of the social worker's role in divorce was through conciliation courts created by many jurisdictions when they adopted no-fault legislation. These courts were designed to provide "short-contact marital counseling service for couples on the verge of separation and divorce."[17] The proponents of such courts justified them on the ground that divorce was a social problem requiring state services to ease the crisis. These services could be provided by social workers, giving them a new role in the legal system at a time when their role was being limited elsewhere.[18] Conciliation courts thus embodied the notion of a partnership between law and the behavioral sciences.[19]

These courts initially provided reconciliation counseling, but as divorce became more accepted and reconciliation a less important goal, the counseling method was replaced first by a divorce-therapy model and ultimately by the contemporary mediation ideal. As the formal role of social workers evolved, so did their ideology and rhetoric. Consistent throughout the evolution of social workers' involvement with divorce, however, has been their perception that their appropriate function is to make divorce as conflict-free as possible, or at least to manage the conflict appropriately.[20]

Changing Social Work Views

Under early social work ideology, divorce was viewed as pathological.[21] Marriage was to last forever, unless there was legally recognized fault. Divorce was to be avoided if at all possible, and the responsibility of the helping professions was to counsel reconciliation. Under no-fault divorce, by contrast, social workers have moved away from the goal of formally reconciling the couple to reconciling them to their new postdivorce relationship and status. The helping professions adapted to the change in legal rules by creating their own view of reconciling or rehabilitating "the family," in which both parents would continue to "co-parent" after divorce.[22]

Currently, the language of the helping professions portrays divorce as an "emotional crisis" that must be treated but can also provide some "unique opportunities for growth."[23] In the rhetoric of the social workers, divorce is a crisis within the "family system"[24]—a type of "situational" crisis to be "managed."[25] Although the profession no longer sees divorce as pathological, a negative impact on the family system is viewed as inevitable. The focus of the helping professional, under this view of divorce, is on both alleviating the initial "trauma" of divorce and managing the "external variables" that may affect the family's future "response and adjustment to divorce."

The goal of the helping professional is to bring the parties to the recognition that the "structural dimensions" of their former marital system have not disappeared but must be reshaped into a new, though limited, "post-dissolution organization." This new organization is based on the relationship between the parents—now ex-spouses—with parent-child relationships as "sub-systems" within this paradigm.[26] Divorce requires parents to "decouple from their former marital and nuclear roles and begin to recouple at a level of shared parenting responsibilities."[27]

In this framework, the role of the system is to be therapeutic—to facilitate and assist the family in adapting to a new postdivorce family structure.[28] Attorneys, in this context, are viewed as ill equipped to handle the crisis because of their adversarial orientation and the ways in which they impede or defeat the therapeutic ideal.[29] By contrast, social workers and others in the helping professions are in possession or control of the therapeutic process.[30]

Opportunity Seized: The Rhetorical War

As their involvement with divorce cases through conciliation, counseling, and court-ordered custody evaluations increased, social workers rejected the lawyer/social worker partnership that they had initially espoused.[31] Within the context of divorce generally—and disputed custody cases particularly—helping professionals challenged central aspects of legal ideology. With the elimination of fault-based divorce and the advent of their crisis theory of divorce, helping professionals began to assert that adversarial concepts and procedures were inappropriate for resolving divorce and custody cases. As Elkin stated as early as 1973:

> [T]he elimination of 'fault' has made it possible for the Court to
> play a much lesser part in banking the fires of hostility. It is a well-
> known fact in role theory that people cast in the roles of adversar-
> ies probably will live up to those roles. . . . [T]he elimination of
> adversary proceedings eliminated adversary roles and therefore
> reduced the need to fulfill antagonistic roles and the need to strike
> out at each other.[32]

Social workers objected to the very nature of the adversarial process, asserting that it was unnecessary, inappropriate, and indicative of the out-
moded notions of "winning" or "losing" custody. Divorce was a crisis
to be worked through; conflict was to be recognized and managed.
Spouses (with the aid of a social worker) were to be self-determining
and exercise their responsibility to each other and their children to settle
their differences so they could function as postdivorce parents. There
simply was no room for such growth in the traditional adversarial
system.[33] Lawyers' use of adversarial procedures was especially criticized for its effect on children.[34] In essence, social workers' attacks
questioned both the appropriateness of the representation ideal and adversariness as a process by which fact-finding and decision-making occur. For example, one commentator stated:

> Lawyers represent their clients to the best of their abilities, regard-
> less of the effect that might have on the other party. Thus, they
> tend to push their particular client to win every possible advan-
> tage. This provides the couple with another arena in which to bat-
> tle out the issues that led to the divorce at the same time that they
> are trying to negotiate a settlement.[35]

Other authors have observed:

> In addition to the universal and unconscious distortions and mis-
> understandings of relationships by each individual, in custody
> evaluations everyone is consciously distorting and misinterpreting.
> The situation precludes total honesty. Each parent is trying to
> present him or herself as the best, the other as the worst, and will
> often censor or distort information to achieve that goal.[36]

The helping professions tend to distinguish two aspects of divorce:
the emotional divorce, which involves "feelings," and the legal divorce,
which involves a division of property, a determination of support, and a
decision about custody.[37] Social workers view the legal divorce as secondary to the emotional divorce. Thus, once an emotional divorce has
occurred, the legal divorce is *pro forma;* conversely, without an emo-

tional divorce, no true separation can or will occur, and the parties will continue to battle throughout and after the legal divorce. Some form of counseling, therapy, or mediation is seen as essential to a resolution of these emotional issues,[38] with postdivorce shared parenting as the optimal goal.

In this regard, social workers argued that an adversarial role was unnecessary: lawyers were not needed to prove grounds for divorce as they had been under the fault-based system. Similarly, social workers viewed lawyers as unconcerned with, and incompetent to perform, the needed therapeutic function.[39]

Lawyers could not be discarded altogether, however, as some issues still needed legal resolution. The social work literature explicitly expressed the competition between the professions, with legal personnel cast as inappropriate decision-makers in custody cases due to their lack of training in child development and psychology. As one article boldly stated, "The judge and the lawyers are not qualified to make a determination as to the best placement for a child considering emotional factors. Judges can evaluate financial and physical circumstances—as can almost any layman."[40] Some commentators are more generous to judges even while criticizing them:

> Although it can be assumed optimistically that most judges are
> concerned, sensitive, intelligent people who want the best for fam-
> ilies, it can also safely be assumed that many of them have limited
> training in child development, women's issues, psychosocial as-
> sessment, or family relations. The reality is that the exercise of ju-
> dicial discretion is far less a product of the judge's learning than of
> his or her temperament, background, interests, and biases.[41]

Although it was initially thought that no-fault divorce would eliminate conflict,[42] social workers' involvement with the system convinced them that this legal change had no such transformative effect. In the custody area, in particular, conflict was still apparent. One article stated, for example:

> The agency's direct involvement in the divorce process through
> the preparation of child custody evaluations only served to
> strengthen the staff's concern with the frequency of unsatisfactory
> outcomes. Even the most arduous, comprehensive, and conciliato-
> rily drafted custody evaluation was unsuccessful in significantly
> reducing the competitiveness, acrimony, and pain within the fam-
> ily system. There continued to be a winner, a loser, and ongoing
> stress.[43]

Moreover, the mental health workers, philosophically geared toward cooperation and compromise, experienced great frustration working within a legal system that required the choice of one parent over another and that promoted one relationship while "terminating" another.[44] In the task of performing custody evaluations, for example, even the most carefully expressed adverse recommendation might produce pain and anger.[45]

Social workers' disenchantment with the conflict-reducing potential of no-fault divorce led them toward mediation. Consider the following report about a private agency's transition to a mediation model:

> The agency was uncomfortable in its role [of performing evaluations for use in court] which too often resulted in prolonging, sometimes intensifying, and too seldom resolving the agony of the family. A hypothesis evolved: it was not the characteristics of the decision itself that generated failures but rather the identity of the decision makers. The courts could not hope to *resolve* parental disputes if they did not have the cooperation of the family.
>
> When parents accepted responsibility for restructuring the family, when they used their energy to create a resolution, and when they had an investment in making that resolution work, the outcome had the greatest hope of becoming a true resolution.[46]

Another commentator reported:

> In undertaking the role of divorce mediator, social workers must first overcome the difficulty of being party to a family's breakup. Most social workers see their role as a supportive one and use their professional skills in assisting families to resolve their problems and stay together. . . .
>
> Once divorce is inevitable, the social worker's role changes to one of attempting to make the separation as painless as possible, to help the couple maintain their individual dignity, and to assist the children to make the transition by reducing the conflict inherent in the process of divorce.[47]

Social workers' criticisms of the existing no-fault system formed the basis of calls for an alternative system, reflecting even more procedural and substantive changes, such as mediation and the establishment of a shared-parenting norm. These reforms were urged in rhetoric that embodied their view of litigation, conflict, and what is desirable in the postdivorce family.[48]

The calls for change were accompanied by assertions about what was "really" happening in the divorce context; that reality was psychological, not legal, in its focus. According to mental health professionals, the desire to litigate divorce issues, particularly custody, is the product of unresolved feelings about the termination of the marriage. This theme is strongly presented in the very influential work of Wallerstein & Kelly detailed in chapter 7, in which the authors state:

> Psychologically, an individual's rage against an ex-spouse, often expressed in litigation in which the child is the pawn, can apparently remain undiminished by the passage of time or by distance. The fight for a child may serve profound psychological needs in a parent, including the warding off of severe depression and other forms of pathological disorganization.[49]

Intervention by a helping professional is necessary to assist a couple in resolving these feelings, so that they do not engage in protracted litigation as an extension of their emotional battles. The helping professionals' view is that litigation is harmful to all, particularly children, and that it is usually undertaken without any true legal or factual justification. The literature recognizes few valid bases for custody battles. One commentator expressed this sentiment thus:

> Parents who contest custody are usually not emotionally divorced from each other: their struggles with one another are not dead but have disguised themselves as a custody dispute. . . . Custody/visitation disputes are essentially unresolved family conflicts exacerbated by the breakup of the family and the adversarial court procedures. . . .[50]

Moreover, results achieved under a sole-custody legal doctrine were objectionable from the viewpoint of social workers' "family-systems" theory. Rather than focusing on the best parent, the social worker concentrated on how to "restructure" the family.[51] As one advocate of restructuring argued:

> Reorganization is clearly the goal: Just as the relationship between married spouses is a critical determinant of family interaction, so, too, is the relationship between divorced spouses critical to divorced family reorganization and interaction. . . . The [stressful] process of coparental redefinition requires that divorced spouses separate their spousal and parental roles, terminating the former while redefining the latter. This very difficult and somewhat paradoxical process forms the nucleus of divorced family reorganization and redefinition.[52]

Restructuring meant allowing both parents to continue their parental relationship with the children.[53] When forced to choose between parents, helping professionals preferred the parent who would most freely allow the child access to the other parent.[54] The notion of "the most generous parent" became synonymous with the determination of who was the better parent.[55]

Given social workers' assumptions, their criticisms of the legal system, and their characterization of divorce, it is no surprise that mediation by those trained in the helping professions emerged as the logical procedural solution.[56] If disputed custody was really an emotional event, and the legal system and lawyers had no ability to address the problems, then a new process and new personnel were necessary. Social workers' criticisms of legal decision-makers, processes, and results were essential to the formulation of the mediation ideal.[57]

Language has played a critical role in the reform process that has shifted decision-making authority to mediators and the helping professions. The rhetoric employed criticized the traditional system and established an alternative that called for skills possessed by helping professionals. Yet the rhetoric has occasioned more than a transfer, formal or informal, of responsibility for making the ultimate decision in contested cases. It has invoked changes in the substantive rules by which cases are resolved. The domination of social work ideology and rhetoric now appears complete. It is inconceivable that one could seriously discuss custody policy and practice today without both using the rhetoric and addressing the concepts and values of the helping professions.

The Manner of Appropriation: The Use of Narrative Strategies and the Intersection of Other Interests

I believe that the rhetoric and strategy of the helping professions have been successful for two related reasons. First, the helping professions have presented their arguments in the form of "stories" containing powerful images that are readily understood by those not familiar with the custody decision-making process. Second, the images that they project intersect and are compatible with the interests of significant societal groups that have facilitated the changes suggested by the stories.

Narrative Strategies

As with property reform (detailed in chapters 3 and 4), one of the significant methods by which equality ideals became dominant in the custody area was through the construction and manipulation of rhetorical visions or narratives—stories with a beginning, a middle, and an end. There is competition and drama—tension and resolution—in these narratives. Their "morals" are ways of legitimating one type of substantive and procedural result to the exclusion of others. In describing or illustrating a "problem," they also suggest the "solution." This form of presentation makes the professional standards of the helping professions and the legal system concrete, understandable, and susceptible to positive action. This rhetorical strategy operates by presenting simplistic, dichotomous images: negative images, or "horror stories," regarding the existing (lawyer-controlled) divorce practice and corresponding positive images, or "fairy tales," of an idealized (controlled by the social worker) process for purer and better decision-making.

An additional characteristic of these narratives operated to the helping professions' advantage in securing changes: they were cast in terms of mere substitution of decision-makers rather than alteration of results. They focused on divorce as a discrete event that had to be made less volatile through the use of trained mediators. These narratives either assumed or ignored and obscured the desirability of the substantive goal of shared parenting. The narratives confined the discussion to the desirability of a change in procedure without revealing that this would also produce a change in substance compatible with the new decision-makers' professional ideology and norms.

The use of rhetorical devices serves the institutional interests of those in the mediation business who wish to stake out an area for their own control. Their language, which is cast as neutral and professional, is political. As professor Edelman asserted in his early work on linguistic theory:

> With [language] we not only describe reality but create our own realities. . . . It is a commonplace of linguistic theory that language, thought, and action shape each other. Language is always an intrinsic part of some particular social situation; it is never an independent instrument or simply a tool for description. By naively perceiving it as a tool, we mask its profound part in creating social relationships and in evoking the roles and the "selves" of those relationships. . . .
>
> The most fundamental and long-lasting influences upon political beliefs flow . . . from language that is not perceived as political at all. . . . The special language of the helping professions, which we are socialized to see as professional and as nonpolitical, is a major example of this level of politics. . . .[58]

This fact has been obscured, however, because their rhetoric has confined the debate to a procedural level.

The Horror Story

The image of the legal system constructed by the helping professions is adversarial, combative, and productive of divisions, misunderstandings, and hostility. These negative characterizations are understood to be the inevitable products of a system controlled by attorneys and the judiciary. Social workers assert that lawyers focus on rights, claims, due process, and other things "peripheral" to the real issues.

Those who flock to mediation as the ideal decision-making mechanism accuse lawyers and the adversary system of increasing trauma, escalating conflict, obstructing communication, failing to perceive the need for negotiation and counseling, and generally interfering with the development of a process that could help the parties. In their vision, the adversarial system, with its emphasis on conflict and rationality, is inherently unresponsive to the "emotions" and "feelings" associated with the divorce process,[59] feelings which social workers believe are more important and worthy of concern.

Lawyers in general and judges in particular are viewed as poorly trained to deal with the psychological aspects of divorce. Blinder accused lawyers of suffering from "militant tunnel-vision advocacy." His view of the different roles of attorney and social worker is so remarkable that it is worth quoting in full:

> In short, the attorney has an obligation to point out to the client that the manifest reasons s/he seeks a divorce may not be the real ones, and that need for professional guidance may not end with marital dissolution. It is the task of the family therapist to help people make a success of their marriage. Should that be impossible, the therapist may still be able to assist the attorney in the latter's responsibility to help the couple at least make a success of their divorce. Attorneys by temperament and training are inclined to see marital and child custody problems as residing entirely within their opponent's client, leaving their own client blameless. The family therapist has the obligation to help the attorney recognize that such problems usually reside not *within* but *between* the contesting parties. I know of no field of law where the tools of militant tunnel-vision advocacy are less appropriate.[60]

Lawyers and judges are seen as acting on their own biases and values in determining what is in the best interest of the child.[61] A related criticism is that lawyers replace the parties in the negotiation process and thereby fail to enhance the conflict-management skills of the parties and to produce agreements to which the parties are committed. Indeed, McKenry views mediation as the only "responsible" choice for couples:

> In the adversary system, couples relinquish nearly all responsibility for decisions about the settlement to their respective attorneys and communicate with each other by proxy. Couples involved in divorce mediation decide on the issues of their divorce settlement themselves. The partners work together under the guidance of an impartial mediator and according to the marital mediation rules of the association.[62]

Lawyers are criticized for dwelling on the past, laying blame, finding fault, and failing to focus on future conduct as do mediators.[63] In this way, social workers' rhetoric lays the basis for their claim to control of the process.

Even social workers and mediators who are friendly to lawyers cannot seem to avoid a negative, stereotypical characterization of them. In a recent article advocating a close working relationship between the professions, one author described how lawyers are committed to "rationality, rights, and conflict solution," whereas social workers are concerned with "feelings, needs, and growth through relationship."[64] In the social work world, of course, to accuse someone of rationality or intellectualism is a criticism, implying an insensitivity to more important emotional concerns.[65]

The generic horror story therefore involves a husband, wife and child(ren) who enter the divorce process, employing two lawyers (his and hers).[66] There is escalating bitterness, pain and suffering. More and more money is expended. The child(ren) is(are) particularly hurt by the process, particularly since he/she(they) lose(s) a parent in the process (the "noncustodial" parent). It is a process in which there are "winners" and "losers." In other words, it seems inevitable that there will be an unhappy ending to this narrative.

The Fairy Tale

In contrast to the negative images embodied in the horror stories describing the legal process, the helping professions present themselves as a distinct and preferable alternative. The ideal is established rhetorically.

Social workers view divorce as occasioning the birth of an ongoing, albeit different, relationship, with mediators and social workers as its midwives and monitors. "Let's talk about it" seems to be the ideal, and the talk is envisioned as continuing for decades. The continued involvement is not only with each other but with the legal system as well. This ideal is obviously very different from the traditional legal system, which seeks an end or termination of significant interaction at divorce: a division, a distribution, or allocation of the things acquired during marriage—an emancipatory model—and with its "ending," the permission for a "new life" for the participants and the withdrawal of active legal interference in their relationship.

The helping professions' ideal process "avoids" or "reduces" conflict and is typified by mediation. Helping professionals believe that mediation,[67] employing a therapeutic process, is within their exclusive domain because lawyers, unlike social workers, ignore the underlying causes of divorce and give little regard to the "real reason" for it. Therapeutic skills can facilitate acceptance of the divorce and foster a positive approach to the crisis.

Lawyers' skills are downgraded and social workers' and mediators' skills are mystified and reified:

> Lawyers or others with legal experience have much to offer, but skills in behavioral science are lacking. It is generally easier for one trained in behavioral sciences to acquire legal and other knowledge required for mediation, than for the legally trained person to gain knowledge and a feel for behavioral science and counseling skills.[68]

In this way, social workers and mediators set apart the concerns of the adversarial system and subordinate them to the more important concerns of their own professions. Caring, sharing, mental health, and concern for future function, they assert, are their exclusive preserve and cannot be attained through the adversarial process.

In this contrasting generic fairy-tale narrative, husband, wife, and child(ren) consult not two lawyers but one mediator; only one is necessary because the process is nonadversarial. The process is characterized by cooperation, caring, and acceptance.[69] It costs less money and produces a fairer result. This is obviously a narrative with a happy ending.

INTERSECTION WITH OTHER INTERESTS

Also significant in regard to the success of the transformation of custody decision-making is the fact that the rhetoric of social workers and mediators intersected with and incorporated the concerns and assumptions of several other groups concerned with custody policy. This overlap assisted the mediators' discourse in gaining dominance. The helping professions' views on mediation, for example, have empowered fathers and fathers'-rights groups. The rhetoric has offered fathers' groups a legitimate way to argue for their political goal of removing custody cases from the courts, which they view as favoring women. Fathers'-rights groups see mediators as more malleable than judges and attorneys, who are concerned with laws and rights. They also see mediators as less powerful and exacting and less likely to focus on embarrassing child-support issues when custody and visitation problems exist. In fact, most mediators do not feel competent to address the economic aspects of divorce. Setting custody in a mediation context, therefore, ensures it is isolated from economic considerations, a result that should be of some concern since the ability to parent children adequately is somewhat related to material circumstances. It is no wonder that within the fathers'-rights discourse, mediators are the preferred decision-makers.[70]

Some of the nonprocedural implications of the change in process begin to emerge in the political use by various groups of the helping professions' concepts. There is still no careful or developed assessment of the shared-parenting norm, however. Rather, the shared-parenting norm is presented as the solution to identified problems. For example, fathers'-rights groups have pushed for mediation and joint custody because they claim these innovations will encourage men, who now default in alarming numbers, to pay their child support.[71] These groups indicate that the legion of fathers who never bother to visit their children will flock to see them if they are empowered with unilaterally exercisable rights with regard to their children.[72] Ironically, the failure of divorced fathers is used as one of the major arguments for giving men more control and power over children and, through them, over their mothers' lives.[73] Joint custody or shared parenting, however, empowers fathers as a group without requiring any demonstration of responsibility. I consider this inappropriate. In no other area does the law reward those who have failed in their duties as an incentive for them to change their behavior.

The rhetoric of mediators also intersects with and complements the concerns of members of the legal profession. This convergence is probably one of the most significant factors in the success of the helping professions' reforms. Mediators have been empowered by judges and court administrators who dislike custody decision-making under the best-interest test or who believe that such cases clog up the system. The substantive implications may be lost and the discussion focused merely on the transfer of troublesome custody issues to an "alternative" system.[74] This is particularly true when the alternative system is characterized as "more humane and caring" and appears to resolve everyone's problems.

Further, family-law attorneys who are uncomfortable in courtroom settings or bored with their profession may find it attractive to envision themselves as mediators, employing a whole new set of mechanisms that will enhance their prestige, their self-worth, and the quality of what they do on a day-to-day basis. There is a mystique about mediation that many find compelling. Mediators do not choose sides but are counsel for the situation. Mediators are disinterested advisors whose only role is to assist the family in making decisions. Family lawyers have a bad image in the press, in the eyes of the public, and in their own eyes;[75] mediation may be a way of rehabilitating that image.

Legislatures also have found the reallocation of decision-making power attractive. The reallocation can be accomplished by using existing court-associated personnel—the social workers who previously performed custody investigations can now try their hands at mediation. Further, because the goal of shared parenting leads to equal division, or joint custody, it is consistent with the recent trend in all of family law toward mathematical formulas for decision-making.

To those uncertain about or upset with the function of the present family-law system, the mediators' vision presents a more coherent and more encompassing ideal embodying deeply held beliefs and assumptions. In the procedural context, it offers a process free of conflict. In the substantive context, it appeals to ideals of equality, sharing, and caring. The mediators' view is also one that seems distinctly utopian. Its underlying premise is that one can seek personal happiness and fulfillment by terminating a marriage relationship, yet not lose any of the benefits that marriage provides. The hidden message is that divorce can be painless. One can retain one's children, even one's "family," although the family structure may be slightly altered. It is a grand dream: everybody wins, nobody loses.

Assessing the Narratives

The issue arises why anyone (except those involved) should care about the rhetorical competition I have described between lawyers and social workers in this area. In fact, some lawyers join the mediators and fight for the very reforms that will take divorce and custody decision-making out of the legal system.[76] The rhetorical competition I have described has important implications for many people who are or will be involved in the family-law process, particularly custodial mothers. The ideological shifts described may in fact result in a process that produces bad decisions for many women and children.[77] Joint custody can be a disaster if parents are unwilling or unable to cooperate.[78] Such an arrangement may give a man continued control over his children (and through the children, control over his ex-wife's life) yet not result in increased assumption of responsibility on his part. Anecdotal evidence indicates that many women view joint custody as "losing"—whereas many man view it as "winning"—the divorce wars;[79] as a result, many women bargain away needed property and support benefits to avoid the risk of "losing" their children. The negative implications of the shift to a therapeutic model and mediation remain largely unexplored.

Proponents of the therapeutic model have defused possible political controversy and opposition to these changes by casting themselves as neutral, disinterested professionals in their advocacy of mediation and the substantive goal of shared parenting. But they are not neutral. They have an institutional and professional bias for certain procedural and substantive results that promote their own interests and that will produce changes designed to enhance and ensure their continued centrality in custody decision-making.

The discourse of the helping professions has created rather than reflected reality. In part, helping professionals have been successful in appropriating the divorce business for themselves because, in the abstract, they offer hope to those who have been hurt by divorce and custody battles. The "reality" that they construct through their rhetoric is one that many want to believe exists.

The realistic assessment of the "fairy-tale" narrative, however, is that there will be no happy ending; in fact, there will be no ending at all. The narrative assumes an ongoing relationship between the spouses, not an ending—a fact that is not apparent in the presentation of the typical adversary system versus mediation.

The costs associated with such nonendings are also hidden. Traditional divorce was an emancipatory process that terminated the relationship and freed lives for rebuilding. The social workers' ideal of an ongoing coparental relationship may leave little room for the formation of new relationships by parents or by children. Children may in fact suffer more from these nonendings.[80] They may never be able to overcome the quite typical fantasy that mommy and daddy will get back together. It is not clear that nonendings will in fact be "happy" in any significant number of family situations.

Nonendings do benefit mediators, however, who assert that only they can achieve reorganization of families (the process that produces happy nonendings). In the view of the social worker, mediation is in the

first instance designated as a superior process[81]—one based on infor-
mality that can, therefore, give full protection to the privacy and autonomy of the parties by allowing them to make important decisions for
themselves. The ideal process takes place within a context of open communication and protects the parties against having issues decided for
them through lawyers' adversarial tricks.

Yet the supposed benefits of mediation are not all process-related. It
is also argued that the purpose of mediation—to reorient the parties toward one another—is substantially different from, and superior to, the
legal ideal. Mediation discourages the focus on legal rights and seeks to
help the divorcing parties achieve a new and shared postdivorce relationship through which each redirects his or her attitude and disposition toward the other for postdivorce shared parenting. The ideal product of the process, in the rhetoric of the helping professions, is a
restructuring of the adults' relationship rather than its termination.

Some processes, according to the helping professions, facilitate the
adjustment of the "family system" for postdivorce parenting; others,
such as adversarial processes, interfere with it. The helping professions
believe that the process for awarding sole custody, for example, is indicative of the win/lose mentality that social workers seek so desperately to
purge from the system. Implicitly, within the helping professions' rhetorical framework, the mediator/social worker is the appropriate, preferred decision-maker who dispenses the appropriate, preferred result.
The social worker's old role as dispenser of "treatment" to deter divorce
or, failing this, of advisor to the court about what placement would be
in the best interest of the child has evolved into a new role. Social workers are now in charge of reordering and maintaining the family system.
Their role has evolved into one that begins by managing the initial
trauma, then attempts to achieve acceptance of the changes caused by
the divorce, and ultimately seeks to restructure the family from "married couple with children" to "divorced co-parents."

Although "system stability" has remained a constant goal under early
and contemporary social work practice, the new ideal focuses on build-
ing the postdivorce relationship between both parents rather than ensuring that there is one custodial parent with whom the children have a
primary relationship. In this process, the relationship of the noncustodial parent to his or her children has assumed great importance, and fa-
cilitating continual contact between children and noncustodial parents
is the paramount pragmatic goal.[82]

The implications of this approach are enormous. Not only does this
represent a serious decision about who it is that ultimately makes cus-

tody decisions—judge, attorney, or mediator/social worker—but, because of the nature of the mediator/shared-parenting ideal, adoption of this approach represents a significant opportunity for continuous and substantial intervention by social workers or other court-associated personnel. The goals of the helping professions are at odds with the traditional legal goal of divorce. Nothing is "terminated" except the formal marital bond between the adults. Because the family unit theoretically continues, it may often be in need of the services and communication skills provided by the mediator alternative to the adversarial system. Potentially, therefore, the legal system's involvement will not end either, at least until all the children reach adulthood. Coercive and continuous supervision of the restructured unit is compatible with this view. There are no legal or doctrinal impediments to reactivating the mediation system.[83] If things are not operating to the satisfaction of one ex-spouse, the mediation mechanism can be reengaged to work things out.

This narrative nonending has been uncritically incorporated into reform rhetoric concerning the legal system. Recent changes in custody rules, particularly those setting forth presumptions of joint custody, are consistent with the rhetoric and the nonending it advocates. The acceptance of this nontermination ideal is also associated to some extent with the imposition of other ideals onto family law, including the goals of equality, gender neutrality, and social restructuring. Concern with these abstract goals may overtake the desire to reach workable and practical decisions upon divorce. The entire area is permeated with symbolism that relates only tangentially to the realities of divorce.

Ultimately, the helping professions' discourse has encompassed and absorbed traditional legal dialogue concerning custody. "Sharing" became identified as the public and political language of the escalating debate over the appropriate concept and process for resolving custody disputes.[84] The political victory of the helping professions is evident in the conferring of legally significant rights and obligations, through the explicit delegation of decision-making authority, upon the social workers and mediators. The legislature and the judiciary have delegated this power both on an institutional level, by creating mandatory mediation or counseling services staffed with social workers and connected to the court system, and in individual cases, in which judges seek and accept the advice of "experts" in the helping profession. This formal recognition of the helping professions' role places the state's imprimatur on their appropriation of custody decision-making.

THE POLITICS OF CUSTODY

The rhetorical symbolism employed by social workers and mediators is politically powerful. It empowers the helpers and may allow them to eclipse the interests of those who are designated as the very ones to be helped. For example, although the helping professions' vision portrays mediation as allowing custody decisions to be made with sharing and caring rather than with conflict and contention, mediation may in fact merely hide rather than eliminate conflict, allowing the stronger of the two parents to dominate and control the weaker.[85]

The adoption of the mediators' image has important substantive implications with significant political and social ramifications. One of the most harmful assumptions underlying social workers' discourse is that a parent who seeks sole custody of a child has some illegitimate motivation.[86] Mediators may acknowledge exceptions to this generalization in situations in which one parent is a drunkard or drug addict or in which a child is abused, but the general assumption is that the parent who is willing to live up to the ideal of shared custody and control is the one with the child's real interests at heart.

Mediation advocates often characterize opposition to shared custody as pathological.[87] The assumption in the social workers' discourse is that the parent who rejects the shared-parenting ideal and seeks sole custody of his or her child has an illegitimate motive. A mother who resists sharing her child with her ex-husband is characterized as having "issue overlay"; she protests too much.[88] Such women may be characterized as clinging and overly dependent on their roles as wives and mothers; social workers and mediators assert that these women can be helped through the mediation process only if they are cooperative. Other women are seen as greedy, merely using the children in order to get larger property settlements; it is claimed that an "effective" mediator can block these women from achieving their evil ends. A third stereotype focuses on vindictive mothers who use the children to get back at their ex-husbands; they are perceived as the type of women who should be punished by having their children taken away and sole custody awarded to the fathers.

Lost in the rhetoric of the social worker are real concerns. There is little or no appreciation of the many real problems that joint custody and the ideal of sharing and caring can cause. The prospect of a continued relationship with an ex-spouse may be horrifying to contemplate,[89] but the sharing ideal assumes that a relationship between the noncustodial parent and the child cannot proceed without it. Also unsettling is the extent to which allegations of mistreatment, abuse, or neglect on the part of husbands toward either their wives or children are trivialized, masked, or lost amid the psychological rhetoric that reduces mothers' desires to have custody and control of their children to pathology.[90]

We should be deeply skeptical of these views on women and mothers. They are not accurate, and the visions they present are deeply misogynous. In a recent survey of the literature on mental health professionals published between 1970 and 1982, one author found "mother-blaming" in "epidemic proportions":

> In the 125 articles in [the] study, mothers were held responsible for 72 different types of pathological disorder in their children. . . . [N]ot a single mother was ever described as emotionally healthy, although some father-child [relationships] were described as ideal.[91]

Contrary to the rhetorical vision of much of the helping professions, most mothers love their children and would not willfully deprive them of contact with a caring and responsible father. In fact, if the children are old enough to assert their own interests, it is unlikely that mothers could deprive them of contact with their fathers even if they wanted to. By making these observations, I do not mean to suggest that abuses never occur but rather to point out that they are not typical, or even common, and that it is irrational to base custody policy on the deviant rather than the typical postdivorce situation.

Because social workers and others sympathetic to mediation have created and controlled the presentation of both narratives, the real nature of the competition between the legal and therapeutic models has been hidden. Notably, there are no parallel scenarios involving vindictive or greedy husbands in the mediation literature. No alternative narrative sympathetic to the single parent or sole custody and control has gained any credibility in the literature. Nor do many stories assign different characters to the stock "victim" and "villain" roles.

Further, by branding opposition to mediation and joint custody as the manifestation of a psychological problem to which mediation is itself the solution, mediation rhetoric forecloses any effective expression of women's legitimate concerns. As things now stand, the cries of protest over the imposition of a joint-custody or shared-parenting solution from mothers who will be assuming primary care for their children (but sharing control) are attributed to the fact that these mothers have not accomplished an "emotional divorce." As soon as they are able to get over "their issues" they will be able to begin "rational problem solving" and will cooperate agreeably.

Social workers' discourse accepts without criticism the superiority of "rational decision making" within the new, reconstructed family structure. Through this method the "vindictive" woman is thwarted and the "victimized" man allowed to continue to operate in *pater familias* (in an altered form, of course) by being given "equal rights" without the formal imposition of responsibility. Helping professionals believe this approach remedies the pro-mother imbalance that has existed in custody decision making.

The important substantive implications of these reforms for divorce and child-custody cases are obscured by viewing mediation simply as an "alternative procedure" that is preferable to settlement negotiations previously performed by attorneys. Such a perspective misses the more fundamental challenges mediation presents to central aspects of the legal model, particularly the traditional notion that representation by competing adversaries is the most reliable method of establishing the necessary facts upon which to base subsequent decision-making. The ability of helping professions to label divorce a psychosocial crisis has been pivotal in this regard: what was once a legal event handled through legal procedures by lawyers and judges has become an emotional crisis to be managed by mental health professionals. That substantive changes have resulted from this procedural shift should not be surprising. This trend should be reversed.

PART THREE
Abdicating Equality

T E N

Alternative Visions from Discarded Discourses

[T]he United States has less economic equality than Sweden or Japan, at least in part because American cultural values and political structures do not foster it. . . . [T]here are no necessary or automatic links between political equality and economic equality. The United States has experienced steady movement toward political equality yet relatively little change in the distribution of economic resources. . . .

Ironically, the strong U.S. commitment to political equality and the strong antipathy to established authority limit the state's ability to "enforce" equality. The U.S. government is weak; it would have trouble launching an ambitious redistributive effort, and few people appear to want it to do so. Americans endorse equality of opportunity, an ideal that fits well with the individualistic, achievement-oriented principles of free-market capitalism. This view is reflected in the strong American commitment to public education. Concern for opportunity instead of condition delayed the introduction of a system of comprehensive health care until the mid-1960s. . . .

The United States also has faced a troubling irony throughout its history: although it encompasses an extraordinary diversity of ethnic, racial, religious, and regional groups . . . it has always preferred to address equality issues in highly individualistic terms. Group-based claims do not fare well in the American political system.

Verba et al.*

ALTERNATIVE VISIONS

Substantial agreement exists among legal and other professional groups that changes in the area of divorce, property distribution, and

*VERBA & KELMAN, ORREN, MIYAKE, WATANUKI, KABASHIMA & FERREE, *ELITES AND THE IDEA OF EQUALITY* 55 (1987).

child custody have not only been proper and appropriate but progressive and far-reaching. There may be some "minor" adjustments or "tinkering" necessary, but equality is clearly recognized to be the fundamental organizing concept and desirable goal. Such conclusions are also consistent with mainstream liberal feminist rhetoric. There seem to be few oppositional groups. The way in which the reforms were generated and the symbolic terms in which they were couched, in addition to the difficulty of articulating an effective critique of "equality" in the family-law context, combine to place these reforms beyond popular criticism. Far from representing substantial challenges to the concepts underlying the traditional family, however, family-law reforms have simply reinforced old values, adapting patriarchal objectives and structures of control to contemporary circumstances. Both the old and the reformed rules operate to the comparative disadvantage of divorcing women and their children because they are premised on the two-parent, patriarchal model as the "normal" family form.

The newly-fashioned gender-neutral law creates an appearance of equality, but the consequences of divorce are far from equally borne. From a practical perspective, divorce was never equally available to women and men under the fault system because of men's comparative economic superiority, which allowed them much greater freedom to leave unsatisfying intimate relationships. This remains true today. Despite the fact that each spouse has a legal right to unilaterally terminate the marriage bond, the costs—both economic and, given custody reforms, emotional—which attend divorce are far more profound for women than men. Thus, in spite of the illusion of easily available divorce created by formal law, it is still freer for some than for others.

Even the most cursory review of data like that gathered by Lenore Weitzman[1] supports the contention that divorce is an economically advantageous enterprise for men but disastrous for women and children. Through the application of a business, contractual, partnership model, dependency and need are obscured. Changes in the economic rules governing divorce certainly were not designed to be responsive to the needs of many women and children. Furthermore, were the economic realities of divorce not sufficient disincentive to women contemplating an exit from marriage, the fear of loss of custody or the prospect of a continued, postdivorce shared-parenting relationship with an ex-husband now looms as well. Contemporary custody discourse trivializes women's emotional investment in their primary caretaking relationship with their children. It is perhaps on this level that reformist discourse has been least sensitive to women's reality.

Symbolic ideals have overshadowed more instrumental concerns in divorce reform. They have done so because they have ignored women's connection to children in an attempt to cast them as unencumbered, equally-empowered market actors. Perhaps in some future, more distant time, the transformative aspects of these symbolic reforms may begin to bear fruit; however, more than a decade after their implementation, such changes are more illusionary and rhetorical than real. The casualties are clear—scores of women and children forced to endure "equality" today for the tenuous prospect of gender equity decades away.

Alternative visions, not premised on symbolically satisfying notions of grand concepts such as equality, were available that might have resulted in rules very different from those adopted in recent years in the majority of jurisdictions. They are much less ambitious and much more focused, and reflect the unequal "reality" of many women's lives. The proposals reference less-grand social goals about which many people can agree, such as the encouragement of nurturing and care for children. I do not suggest that these are perfect or even permanent solutions, but they reflect my belief that legal policy-making involves more than the uncritical imposition of superficial social ideals, that the articulation and imposition of norms through law has profound political and moral implications.

Alternative Solutions
Property Division at Divorce

Although equality in the ongoing family seems to be viewed as a key for women's entry into the market, feminist theory has for the most part neglected divorce as a distinct subject of inquiry. Of course, divorce does present the same sort of questions about access to market participation for women with domestic responsibilities as for those involved in ongoing marriage, but the problems associated with combining work and family are exacerbated. The circumstances that would make equal access to market institutions a viable reality for a divorced woman are more complicated than those presented in the context of an ongoing family with both spouses present. The idealized feminist solution of shared, equal responsibility for domestic chores is hard to implement when the family unit only has one adult in residence. The chores still have to be done, children must be cared for, and a home must be established and maintained, but there are no longer two adults to divide the burdens. If women assume these responsibilities after divorce, as they do in the overwhelming majority of cases, they may need more assets or financial resources than their ex-spouses to have effective access to market opportunities. This need is further complicated by the fact that a woman is statistically likely to earn far less than her ex-spouse after divorce even if she is working. To achieve equality of result, it might thus be necessary to treat the spouses differently when distributing the assets of the marriage. Perhaps even postdivorce income should be allocated as "alimony" or "property" to ensure adequate future care of children.[2]

To be satisfied with or to insist upon rule-equality in fashioning the economic rules to be applied at divorce is to overlook the serious toll that an egalitarian ideology takes on women who must function in an unequal world, which requires that they meet greater demands with fewer resources. It also elevates a simplified ideal to the status of a rule of decision, and obscures the real issues in divorce. Feminists, consistent with their desire to assist women, should be advocating the need for unequal treatment—for result-equality—in divorce.

As it currently stands, the partnership concept of sharing responsibility and contribution is typically translated into assuming equal economic responsibility after divorce, a result that is unrealistic, even cruel, given the material situation of many women. The problem is not that the idea of sharing financial responsibility between husband and wife is inherently unreasonable or unfair, but rather that sharing expectations must be tempered by reference to the statistical evidence indicating that equality in the financial circumstances of men and women does not exist. Shared responsibility should not be equated with equal responsibility.[3] Furthermore, as recent studies have shown, two decades of the women's movement have not substantially improved the position of women and children. As Victor Fuchs has argued:

> The advocates of comparable worth are correct on one score: society does put a lower value on the work that women do. But they are incorrect in thinking that this results from some flaw in the market. . . .
>
> Historically, women have been disadvantaged [in] many ways—by law, by religion, by custom, and by prejudice. These handicaps are gradually being eliminated. In contemporary America, the greatest barrier to economic equality is children. Most women want to bear children and are concerned about their well-being once they are born. Whether this "maternal instinct" is primarily biological or some complex interaction of biology and culture, is not critical for framing public policy. What is important is that the "propensity to mother" is present and strong, and puts

women at a disadvantage. I conclude that the fairest, most efficient, most effective way to help women is through their children.

Child-centered policies have another advantage: they help children directly. This appeals to my sense of equity because they are
the group that has been most adversely affected by recent social
and economic trends. The "feminization" of poverty . . . is
[largely] illusory, at least for white women. But the "juveniliza-
tion" of poverty is very real for children of all races.[4]

Fuchs makes three major recommendations in the form of general
principles:

1. Child-centered policies are preferable to labor market interven-
   tions.
2. The child-centered benefits should be widely available—not
   conditioned on marital status, employment status, or income.
3. The cost of the programs should be borne by the entire society
   through broad-based progressive taxes, not distributed
   through arbitrary methods with euphemistic names like "em-
   ployer provided" daycare.[5]

Principles such as these recognize and accomodate the positive and lasting nature of mothers' ties to their children, which are evident in our
culture and consistently borne out by statistics. They do not rest on
empty ideals such as equality.

The ramifications of our continued symbolic adherence to equality in
reforming family law have been significant. A commitment to equality
initially encouraged its proponents to minimize or deny differences between the individuals for whom they asserted they spoke—women—
and the individuals they perceived to be in superior positions—men.
Contribution was adopted as the justification for modern economic
rules because it *is* an equalizing concept, while *need* demands an ac-
knowledgment and evaluation of differences.

Overreliance on symbolic concerns has created several difficulties.
The contribution concept has impeded the development of instrumental rules and implementation of principles such as those suggested by
Fuchs that directly address practical problems. Arguing that housework
and child care are "equal" to monetary contributions and are therefore
entitled to equal recognition when property is divided, of course, could
be viewed as one way of dealing with need in the overall context of the
equality concept. Need is disguised, but not abandoned.[6] But this is not
satisfactory if there is a conceptual limitation on the notion of contribution. If the assumption is that contributions are to be considered as of

equal value, therefore deserving no more than an equal share of the property the equality solution must be considered inadequate for addressing the problem of need. So limited, equal divisions would fail to satisfy need in the overwhelming majority of cases.

One scholar who recently analyzed property divisions at divorce under equitable distribution statutes found that even when the presumption for a 50/50 division is not explicitly a part of the statutory scheme, courts seldom deviated from an equal property division except in extraordinary cases, which usually involved a spouse with poor health. Furthermore, when deviation did occur, it was usually minimal, involving a 60/40 distribution of assets. She concluded that courts are not using property distribution to address postdivorce financial disparity between spouses despite express statutory authority providing for consideration of such need-based factors.[7] As to the ability of equal divisions to satisfy need, it should be apparent to the reader by now that need cannot be alleviated by equal divisions so long as other factors between men and women remain unequal.

Perhaps the inescapable fact of need underlies the current battle to expand the concept of property. By categorizing education or goodwill in a business as property, the division question can be neatly resolved by imposing the equality model with its theoretical tenets of contribution and right. The present articulation of the argument urging that future income constitutes property in some circumstances is confined to relatively few fact situations, but as the argument gains adherents, the concept may be expanded as a way of dealing with need within the framework of equality. Earlier reformers, for example, hoped to lessen the negative stereotypes concerning the dependency of women associated with *alimony* by substituting the term *maintenance.* How much better for the image of woman as independent and equal if future salary or earnings could be characterized as property and therefore be subject to equal division as a matter of right.[8] Maintenance (nee, alimony) would be further transformed from a concept based on need, with its negative implications of dependency and market inferiority, to one consistent with equality, with its positive concepts of contribution and partnership. The difficulty with this resolution is that it only applies to those cases where a "contribution" has been made to acquiring the degree or the good-will.

The concept of need is the often-unstated argument that underlies all the arguments in the property division area. Because it is disguised, however, the solutions which are proposed can fail to deal effectively with the problem of need. To emerge from a divorce in a position that even begins to put them on a par with their husbands, many women need to receive more in property division than the strict equality concept will allow.

At a minimum, the family home should follow custody of the children, and alimony should routinely be used to offset future economic *and* noneconomic difficulties caused to the child-caring unit by market and child-care responsibilities. In this way it is possible to formally adhere to basic feminist goals, such as gender neutrality, while still focusing divorce legislation on specific circumstances that might make the future difficult for the parent who leaves the marriage with custodial obligations. A rule that affirmatively favored custodial parents in dividing assets, for example, could apply to either men or women. The difference in treatment would depend on the role they assumed after divorce, and would compensate them for the inherent inequality of their positions. This approach would force policy- and lawmakers to inquire into and specifically define what factors should be considered fundamental in making allocation decisions during divorce, either because those factors can be used to predict future problems or because they are manifestations of existing inequities that can be traced to societal conditions.

It is difficult to believe that the articulation of such specific desired results would not generate support for such reforms even if appeals to a generalized sense of fairness could not. There is now a great deal of concern about the way that divorce has led to large numbers of women and children slipping into poverty. The irony of the current direction of divorce reform is that its focus on equality ultimately impedes the development of doctrine that would more effectively represent a perspective that places those women at the center of concern. Consider Weitzman's approach in *The Divorce Revolution.*[9] She apparently sees no way within her equality-based theoretical framework to avoid having to ultimately "split" the house. As I have observed elsewhere, this illustrates a peculiar inconsistency in her policy recommendations.[10] In some areas Weitzman accepts the idea that women who arrange their lives within marriage to their detriment in regard to market participation should be compensated. But, she can only see "parenthood" as being similarly "detrimental" to a certain degree or, more correctly, up to a certain point in time—when all the children are eighteen. Such results can be understood as attending the partnership paradigm: by its concentration on adults, children are ignored. In part, this is because of the reluctance to view children (metaphorically) as ongoing "liabilities" following partnership dissolution. While the "children-as-liabilities" metaphor creates cognitive dissonance, the failure to develop a theory of family law around the analytical constructs of "need" and "dependency" has resulted in inequities which plague women in their (in)ability to provide for themselves and their children after divorce. Indeed, Weitzman herself illustrates most poignantly how much women have lost in the divorce reform game:

> The changes in the rules for dividing property have had a major impact. Before 1970, under the old law, the innocent plaintiff, usually the wife, was typically awarded a significantly larger share of the marital assets. In 1968 wives were awarded more than half (60 percent or more) of the property in both San Francisco and Los Angeles cases. Most of these awards allowed the wife to keep the family home and its furnishings which often constituted the single most valuable family asset.[11]

One difficulty with a set of rules that organizes economic allocations around custody of children might be the possibility that this principle would greatly increase the number of contested custody cases. As noted in previous chapters, there is some evidence that men have used the threat of a custody battle to gain economic concessions. In order to ensure that this does not occur, it is essential that custody rules be reformed so that they are more predictable and easy and inexpensive to administer. In fashioning this pragmatic rationale for clearer custody standards, of course, I assume that the more determinative rules that are fashioned should reflect the value of nurturing and care for children typically associated with the primary caretaker.

Articulating Custody Standards and Rules
The Role of Law: Creating a New Rule from the Discarded Discourses

As it has evolved, legal doctrine cannot adequately address the difficult problems inherent in custody decision making. The best-interest-of-the-child test must be replaced. The task is to find a rule that both avoids making moralizing choices between parents and is determinate enough to be applied within the traditional legal system. The rule would have to eliminate the need for predictions about the future psychological well-being of children or speculations about how best to ensure their developmental potential.[12] It must remove the potentially abusive social worker/mediator, yet guard against potentially abusive lawyers or judges. Thus, what we need is a more definite rule that will nonetheless have at its core an appreciation of what we as a society agree will be in the best interests of children.

One recent suggestion is that custody courts should apply a "primary-caretaker" rule.[13] This rule has been characterized in different ways,[14] but the essence of the primary-caretaker standard is that children need day-to-day care, and that the parent who has performed this primary care during the marriage should get custody.[15]

In supporting this test, it is my belief that there are qualitative differences between the contributions of primary caretakers (typically mothers) and primary earners (typically fathers) to the upbringing of their children. The income contributions fathers make for their families cannot be classified as "sacrifices." In the process of generating family income, fathers are simultaneously establishing themselves in their professions, a benefit they retain throughout their careers. Although this undeniably affords advantages to the entire family during marriage, the sharing of the benefit generally diminishes significantly at divorce, as evidenced by data relative to fathers' postdivorce child-support payment patterns.

By contrast, mothers' sacrifices in providing daily care to children yield no collateral advantages, except in terms of the attachment that forms between mother and child. Children consume the services mothers provide to them, with the years spent in child-rearing representing a depletable amount of the mother's nonrenewable resources. Similarly, the time a woman spends away from career development probably disadvantages her throughout her work life. As Fuchs has pointed out:

> [W]omen's weaker economic position results primarily from conflicts between career and family, conflicts that are stronger for women [than] for men. More specifically, many different kinds of evidence suggest that *on average* women feel a stronger desire for children than men do and a greater concern for their welfare after they are born. This desire and this concern create an economic disadvantage for women which is strongest at ages 25 to 45, but the effects remain throughout life.[16] (Emphasis in original)

The primary-caretaker standard would not ignore the less essential, secondary contributions of the other parent. They are rewarded by the establishment of visitation periods with the children. Custody, however, can be viewed as a reward for past caretaking behavior.

The primary-caretaker rule implicitly recognizes that no expert can confidently make the predictions required under the future-oriented best-interest placement, and that past behavior may in fact be the best indication we have of commitment to the future care and concern for children. I think it is essential that only the past performance of the parents be considered. Helping professionals should not speculate about which parent would be able to produce the best future environment for the child. The only relevant inquiry should be which parent has already adapted his or her life and interests to accommodate the demands of the child.

Further, in determining custody there should be no speculation as to the quality or extent of emotional bonding between parents and children. The primary-caretaker test assumes that these bonds exist between the primary caretaking parent and the child; they are evidenced by the caretaker's sacrifice and devotion to the child. The test also assumes that the child reciprocates this devotion.

In addition, I would apply the rule to all contested custody cases, not just to those involving children of tender years, as is sometimes recommended. I believe that limiting the rule to children under the age of seven unrealistically assumes that nurturing ends when a child begins school. This limitation would also send the message that if a parent fails to nurture during a child's early years, he need not worry, because there will be no negative consequences with respect to later custody determinations.

In my opinion, a major advantage of the primary-caretaker rule is that it is particularly susceptible to legal analysis because it involves past fact-finding, an inquiry traditionally performed by courts. It has the benefit, therefore, of being a rule that judges can comfortably apply and that lawyers can easily understand and use. More importantly, however, the criterion for selecting a custodial parent is clear enough that in most instances parents will be able to predict what the result would be if they litigated the custody issue. Such predictability reduces the need for litigation. Avoidance of litigation does more than save the system from an overload of family-law cases. Custody disputes are expensive and time-consuming for the parties to litigate. The current set of rules, which requires individualized hearings to determine a plethora of facts and to parade a bevy of experts on the issue of what is in a child's best interest,[17] does not provide "justice," particularly for women, who tend to be less well-off economically than their husbands, and who cannot afford such expensive procedures.[18]

Further, the mere fact that both parents work does not, in the vast majority of cases, mean that both are primary caretakers (or that neither is). This is an additional benefit of the primary-caretaker rule: appropriate application should seldom result in very different parental sacrifices being considered equal.[19] It is important to take into account that although most mothers work, they choose careers (or, more likely, "jobs") that accommodate their children in ways most fathers do not.[20]

Their jobs are usually the ones that must be flexible enough to permit time off—initially for the bearing and breast feeding of an infant and later for other day-to-day obligations such as school conferences or the care of a sick child. Thus, even though both parents work, mothers' career sacrifices for their children would often qualify them as the primary caretakers.

In addition, one further advantage of the primary-caretaker rule is that the evidence on which it relies can be gleaned in open court according to our notions of due process and publicly accountable decision making.[21] It avoids the need for speculative assessments about psychological consequences of attributes and refocuses responsibility for the decision on the parents and, if they can't agree, on the judge who must make the factual finding as to who has cared for the child. Therefore, the rule takes decision making away from the helping professionals.

One possible objection to this test is that it will produce even more maternal-custody arrangements than has the best-interest test. Such criticism shows how far we have strayed in the United States from real concern for children to a desire to adhere to simplistic notion of equality between spouses at divorce. Even if this conclusion is valid, it should not be the basis for rejecting the test. The primary-caretaker test is not designed to remove the potential for fathers to obtain custody at divorce. The rule is gender-neutral on its face. As with most gender-neutral rules, its impact may not be gender-neutral, but this result only reflects the fact that women are the primary nurturers of children in our society.[22]

The rule may currently operate to the advantage of mothers, but, if we value nurturing behavior, then rewarding those who nurture seems only fair. If fathers are left out, they can change their behavior and begin making sacrifices in their careers and devoting their time during the marriage to the primary care and nurturing of children. Men can exercise the same "free" choice that women traditionally have in these matters, adjusting their outside activities to care for their children. Men who choose not to devote their time and attention to the children during the marriage but wish to care for them after the marriage ends can bargain against the mother's entitlement as primary caretaker by making financial or emotional concessions at divorce. In cases in which both parents acted as true primary caretakers, I predict that few custody battles would ensue and the cooperative patterns concerning the children established during the marriage would continue.

The system should reward demonstrated care and concern for children. If we merely want to further the goal of symbolic equality between parents, custody could be decided by the flip of a coin.[23] If we aspire beyond rhetoric, however, we need a more sensitive and realistic rule. The primary-caretaker test is an attempt to ensure a good future for children in our culture. It encourages nurturing and concern for children in a concrete way. The positive message that the rule sends to parents about what is valued by the legal system and by society at large is clear and unambiguous.

One other very important rule must be firmly established. As it now stands, custody determinations are modifiable decisions until the child reaches the age of majority. This means that the potential for reconsideration can haunt a custodian and the threat that she may lose her child may continue to influence her choices and options. The modifiability of custody orders provides the basis for ongoing threats and coercion by a disgruntled ex-spouse. This should end. Merely because a divorce occurred sometime in the past is not a sufficient basis for continued state interference with parental prerogatives and functioning. The legal system should initially award custody based on factors that encourage nurturing and care of children. After the initial determination, however, the law should leave subsequent decision making over the course of the child's minority to parents, the most interested parties. Absent abusive situations, parents should be left to work out arrangements concerning their children. If the law takes this approach, then the legal system will fulfill its responsibility by making an initial custody determination when the parties cannot agree, and the basis for ongoing coercive intervention will clearly terminate with the marriage.

The Child's Advocate

In spite of the problems with the idea of child advocacy addressed in chapter 6, I do think that legal advocates could perform two valuable functions in custody decision making as it occurs today. Both are valuable professional and political functions. First, I envision in individual cases that a child advocate could bring legal values, such as due process and a preference for public decision making, back into a process that has become so informal and nonlegal as to often operate according to the whims of politically unaccountable professionals, or to be driven by professional fads and biases. Second, the potential child advocate could perform a public function by lobbying for the replacement of the best-interest test with a more determinative substantive rule—one more susceptible to the protections of traditional legal decision making and more responsive to actual caretaking responsibilities, such as the primary-caretaker rule, which rewards past care and concern for children and minimizes the role and power of the helping professionals in custody decision making.

There have always been voices of doubt raised about the effectiveness of the current system, given its reliance on predictions about the future well-being of children based on scanty evidence of questionable validity. The legal advocate could best serve the interests of children by not viewing him or herself as only a part of a best-interest team. The legal advocate should not be aligned with any other professional but should remain skeptical and critical of them all. The helping professional experts would be presumed to be useful *only* in weeding out or identifying those parents who are *clearly unfit* to care for their children. Providing that the tests and methods of such professionals are reliable, they can tell us who falls below a legally defined bright line. Their opinions as to the superior parent—the one who most resembles their professional ideal and who, in current practice, would receive the best-interest recommendation—should be viewed as just opinions. At most, they would be entitled to no more respect than any other opinions; optimally they would be excluded as irrelevant in most custody determinations.

The legal advocate's function would, in those few cases where it was necessary, ensure that the helping professional's opinion was not overvalued in relation to information more relevant to the determination of who had acted as the primary caretaker—that supplied by teachers, neighbors, and others who had had more extensive exposure to the individual child. The legal advocate would act as a check on the private, informal decision-making process. In this way professional biases such as the current ones favoring shared parenting or creating a custody preference for the most generous parent would be recognized as ideological and be subjected to vigorous and critical probing. This, I assert, would unequivocally be in children's best interest.

When an expert testifies, the expert's education and experience would be explored by the legal advocate. Supervision and a critical assessment of the fact-gathering process of the mental health professional would be essential functions for the legal advocate in fulfilling his or her responsibility to the child. The goal would be to expose, and thus examine, the process of reaching a nonlegal professional opinion. What has been lost under current practice are legal procedural values—due process, adherence to clear standards, the right to cross-examination—in addition to the undervaluing of nurturing and caretaking. The current referral to nonlegal personnel may make us feel easier because we can believe that some other profession is appropriately taking care of the custody business, but that illusion may not work in the best interest of the children.

CURBING DISCOURSES
Use of Social Science Data

Custody questions are by their very nature moral, legal, and political questions. While social science data may help in discussing the contours and content of moral philosophy, the dimensions of legal regulation, or the wisdom of a political choice, it is essential that legal policymakers realize that social science alone cannot provide definitive answers. We should not allow those who would offer us values disguised as social science facts to claim that they (and their data) provide the answers we seek. Just as law is influenced by the culture, beliefs, and institutions in which it is located and not derived from abstract notions of universal truth, so, too, are social science conclusions thoroughly embedded in the culture and the professional practices which produce them. Social science research is no more than additional data to be carefully used in conjunction with other data to shape or question legal policy.

In the area of custody policy, no one substantive position is necessarily better, in any absolute or abstract sense, than any other. Choices in this area must and will be made. But no one can legitimately claim to deserve more credibility because his or her arguments are based on abstract truth. In chapters 7 and 8, I described the ways that social science data can be misused by legal policymakers and the way that it may reflect the biases of individual social scientists. The data are not value-free, nor are they used in a value-free manner. Both the generation and the use of social science data reflect the context in which the data are produced.

This context includes the often-unquestioned acceptance of concepts such as *androgyny, mental health,* and *moral development,* terms that demonstrate a cultural predisposition for images that conform to the ideal of self-contained individualism. This paradigmatic ideal, however, was generated in the context of liberalism, capitalism, and male dominance. Our view of the ideal and its desirability should not be ahistorical. Self-interested individuality does not represent a natural exalted state to which we should all aspire.

In addition, legal policymakers should be very skeptical about the production of knowledge in other disciplines. There are conflicts in all disciplines, as well as boundaries and unavoidable responses to sociocultural forces that shape knowledge.[24] The law has recognized this in regard to its own production of knowledge; so, too, it should be skeptical of other productions.

Use of "Alternative" Decision-Makers

In chapter 9, I detailed how important substantive implications for divorce and child-custody cases are obscured by viewing mediation simply as an alternative procedure that is preferable to settlement negotiations previously performed by attorneys. Such a perspective misses the more fundamental challenges mediation presents to central aspects of the legal model, particularly the traditional notion that representation by competing adversaries is the most reliable method of establishing the necessary facts upon which to base subsequent decision making. The ability of the helping professions to label divorce a psychosocial crisis has been pivotal in this regard—what was once a legal event handled through legal procedures by lawyers and judges has become an emotional crisis to be managed by mental health professionals. That substantive changes have resulted from this procedural shift should not be surprising. This trend should be reversed.

Custodial mothers have had no spokesperson in the legal arenas. Feminist groups might have picked up their cause. However, mothers' desire for sole custody or claims for preferential consideration based on maternal status or on the functions they stereotypically perform are incompatible with the symbolic presentation of equality by liberal mainstream feminism. Lawyers are another group of potential spokespersons for the perspective of custodial mothers that past parenting behavior is the relevant consideration. Yet they, too, have failed to present mothers' concerns. Indeed, family-law specialists seem to favor transferring decision making from judges, attorneys, and the legal system to mediators and social workers.[25]

Custodial mothers' experience as primary caregivers during marriage and after divorce should have figured significantly in the establishment of new rules to govern the process and content of custody decision making. Yet because of the domination of the social workers' rhetoric, which asserted the inherent shared nature of parenting, custodial mothers' concerns were minimized or ignored. Joint custody is seen as nothing more than a continuation of patterns of shared parenting within marriage. In most ongoing marriages, however, one parent, normally the mother, assumes day-to-day primary care.[26] Shared parenting in these situations seldom means equally divided responsibility and control; typically one parent sacrifices more than the other in order to care for the child. The sense of sharing in this context is not based on the actual assumption of divided responsibilities by the parents. Rather, the shared parenting can be viewed as based on the relationship between the parents who, because of the intimacy of their situation, share the potential for jointly exercising important decision making responsibility for their children. Yet an unrealistic and idealized vision of shared parenting independent of the relationship (or lack thereof) between parents is now imposed on couples after divorce. This vision assumes that they will work out their relationship to make shared parenting successful.

It is one thing for divorcing parents voluntarily to choose the shared-parenting ideal, but quite another to impose it on parents who do not or cannot live up to its demands. There may be substantial costs to treating the deviant as the norm and fashioning rights outside the context of responsibility. In the divorce context, this amounts to furthering the interests of noncaretaking fathers over the objections and, in many instances, against the interests of caretaking mothers. The legal system should not participate in, let alone facilitate, this unjust result.

We must ask a number of questions. Why are we as a society condoning imposition of this ideal? Don't we, and the legal system, have a responsibility for the form and content of these decisions? The mediators' interest in the acceptance of this alternative system is clear, but why should those of us who are lawyers and family-law policymakers acquiesce in this transfer of decision making power? Are we comfortable with the social workers' assertions that mediation is a superior process and shared parenting the appropriate goal? For lawyers, the central question may be whether there is any role for law—for a legalistic approach—in the custody area. Further, we should consider whether the legal model, although imperfect, may be superior to the therapeutic model.

A legal model that relies on both legislative and judicial institutional roles in formulating custody rules would have to give some credence to traditional legal values such as procedural due process: the right to a hearing, the right to cross-examine witnesses, and so on. Mediators are free to criticize or to ignore these aspects of the adversary system. Yet these legalisms are not vestiges of an arcane system; they embody a consensus about important values in our society. In fact, because there seems to be greater consensus about the importance of due-process values than about what constitutes an ideal (or even an acceptable) family, shouldn't custody decision making rules comport with *these* values? The public nature of the legal process means that the basis for decisions will be explained, debated, and publicly considered. This process may not be foolproof, but it is better than one in which substantive rules and standards evolve and are implemented behind closed office doors without any possibility of checks from the political system.

CONCLUSION

Confined by images of equality, liberal feminists historically have used two compelling images in their attempts to gain access to powerful social institutions. These images initially appear to be complementary. The first image is a negative one: the image of woman as the victim of existing institutions. This image has been useful in convincing large numbers of both women and sympathetic men that women have indeed been oppressed in this society, and that women need and deserve laws removing this oppression from their social, legal, and political experiences. The second image is a positive one: the image of equal treatment. Equality has emerged as a potent ideal with which to rectify the victimization of women in society, and to that extent it complements the image of woman as victim. Equality rhetoric can be used both as an organizational tool and as the basis for proposing specific formal changes in the laws.

Because of its practical political uses, it is hardly surprising that the victim/equality imagery has sometimes been overdrawn in liberal feminist arguments. In the context of marriage and divorce reform, however, these exaggerations have had unfortunate consequences. The divorce-reform process discussed in this book is an example of a situation where an interest group with societal concerns that encompass specific legislative problems, but also extend far beyond them, directly articulated reform goals in legal abstractions in an attempt to implement these broader concerns. This group, because of its composition, was viewed as uniquely legitimate within the political process; it represented the interests of women and was therefore seen as the appropriate purveyor of solutions to the problems that were being addressed.

The liberal feminists used the ideology of equality both to attack the existing rules, demonstrating the need for reform, and to supply the theoretical underpinnings that shaped the formal content of the reform rules. The liberal feminist equality ideology gave the reform rules legitimacy as it simultaneously removed legitimacy from the rules that were to be replaced. Actions subsequently taken by legal institutions will have the appearance of neutrality and fairness insofar as they are consistent with the reformed rules.[27] Because of the legitimacy conferred by the prevailing ideology during the crucial political process, the substantive rules are viewed both as unbiased and as actually operating to confer equality before the law. The individuals, groups, and interests that were perceived as disadvantaged under the old rules are now viewed as having been vindicated through the process of reform. The formal bias in the system, as represented by the old rules, has been removed, and the once-disadvantaged can no longer complain about results, because the system now treats them neutrally and equally under the law.

However, if one rejects the comprehensiveness of the "equal" and "victim" stereotypes of women and marriage, one must confront the fact that there are many women whose circumstances have not been addressed by equality legislation and who will not benefit from the reforms. In addition, once children are included in the equation, it becomes even clearer that equality just doesn't add up to needed reform. The changes, however, have been potent and powerful on a symbolic level, and this has operated to frustrate more instrumental concerns and resulted in the generation of reforms that cause great damage to women and children.

The rhetoric of equality is too easily appropriated and utilized to gain support for antifeminist measures. Equality rhetoric is a rhetoric that belongs both to no one, and to everyone. For this reason alone, it would seem time to abandon equality.

Notes

CHAPTER ONE

1. ROBERT MERTON, THEORETICAL SOCIOLOGY 68 (1967).

2. Geertz states in regard to grand anthropological concepts: "If anthropological interpretation is constructing a reading of what happens, then to divorce it from what happens—from what, in this time or that place, specific people say, what they do, what is done to them, from the whole vast business of the world—is to divorce it from its applications and render it vacant. A good interpretation of anything—a poem, a person, a history, a ritual, an institution, a society—takes us into the heart of that of which it is the interpretation." CLIFFORD GEERTZ, THE INTERPRETATION OF CULTURES 18 (1973).

3. J. B. White, *Law as Rhetoric, Rhetoric as Law,* 52 U. CHI. L. REV. 684 (1985).

4. *Id.* at 695.

5. Grand theory represents a belief that there is a "truth" to be discovered, a rejection of the idea that theory is constantly in process. *See* CHRIS WEEDON, FEMINIST PRACTICE AND POSTSTRUCTURALIST THEORY 11 (1987), where the author defines her feminist project as "hold[ing] on to feminism as a politics and mobiliz[ing] theory in order to develop strategies for change on behalf of feminist interests," rather than coming up with a "definitive feminist theory—a totalizing theory of patriarchy."

6. CAROL SMART, FEMINISM AND THE POWER OF LAW 71 (1989). *See also* West, *Jurisprudence and Gender,* 55 U. CHI. L. REV. 1 (1988) (the need for a more experience-based jurisprudence). *But cf.* Olsen, *Feminist Theory in Grand Style,* 89 COLUM. L. REV. 1147, 1166–77, for a defense of grand theorizing in the context of reviewing the work of Catherine MacKinnon.

7. *See* MacKinnon, *Feminism, Marxism, Method and the State: An Agenda for Theory,* 1982 SIGNS 227–56, at 239–40, where she discusses the political implications of method. *See also* Fineman & Opie, *The Uses of Social Science Data in Legal Policymaking: Custody Determinations at Divorce,* 1987 WIS. L. REV. 107.

8. *See* Fineman, *Illusive Equality: On Weitzman's Divorce Revolution,* 1986 AM. B. FOUND. RES. J. 781, where I further discuss and criticize this tendency.

9. Two excellent illustrations of works that analyze the interplay between formal legal developments and their application in practice are Girdner, *Child Custody Determination: Ideological Dimensions of a Social Problem,* in REDEFINING SOCIAL PROBLEMS 165 (E. Seidman & J. Rappaport eds. 1986), and McCann, *Battered Women and the Law: The Limits of the Legislation,* in WOMEN IN LAW: EXPLORATIONS IN LAW, FAMILY AND SEXUALITY (J. Brophy & C. Smart eds. 1985).

10. No-fault divorce reform is a good example of this phenomenon. Prior to the passage of these statutes, it was widely accepted practice for lawyers to counsel clients on how to "create" grounds for divorce. *See* L. FRIEDMAN, A HISTORY OF AMERICAN LAW 179–84 (1973). Thus, rather than representing any legal "change," no-fault reforms actually mirrored existing practice.

11. For a particularly potent example of the persistence of this idea, it is illuminating to trace these assertions of pathology in single-parent families over the twenty-year period after the issuance of the Moynihan Report (*See The Negro Family: The Case for National Action,* in THE MOYNIHAN REPORT AND THE POLITICS OF CONTROVERSY [L. Rainwater & W. L. Yancy eds. 1967] *see also* MOYNIHAN, FAMILY AND NATION [1986]) to the 1986 presentation of the problems of the black family in Bill Moyers' documentary, *The Vanishing Family: Crisis in Black America* (narrated by Bill Moyers, Columbia Broadcasting System [CBS] Special Report, January 1986).

CHAPTER TWO

1. Fineman, *Beginnings and Endings: The Effect of the Law on Forms and Consequences of Family Relations,* in CHALLENGES OF THE 80S: FAMILIES FACE THE FUTURE 26 (Nickols & Engelbrecht eds. 1981). Proceedings of the Fourth Annual Conference of the Family Study Center, Stillwater: Oklahoma State University [hereinafter CHALLENGES].

2. *See* M. GROSSBERG, GOVERNING THE HEARTH 250–53 (1985).

3. *See e.g.,* Freed & Foster, *Marital Property Reform in New York: Partnership of Co-Equals?,* 8 FAM. L.Q. 169 (1974). This concept can be traced to nineteenth- and early twentieth-century feminist theory. *See* JOHN STUART MILL, *The Subjection of Women,* in THREE ESSAYS 427–548 (1975). In American law, the partnership model has long been urged as a way of limiting judicial discretion. *See* Daggett, *Divisions of Property Upon Dissolution of Marriage,* 6 LAW & CONTEMP. PROBS. 225, 229 (1939).

4. *See* Freed & Foster, *supra* note 3.

5. *See* M. GLENDON, THE NEW FAMILY AND THE NEW PROPERTY (1981).

6. *Id.* at 104–6. *See also* Glendon, *Modern Marriage Law and Its Underlying Assumptions: The New Marriage and the New Property,* 13 FAM. L.Q. 441 (1980).

7. Glendon suggested that the sources of "standing and security" in society have shifted from family to work. GLENDON, *supra* note 5, at 101–18; Cantwell, *Man + Woman + Property = ?,* PROB. LAW. 9–10 (1980). That is, as employment relationships have moved away from concepts of termination-at-will, becoming more secure and predictable, family relationships—particularly husband/wife relationships—have become tenuous and insecure because of the availability of termination-at-will (i.e., no-fault divorce). Glendon has said that the only employment situation in which termination-at-will "applies more than ever is the unpaid labor force, namely, homemakers." Glendon, *The New Family and The New Property,* 53 TUL. L. REV. 697, 701 (1979). *See also* Fineman, *Beginnings and Endings: The Effect of the Law on Forms and Consequences of Family Relations,* in CHALLENGES, *supra* note 1.

8. Modern no-fault legislation began to spread after California enacted a No-fault Law in 1969. The Uniform Marriage and Divorce Act, promulgated in 1970, embodied the concept of irretrievable breakdown as the sole basis for dissolution. *See* Unif. Marriage and Divorce Act § 305. By 1990, all states had passed some form of no-fault legislation. *See* Freed & Foster, *Divorce in the Fifty States: An Overview,* 14 FAM. L.Q. 229 (1981).

9. *See* N. BASCH, IN THE EYES OF THE LAW (1982).

10. *See* J. POLE, THE PURSUIT OF EQUALITY IN AMERICAN HISTORY (1978), particularly the introductory material and the chapter on women. Easton, *Feminism and the Contemporary Family,* SOCIALIST REV., no. 39, 1978, at 39 asserts that the family was a subordinate theme in nineteenth- and early twentieth-century America. The focus then was on the exclusion of women from public life. Only during the 1960s and 1970s did feminists begin

to focus on "patriarchy." The author asserts that women are now dealing with new forms of male dominance, forms without names. *Id.* at 11.

11. *See* Dow, *Sexual Equality, The ERA and the Court—A Tale of Two Failures,* 13 N.M.L. Rev. 53 (1983).

12. Formal equality has been useful in some areas, such as the right to vote, when "differences" are deemed no longer relevant. Perception of differences changes over time. Bernard, *Sex Differences, An Overview,* in Beyond Sex-Role Stereotypes 10, 13–14 (A. Kaplan & J. Bean eds. 1976). Arguments that women should be treated as equals to men, if the result is also viewed as exposing women to harmful consequences because they are not in fact the same, have occasionally failed. Instead, society has in some circumstances sought to devise protective rules and laws that recognized these perceived fundamental differences. Historically, this has been a dilemma in the imposition of the equality concept. *See* J. Baer, The Chains of Protection: The Judicial Response to Women's Labor Legislation (1978).

13. *See* Muller v. Oregon, 208 U.S. 412, 244 (1908) (limited working hours for women upheld because of their weaker physical nature and their need to be protected). *See also* Kanowitz, *Benign Sex Discrimination: Its Troubles and Their Cure,* 31 Hastings L.J. 1379 (1980).

14. *See* International Union v. Johnson Controls, Inc., 680 F. Supp. 309, 886, F.2d 871, *cert. granted,* 58 U.S.L.W. 3614 (1990).

15. It has been argued that "[t]he liberal critique of legal inequality between men and women is an important and necessary aspect of the feminist position, but it is not by itself an adequate base for feminist theory. A theory of women's liberation must come to grips with the structural inadequacies of existing institutions." K. Ferguson, Self, Society and Womankind: The Dialectic of Liberation 3–18, 19 n.6 (1980). This statement may be viewed as the basis for urging the need for unequal rules. This theme is repeated in a student note which is critical of laws that merely protect women's attempt to adopt men's roles (the assimilation goal). The author argues that definitions and strategies relating to women should be expanded so as to encompass socially created handicaps capable of legal remedies. Note, *Toward a Redefinition of Sexual Equality,* 95 Harv. L. Rev. 487 (1981). "Rule-equality," the formal sameness of treatment of individuals, however, has been an ideal throughout American history. It is a resilient ideal. Examples of historic rule-equality measures include women's efforts to acquire the right to vote and to gain access to education and employment opportunities regardless of race or gender.

16. An often-cited early example of the need for rule-equality is Bradwell v. Illinois, 83 U.S. 130, 141 (1873), in which the Supreme Court found that the timidity and delicacy of women made them unfit to practice law.

17. *See generally* P. Zopf, American Women in Poverty (1989); V. Fuchs, Women's Quest for Economic Equality (1988). As Fuchs observes: "Are women better off now than they were in 1960? Are they worse off? A complete answer to this question—one that takes account of feelings of self-worth, autonomy, and other psychological dimensions . . . is probably impossible. The sources of well-being are so numerous—love, work, health, family, friendship, religion—and their interactions so complex as to defy measurement and aggregation. Many women have testified eloquently to their enhanced feelings of self-worth, to their ability to function independently, to an enlarged sense of power and autonomy. At bottom, however, no one can ever quantify another person's misery or joy.

"It is possible, however, to address a more restricted set of questions concerning *economic well-being,* which economists usually define as access to goods, services, and leisure. . . . Despite large structural changes in the economy and major antidiscrimination legislation, the economic well-being of women as a whole (in comparison with men) did not improve. The women/men ratio of *money income* almost doubled, but women had less leisure time while men had more, an increase in the proportion of adults not married made more women dependent on their own income, and women's share of financial responsibility for children rose. One group of women, however, did achieve great gains relative to their male counterparts. They were unmarried, white, young, and well educated." *Id.* at 75–76 (emphasis in original).

18. "Conflicts between career and family bear heavily on many women, and their gains in paid work have been offset by loss of leisure and the decline of marriage. Young, white, well-educated, unmarried women have made substantial economic progress relative to their male counterparts, but the price has often included foregoing the opportunity to have a child. For the first time in our nation's history, an entire generation of young people are not replacing themselves. Furthermore, those women who do combine motherhood and paid work face constant pressures to arrange appropriate care for their children and frequent crises when those arrangements go awry." V. FUCHS, *supra* note 17, at 94.

More and more women are working two or more jobs after divorce in order to maintain substantially the same standard of living for themselves and their families as when they were married. *See For Many Women, One Job Just Isn't Enough,* New York Times, 15 Feb. 1990, at A1.

19. G. WOOD, THE CREATION OF THE AMERICAN REPUBLIC 1766–1787, at 70–75 (1969). For the same reasons, equality as an ideal might also have been perceived as problematic to family-law reformers had the mother-child relationship been central to their concerns. This will be more fully discussed in part 2 on child-custody decision making.

20. *See, e.g.,* Orr v. Orr, 440 U.S. 268 (1979) (invalidating on equal protection grounds a state statute permitting alimony awards only to wives).

21. *See also Ex parte* Devine, 398 So.2d 686 (Ala. 1981) (invalidating the tender-years doctrine directing placement of young children with their mothers upon divorce as unconstitutional gender discrimination).

22. As Fuchs observes, "In the early years of the sex-role revolution there was a hope that differences in homemaking and childcare responsibilities would disappear, but this is not occurring on a large scale. There are some households in which the father does as much as or more than the mother, but they are the exception, not the rule. Moreover, almost one child in four is raised in a household without a father or stepfather. Children are still predominantly women's concern." V. FUCHS, *supra* note 17, at 72.

23. *See, e.g.,* Benn & Benn, *Women's Role in American Society: Retrospect and Prospect; Training the Woman to Know Her Place: The Power of Nonconscious Ideology,* in WOMEN'S ROLE IN CONTEMPORARY SOCIETY: THE REPORT OF THE NEW YORK CITY COMMISSION ON HUMAN RIGHTS 101, 107–12 (1970); Mainard, *The Politics of Housework,* in SISTERHOOD IS POWERFUL: AN ANTHOLOGY OF WRITINGS FROM THE WOMEN'S LIBERATION MOVEMENT 447–54 (1970).

24. Mainard, *supra* note 23, at 447–54 (1970).

25. It does not appear that this will occur. As Fuchs observes, "[A] glimpse into the future comes from a survey I have taken among hundreds of undergraduates at Stanford University during recent years. Both women and men say that happy marriages and successful careers are very important in their vision of a good life. Women give slightly more weight to marriage than men do, but the difference is small, and women attached just as much importance to careers as men do. However, when asked what changes they would make in their paid employment if they had young children, more than 60% of the women but less than 10% of the men say they would substantially reduce their hours of work or

quit work entirely for several years. The adverse effect of this withdrawal on occupational choice and financial process in the labor market is obvious. When queried about the results, the women explain that they define 'successful career' differently from the men—with more emphasis on personal satisfaction than on making money or achieving power." V. FUCHS, *supra* note 17, at 47.

26. *See generally,* Westen, *The Empty Idea of Equality,* 95 HARV. L. REV. 537 (1982).

27. In a brochure arguing for the adoption of a Wisconsin Equal Rights Amendment, the Wisconsin feminist reformers explicitly made this connection: "[W]ithout a constitutional guarantee that men and women have the same rights and responsibilities, the courts have approved laws that deny equal treatment to one sex or the other. . . ." They then argued that existing laws guaranteeing equal rights for women were inadequate because they left "true equality open to interpretation and debate by allowing them [women] *the special protections and privileges which they now enjoy for the general welfare. . . .* This has meant that state laws discriminating on the basis of sex are still in effect." Wisconsin Women's Political Caucus, *The Wisconsin Equal Rights Amendment* (n.d.) (emphasis in the original). The office listed on the brochure is that of the head of the Governor's Commission on the Status of Women at University of Wisconsin-Extension.

28. *See* S. GETTLEMAN & J. MARKOWITZ, THE COURAGE TO DIVORCE 194 (1974). *See also* J. NOBLE & W. NOBLE, THE CUSTODY TRAP 120–22 (1975), recounting a case in which a mother was ostracized by friends and family because she failed to seek custody.

29. The feminist rhetoric of gender neutrality was particularly susceptible to being employed against women and children by fathers' rights groups as they attacked the notion of motherhood as distinct from parenthood. *See, e.g.,* Everett, *Shared Parenthood in Divorce: The Parental Covenant and Custody Law,* 2 J.L. & RELIGION 85, 85–89 (1984). The fathers' rights groups also argued for the child's "right" to access to both parents and the right of the noncustodial father to be equally involved in postdivorce decisions concerning the child. *Id.* at 88–89. Much of the rhetoric of these groups concerns the importance of fathers in the postdivorce family. *See, e.g.,* FATHERHOOD AND FAMILY POLICY (M. Lamb & A. Sagi eds. 1984); Chambers, *Rethinking the Substantive Rules for Custody Disputes in Divorce,* 83 MICH L. REV. 477, 518–20 (1984).

30. The reformers' publications reflected this. In commenting on WISCONSIN GOVERNOR'S COMMISSION ON THE STATUS OF WOMEN, THAT OLD AMERICAN DREAM AND THE REALITY OR WHY WE NEED MARITAL PROPERTY REFORM (1977), one reformer said that it represented "our very deliberate effort to make our work for equality for women, seem as American as apple pie—seen as being in the mainstream, and not as being strange."

31. In New York, for example, feminist reformers supported a rebuttable presumption of equal distribution of marital property on the pragmatic grounds that such a presumption would bypass the ideological and cultural assumption that a husband's contribution was at least 50 percent, and likely more, if he were the higher wage earner in a double-wage household or the sole wage earner in the marriage. Marcus, *Reflections on the Significance of the Sex/Gender System: Divorce Law Reform in New York,* 42 UNIV. OF MIAMI L. REV. 55, 70 (1987).

32. *See* Sears, Hensler & Speer, *Whites' Opposition to "Busing": Self-Interest or Symbolic Politics?,* 73 AM. POL. SCI. REV. 369 (1979), which indicated that the clearest cases of "symbolic politics" are those that present the symbols most similar to those of original socialization, and they elicit the strongest response. The authors concluded that self-interest is not as strong as symbolic reasons for taking positions.

33. Westen, *supra* note 26, at 575–582. *See also* D. RAE, EQUALITIES (1981).

34. As Fuchs observes, policymaking in this area involves complex questions requiring consideration of many sources of information: "Although the economic perspective is

usually reasoning for good policymaking, it is not sufficient. A full analysis of the problems of gender, for instance, requires perspectives provided by anthropology, biology, the humanities, law, psychology, sociology, and other disciplines.'. . ." V. FUCHS, *supra* note 17, at 6.

35. In this regard, consider the following: "Marriage is also a form of partnership . . . [where] one partner—the woman—is usually at a disadvantage. Suppose women were better than men at producing and caring for children but had no particular desire to do so, while it was men who wanted the children and cared more about their welfare. We would probably still see the same [sexual] division of labor we see now, but men would have to pay dearly for women's services. The present hierarchy of power would be reversed." V. FUCHS, *supra* note 17, at 67–68

36. RAE, *supra* note 33, at 35, identifies three different types of equalities: *simple, segmental,* and *bloc.* Simple equality is a comparison between individuals, while segmental equality is individual equality within a subclass. By contrast, bloc equality is a comparison between groups or blocks, and thus asks for something very different from simple or individual equality. Liberal feminist reform efforts tend to adopt a simple or individual model of equality.

37. *See supra* note 2. For the origins of the tender-years doctrine, see Zainaldin, *The Emergence of a Modern American Family Law: Child Custody, Adoption, and the Courts, 1796–1851,* 73 Nw. U.L. REV. 1038, 1072–74 (1979).

38. *See, e.g.,* Fineman, *Dominant Discourse, Professional Language, and Legal Change in Child Custody Decisionmaking,* 101 HARV. L. REV. 727 (1988); Fineman & Opie, *The Uses of Social Science Data in Legal Policymaking: Custody Determinations at Divorce,* 1987 WIS. L. REV. 107; Chambers, *Rethinking the Substantive Rules for Custody Disputes in Divorce,* 83 MICH. L. REV. 477 (1984); Fineman, *A Reply to David Chambers: (Discussion of the Abuses of Social Science: A Response to Fineman and Opie)* 1987 WIS. L. REV. 165; *Children, Divorce and the Legal System: The Direction for Reform: A Symposium,* 19 COLUM. J.L. & SOC. PROBS. 105 (1985); *The Search for Guidance in Determining the Best Interests of the Child at Divorce: Reconciling the Primary Caretaker and Joint Custody Preferences,* 20 U. RICH. L. REV. (1985); Gordon, *The Children of Divorce: The Trend Toward Joint Custody,* 102 MIL. L. REV. 59 (1983); Scutt, *Principle v. Practice: Defining Equality in Family Property Division on Divorce,* 57 AUSTL. L.J. 143 (1983); *Divorce and the Division of Marital Property in Arkansas—Equal or Equitable?* 35 ARK. L. REV. 671 (1983).

39. Younger, *Marital Regimes: A Story of Compromise and Demoralization, Together with Criticism and Suggestions for Reform,* 67 CORNELL L. REV. 45 (1981).

40. L. WEITZMAN, THE DIVORCE REVOLUTION: THE UNINTENDED SOCIAL AND ECONOMIC CONSEQUENCES FOR WOMEN AND CHILDREN IN AMERICA (1985).

41. H. JACOB, THE SILENT REVOLUTION: THE TRANSFORMATION OF DIVORCE LAW IN THE UNITED STATES (1988).

42. *Id.* at 11.

43. FUNK & WAGNALL, STANDARD DICTIONARY, 688 (1980).

44. *Id.*

45. H. JACOB, *supra* note 41; Jacob concludes that changes in property and custody rules "validated . . . the wife's transition from subordinate to equal [that] occurred gradually both in social fact and in the law." *Id.* at 3.

46. Governor's Commission on the Status of Women, *Fact Sheet* (on file in Wisconsin Legislative Reference Bureau) regarding the 1977 Divorce Reform Act in Wisconsin. One of the Wisconsin reformers described the situation as she saw it during an interview with me: "[In states] just adding a no-fault ground for divorce, women ended up gener-

ally in much worse shape than they were under the old law. And as unpleasant and horrendous as the old law was, it did give women a modicum of protection from just sort of being left in the lurch with minimal to no support and a third of the property because that wouldn't happen to them unless they were the person who was wrong and in order to get a divorce most men were going to have to bargain on the economic issues so that they could, in effect, buy out their wives or the wives who would not consent to the divorce."

A comment by Doris Freed, reported by the Washington Post News Service, indicates this is still a viable perception: "[I]t has been a mistake to give up consent [to divorce] as a trading tool. . . . [U]ntil the courts give better recognition to the financial needs of housewives, women will still need consent as a bargaining chip to defend their interests." Capital Times (Madison, Wis.), 27 July 1982, at 10.

47. *See supra* note 2.

48. The fact that this equality in practice may be an illusion due to contemporary political or economic disparities or that the rules themselves incorporate unrecognized bias, such as that favoring market participation, does not affect this outcome of legitimation. It is the perception of neutrality and equality by those who fashion and implement the rules that is fundamental.

CHAPTER THREE

1. *See, e.g.,* K. FERGUSON, SELF, SOCIETY AND WOMANKIND: THE DIALECTIC OF LIBERATION 4–5 (1980); Jaggar, *Political Philosophies of Women's Liberation,* in FEMINISM AND PHILOSOPHY 6–9 (M. Vetterling-Braggin, F. Elliston & J. English eds. 1977). According to Ferguson, the moderate (liberal) feminists are "[b]est represented by National Organization for Women (N.O.W.) and Women's Equal Action League (W.E.A.L.), and various professional women's groups." The moderates have been defined as "women's rights" advocates who are primarily concerned with bringing women into the mainstream of American life "through reform" in contrast to the more radical "liberationists," whose efforts are directed towards revolutionary social change.

2. Between 1890 and 1930 the female/male wage ratio in the United States jumped from about .45 to .60 and then remained at about that level for half a century. After 1979 women's wages began to rise relative to men's, but even in the mid-1980s the average American woman earned only two-thirds as much as the average man for each hour of work. This wage gap is the most obvious and the most important evidence of economic inequality. . . ." V. FUCHS, WOMEN'S QUEST FOR ECONOMIC EQUALITY 49 (1988).

3. "Women are much more likely to work at a paid job now than they were a generation ago, but the proportion of employed women who work part time has shown no tendency to decline. . . .

"Which women work part time? Not surprisingly, it is those who are married and those who have a small child at home. . . .

"The presence of a young child substantially increases the demand for work in the home, making it more difficult to pursue full time employment. . . . Part time work often provides a compromise solution. Statistical analysis of working women shows that even after controlling for age, education, and similar factors, the presence of a young child increases a woman's probability of working part time by about ten percentage points." V. FUCHS, *supra* note 2, at 44–45 (1988).

4. In his analysis of women's economic position in society, economist Victor Fuchs describes the "costs" associated with children as follows: "Having children entails numerous costs—expenditures for goods and services, time lost from paid work, and so on. In addi-

tion to these well-known, obvious costs, there is another that falls particularly on women in the form of *lower wages*. This happens for several reasons. First, many women leave the labor market during pregnancy, at childbirth, or when their children are young. These child-related interruptions are damaging to subsequent earnings because three out of four births occur to women before the age of 30—the same time that men are gaining the training and experience that lead to higher earnings later in life. Second, even when mothers stay in the labor force, responsibility for children frequently constrains their choice of job: they accept lower wages in exchange for shorter or more flexible hours, location near home, limited out-cf-town travel, and the like. Third, women who devote a great deal of time and energy to child care and associated housework are often less able to devote maximum effort to market work. For instance, when a young child is present, women are more likely than men to be absent from work, even at equal levels of education and wages. According to Reskin and Hartmann, 'The care of children . . . still appears to be largely women's responsibility, and this responsibility undoubtedly conflicts with their entrance into and advancement in a number of occupations that routinely require overtime, job-related travel, or inflexible or irregular hours.'

"Perhaps most important of all, because most young women expect to be mothers, they (and their parents) are less likely than men to invest in wage-enhancing human capital while in school and in their first job or two after leaving school. In the past this has been reflected in choice of major, in uncertainty about pursuing graduate school training, and in a reluctance to experience the long hours and other rigors characteristic of apprenticeships in medicine, law, business, and other financially rewarding occupations. The difference between women and men in this respect is narrowing, partly because the barriers of prejudice are weakening, but also because more women are planning to remain childless and those who do want to become mothers expect to have fewer children and to spend less time with them. V. FUCHS, *supra* note 2, at 60–61 (emphasis in original; citations omitted).

5. In this regard, Fuchs comments as follows: "Under correct conditions in the United States, socialization for the roles of wife and mother can frustrate women's quest for economic equality in at least two ways. First, it affects the choices women make in school and in the labor market, choices that limit their lifetime earning power. Not infrequently, women who have sacrificed market skills and ambitions in favor of home responsibilities find themselves at a severe economic disadvantage later in life as a result of divorce. Second, even when individual women resist socialization, they are likely to encounter difficulties in the labor market simply because they are women and are often evaluated and treated according to gender norms." V. FUCHS, *supra* note 2, at 43.

6. As Fuchs observes: "Residential custody patterns for children of divorced parents are also an indication of women's demand for children. A study of divorces in two California counties between September 1984 and March 1985 revealed that in three-quarters of the families there was joint *legal* custody, but in only 20 percent of the cases was *residential* custody joint between mother and father. In the other 80 percent of cases, the mother was fourteen times as likely as the father to have custody. The authors write, 'To our surprise we are *not* seeing an increase in father custody.'

"What about men? Don't they also desire children and care about their welfare? Of course many do, some more so than the average woman. Each sex has its own distribution of preferences, and these distributions overlap. Although many men care a great deal, *on average* their desire and their caring do not seem to be as strong as women's. Hundreds of thousands of children born to unwed mothers never see their fathers or even know who they are. Many divorced fathers see their children rarely and contribute little or nothing to their support. Maternal abandonment of children is a relatively rare phenomenon, but paternal abandonment is not. When parents divorce and remarry, continuing contact between children and their mothers seems to be more important than contact with their biological fathers. In their study of custodial arrangements following divorce, Maccoby and Mnookin find that the noncustodial mothers tend to maintain closer contact with their children than do noncustodial fathers." V. FUCHS, *supra* note 2, at 69–70. (emphasis in original; citations omitted).

7. Consider the following: "Discrimination against women undoubtedly persists, not only in the labor market but in most economic and social institutions. But the biggest source of women's economic disadvantage—namely, their greater desire for and concern about children—is more fundamental, though it is impossible to say how much results from "nature" and how much result from "nurture." Women's stronger commitment to parenting can be inferred not only from statitistical studies but also from a wide variety of other sources, ranging from literary works to the clinical experience of psychotherapists. Motherhood and fatherhood are not symmetrical, are not simply opposite sides of the same coin. Both are strongly influenced by socialization—but in the case of fathers, socialization is practically the whole story. Motherhood is different. Women make a huge investment in pregnancy, childbearing, and nursing—an investment that is crucial to the perpetuation of the species. The father's investment, in terms of time and energy, is usually much smaller. . . . V. FUCHS, *supra* note 2, at 140–41.

8. *See generally* V. FUCHS, *supra* note 2; P. ZOPF, AMERICAN WOMEN IN POVERTY (1989).

9. "Despite major antidiscrimination legislation and a quarter-century of revolutionary social change, women as a group have not improved their economic well-being relative to men. Unmarried white women who are young and well educated are the only significant exception to this conclusion. . . ." V. FUCHS, *supra* note 2, at 139.

10. Hampton, *Marital Disruption: Some Social and Economic Consequences,* in FIVE THOUSAND AMERICAN FAMILIES—PATTERNS OF ECONOMIC PROGRESS 366 (1974). *See also* Smith, *The Movement of Women into the Labor Force,* in THE SUBTLE REVOLUTION (R. Smith ed. 1979), in which the author detailed the sex segregation of women in low-paying, low-status jobs where they earn 60 percent of the wages earned by men.

11. Hampton, *supra* note 10, at 143.

12. *Id.* The study indicated at least three reasons why this might be so. First, age may not be as good a proxy for experience for women, since they may have been out of the labor force for several years due to family responsibilities. This is less true for the single women in the sample, however, and all the individuals considered have been working at least five years. Second, it is possible that women tend to be in more "dead-end" kinds of jobs, where they have less opportunity to acquire new skills and be promoted. Third, there have been changes in the labor market in recent years which may have benefited younger women more than the older women workers.

13. *Id.* at 144. Part of this may be due to the presence and effects of sexual harassment as an additional form of job discrimination. *See* Crull, *Sexual Harassment and Male Control of Women's Work,* 8 WOMEN, A JOURNAL OF LIBERATION 3 (1982).

14. Fuchs, *supra* note 2, at 3–4.

15. *See* V. FUCHS, *supra* note 2; ZOPF, *supra* note 8.

16. *See* L. WEITZMAN, THE DIVORCE REVOLUTION: THE UNINTENDED SOCIAL AND ECONOMIC CONSEQUENCES FOR WOMEN AND CHILDREN IN AMERICA (1985).

17. *See* Younger, *Marital Regimes: A Story of Compromise and Demoralization, Together with Criticism and Suggestions for Reform,* 67 CORNELL L. REV. 45, 89, n. 328 (1981).

Freed & Foster, *Marital Property Reform in New York: Partnership of Co-Equals?*, 8 FAM. L.Q. (1974) at 176, supported the notion of marriage as a "partnership of co-equals with division of labor that entitles each to a one-half interest in the family assets . . . such a system reflects the contemporary understanding of marriage, and the reasonable expectations of the parties." *See* SEX DISCRIMINATION AND THE LAW: CAUSES AND REMEDIES (B. Babcock, A. Freedman, E. Norton & S. Ross eds. 1975) for a distinction between commercial and marital partnership.

Weyrauch, *Metamorphoses of Marriage*, 13 FAM. L.Q. 415, 418–24, 435 (1980) asserted that the incidents of marriage are governed increasingly by notions of equality of spouses, with spouses viewed as persons entering a voluntary association with equal rights, duties and contributions. He noted that small-business case law aided the evolution of the partnership concept of marriage. Underlying this conception, however, is a fundamental assumption of freedom of will that is not always born out in reality, as noted by Weyrauch. There are problems, also, with how one views children if marriage is a contract. There seem to be conflicting views: they are seen as chattels, assets, or products of the marriage, or as persons who are consumers of marriage and entitled to protection. An additional problem, not mentioned by those advocating the partnership concept, is that expectations which may be reasonable at the time of marriage or during a functioning marriage may appear substantially unreasonable at the time of divorce, when ongoing benefits of support and mutual cooperation are terminated.

The partnership model has long been urged as a way of limiting judicial discretion. In criticizing judicial discretion, one author commented that the "greatest evil is not so bad when certain." Daggett, *Divisions of Property Upon Dissolution of Marriage*, 6 LAW AND CONTEMP. PROBS. 225, 229 (1939). Daggett recommended the concept of partnership based on community-property principles and mandatory equal division. She also believed that community-property states were far ahead of common-law property states. With an economic partnership it would make "no difference whether one contributes more energy to the task with better material results than the other; nor does it matter if one makes no contribution at all." *Id.* at 223.

18. *See* D. RAE, EQUALITIES (1981). The notion of sexual equality is simplistic and formalistic insofar as it means that individuals paired as one man against one woman must be treated the same. *See also* Westen, *The Empty Idea of Equality*, 95 HARV. L. REV. 537 (1982).

19. Questions of dependency and need, and how to cope with them, have plagued American society since its inception. Definitions of dependency have changed as the institutions designated to deal with dependency have changed. Until the twentieth century, the problem of need and dependency was dealt with almost exclusively by the family, by private charity, and by state and local governments. W. ACHENBAUM, OLD AGE IN THE NEW LAND: THE AMERICAN EXPERIENCE SINCE 1790, at 131–41 (1979).

The conflict between public and private solutions to perceived need surfaced in the Mother's Assistance movement in the early twentieth century. Illinois passed the Funds to Parents Act in 1911, which provided poor but competent parents with funds to support their children at home. Within two years, twenty states provided cash relief to widows with children. J. AXINN AND H. LEVIN, SOCIAL WELFARE: A HISTORY OF THE AMERICAN RESPONSE TO NEED 131–35, 144–60 (1975).

When Aid to Dependent Children was made part of the Social Security Act in 1935, the primary goal was to support dependent children at home with their mothers. This policy was reversed in 1967 when Congress established the Work Incentive Program and increased appropriations for day-care centers. This new program required that the employability of mothers as well as fathers be assessed. At the same time, proposals were being made to pay wages to mothers who decided against entering the labor market in order to care for their children. *Id.* at 280–85.

One difficulty with the concept of need is expressed in Rothman, *The State as Parent: Social Policy in the Progressive Era*, in DOING GOOD: THE LIMITS OF BENEVOLENCE 69, 83 (1978): "Progressives were far more attentive to the 'needs' of disadvantaged groups than to their 'rights.' Needs were real and obvious—the poor were overworked and underpaid, living in unhealthy tenements and working in miserable sweat shops. Rights, on the other hand, were 'so-called'—the right of the poor to sleep under the bridge or the laborer to fix his own contract with an all powerful corporation. . . . This [postprogressive] suspicion of benevolence and anti-institutionalism has encouraged and is reinforced by an acute distrust of discretionary authority."

A focus on rights (such as equality) is not, however, an ideal solution: "[T]he expansion of rights solves only part of the problem, for there do remain, like it or not, needs as well, imbalances in economic and social power, in inherited physical constitutions, that demand redress." *Id.* at 92. Rights discourse has also been criticized as unstable, indeterminate, reified, and politically disutile. Tushnet, *An Essay on Rights*, 62 TEX. L. REV. 1363 (1984). This critique has been contextualized and criticized by Professor Patricia Williams in *Alchemical Notes: Reconstructing Ideals from Deconstructed Rights*, 22 HARV. C.R.–C.L. L. REV. 401 (1987).

For a discussion of the changing conception of marriage from status to contract, see *The Course of Change in Family Law*, 5 FAM. L. REP. 4013, 4015 (1979). *See also* M. GLENDON, THE NEW FAMILY AND THE NEW PROPERTY 101–18 (1981); Cantwell, *Man + Woman + Property = ?*, PROB. LAW. 9–10 (1980); M. GLENDON, THE TRANSFORMATION OF FAMILY LAW (1989). *But cf.* Rehbinder, *Status, Contract and the Welfare State*, 23 STAN. L. REV. 941 (1971). In the common law, *status* came to mean a deviation from full legal capacity. *Id.* at 943. Rehbinder asserted that the importance of contract has now vanished from family law, and the movement in that area is more appropriately described as that from contract to status. The state has reduced the political autonomy of classes to formal legal equality through bureaucratization and monopoly. *Id.* at 945–46.

20. There are objections to language that characterizes women as being in need in many areas other than divorce. There are also objections raised that disguising need in an attempt to give status to nonworking women may hurt some other groups of women. For example, one author objected to the present label for spouse benefits under social security—*dependent benefits*—as "degrading." Mayers, *Incremental Change in Social Security Needed to Result in Equal and Fair Treatment of Men and Women*, in A CHALLENGE TO SOCIAL SECURITY: THE CHANGING ROLES OF WOMEN AND MEN IN AMERICAN SOCIETY (Burkhauser & Holden eds. 1982) [hereinafter cited as CHALLENGE TO SOCIAL SECURITY]. Compare Edith Fierst's objections in an article in the same volume: "[I am] offended philosophically by [proposals for] homemaker credits and increased child care drop-out years because they increase the rewards of not being employed. Fair play requires that the woman who works and pays taxes should get more for her efforts than the one who does not. Much as I want the homemaker to be secure in old age, I do not want to give her preference over the working woman." Fierst, *Discussion*, in CHALLENGE TO SOCIAL SECURITY, *supra* at 66, 71.

21. UNIF. MARRIAGE AND DIVORCE ACT § 307, Alternative A. 9A U.L.S. 238 (1977). Maintenance and property division are explicitly linked together in the Act. Section 307(a) Alternative A requires a court to consider "whether apportionment is in lieu of or in addition to maintenance." Maintenance awards are limited to a narrow category of circumstances. The court may grant such awards only if it finds that the spouse seeking

maintenance (1) lacks sufficient property to provide for her needs, and (2) is unable to support herself through appropriate employment or is the custodian of a child whose circumstances make it appropriate that the custodian not be required to seek employment outside the home. *Id.* at Sec. 308(a), 9A U.L.A. 347. The commissioner's comments on the section of the Act governing maintenance explicitly state that the provisions of that section and of the section governing disposition of property have the "dual intention" of "encourag[ing] the court to provide for the financial needs of the spouses by property disposition rather than by an award of maintenance." The comment continues: "only if the available property is insufficient for the purpose and if the spouse who seeks maintenance is unable to secure employment appropriate to his [*sic*] skills and interests or is occupied with child care may an award of maintenance be ordered." *Id.* at § 308, Commissioners' Comment, 9A U.L.A. 161.

22. Title is a fairly easy category for people to understand. If the property belongs to one spouse or the other as evidenced in a formal legal document such as a deed, the distribution follows. An extended version of title considers ownership not only as evidenced in legal title but also as a result of the provision of economic assets to secure the property. This system has increasingly been understood to be unfair as clearly favoring the market actor who has economic assets with which to accumulate property and devaluing the non-economic activities of homemakers. As a result, most common-law states have moved away from a strict title system, and the contemporary way we talk about marriage reflects the societal presumption that homemakers should not be left out merely because they have not made monetary contributions to the accumulation of property.

23. Some sorts of extreme misconduct related to marital breakdown have been found relevant to the distribution issue, even in states which explicitly prohibit consideration of marital misconduct. *See* Blickstein v. Blickstein, 472 N.Y.S.2d 110 (N.Y. App. Div. 1984) (court found fault relevant to equitable distribution in "very rare" situations involving misconduct that "shocks the conscience"); D'Arc v. D'Arc, 395 A.2d 1270 (N.J. Super. Ct. Ch. Div. 1978), *aff'd,* 421 A.2d 602 (N.J. Super. Ct. App. Div. 1980) (court found misconduct relevant where the husband had attempted to arrange his wife's murder). *See also* Stover v. Stover, 696 S.W.2d 750 (Ark. 1985) (Arkansas Supreme Court held that the trial court could go beyond the statutory list of factors bearing on equitable distribution to consider fault where the wife had been convicted of conspiracy to murder her husband). The Texas Family Code, which doesn't explicitly address fault but directs the courts to distribute property in a manner that is "just and right, having due regard for the rights of each party," has been interpreted by the Texas courts to permit consideration of fault. Tex. Fam. Code Ann. Sec. 3.63 (Vernon 1975 & Supp. 1985). The court has deemed evidence of adultery and physical violence by the husband relevant to equitable distribution. Mogford v. Mogford, 616 S.W.2d 936 (Tex. Cir. App. 1981).

Additionally, a conception of "economic fault"—the deliberate dissipation of marital assets—is emerging as a relevant consideration in the distribution decision in many states where marital fault is explicitly deemed irrelevant. Arizona law allows the court to consider "abnormal expenditures, destruction, concealment of fraudulent disposition" of marital property. Ariz. Rev. Stat. Ann. Sec 25.318(a) (Supp. 1984). California law includes an analogous provision. Cal. Civ. Code Sec. 4800 (West Supp. 1985). *See also* Blickstein, *supra,* and Smith v. Smith, 331 S.E.2d 682 (N.C. 1985) (court determined that only financial misconduct can be taken into account in the division of property).

24. This conclusion is based on the materials detailed in part 2 of the book.

25. In spite of a decade of enforcement reforms, collection of child support remains a problem.

26. Noncustodial fathers may not feel the same sort of connection to "adult" children and may not be as responsive to their needs. See, for example, Wallerstein's findings: "[A] father's attitudes and feelings about his children can become blunted by divorce—a finding that took me by surprise and one that is hard to understand. Psychologists, lawyers, and judges used to think that a father's relationship with his children during marriage would, within reasonable limits, predict his attitude toward them after divorce. If he was an attentive, loving, and sensitive father before divorce, those attributes of fathering would continue long after the breakup. . . . But we are finding otherwise. . . . [W]e have seen that a father's commitment to his children does not necessarily carry over into the postdivorce years. . . . [M]any fathers who pay all their child support over the years and maintain close contact with their children draw the line with college. While they can afford it, value education, and have cordial relations with their children, they do not offer even partial support through college. . . . The majority [of these men] have college educations. But when I ask about college for their children, they don't want to discuss it." J. WALLERSTEIN & S. BLAKESLEE, SECOND CHANCES: MEN, WOMEN, AND CHILDREN, A DECADE AFTER DIVORCE (1989) at 158.

27. *See* Fineman, *Implementing Equality: Ideology, Contradiction and Social Change: A Study of Rhetoric and Results in the Regulation of the Consequences of Divorce,* 1983 WIS. L. REV. 789.

28. Westen, *supra* note 18, at 572–82. *See also* D. RAE, *supra* note 18. In 1979, Karen Seal argued that given inequality in the market, feminists in California could have predicted that equal division would have an adverse impact on women. She concluded that the "belief in equality is so fundamental, however, that arguing for more than equal division of assets or income for women could be interpreted as discrimination against men." Seal, *A Decade of No-Fault Divorce,* 1 FAM. ADVOC. 10, 14 (Spring 1979).

29. Weitzman detailed that in the first year after their divorces under the equal-division rules, men in California experienced a 42 percent increase in their standard of living, as measured by income in relation to needs. Divorced women, by contrast, experienced a 73 percent decline. Weitzman, *The Economics of Divorce: Social and Economic Consequences of Property, Alimony and Child Support Awards,* 28 U.C.L.A. L.REV. 1181 (1981).

Earlier studies had also shown this pattern, even if the reported differentiations in positions were not exactly the same as the Weitzman findings. *See* Seal, *supra* note 28. In addition, in 1976 researchers found that while there was a 19 percent decline in a typical husband's income in real money terms, his economic position actually improved by 17 percent when assessed in terms of his needs after divorce. Women's positions, however, showed a decline in income relative to needs of 29 percent. Hoffman & Holmes, *Husbands, Wives, and Divorce,* in FIVE THOUSAND AMERICAN FAMILIES, *supra* note 10, at 27–31 (1976). The Hoffman & Holmes study was available prior to the passage of the Wisconsin reform legislation.

30. As noted in an unpublished article in 1982: "In some cases, an equal division might not fairly reflect the contributions of the parties. In *Kobylack v. Kobylack,* . . . the parties had a marriage of ten years, in which both had maintained careers as if they were not married and had treated their marriage as a partnership. The court determined that the division of the two major marital assets, the residence and the automobile, should be in accordance with the parties' economic contributions to the partnership. Thus, because the court did not want either party to retain a 'monetary advantage merely by the virtue of having been married,' the court based its decision on purely economic considerations. The court determined that the husband's financial contributions to the partnership were two-and-a-half times that of the wife and made a division of the marital property in accordance with that rationale.

"On the other hand, a purely equitable distribution often might result in an equal division. For example, in Jolis v. Jolis, 111 Misc.2d 965, 446 N.Y.S.2d 138 (sup. Ct. 1981), after 41 years of marriage and an affluent lifestyle, the parties had acquired marital assets that included cash, securities, a farm, a New York City co-op, and a Paris studio co-op. The court determined that the marital property should be divided equally, emphasizing the wife's abandonment of a promising career as a singer to be a companion and social asset to her husband, the wife's lack of future income and loss of inheritance rights, and the husband's comfortable financial status." Note, *The North Carolina Act for Equitable Distribution of Marital Property,* 1982 WAKE FOREST L. REV. 735, 752 n. 121.

For such women, the equality model is a form of property reallocation or asset-sharing based on other women's social or cultural disadvantages and not on their own circumstances.

31. One commentator has argued for the separate treatment of the marital home at divorce on the basis of children's and custodial parents' needs. She noted the beginning development in Anglo-American equitable distribution systems of such a separate legal regime for disposition of that property upon divorce and criticized systems which subject the marital home to an equal division as only superficially fair. Comment, *The Marital Home: Equal or Equitable Distribution?,* 50 U. CHI. L. REV. 1089 (1983).

32. To be successful in most jurisdictions, she would have to combine this argument with one or more of the following factors: that she has been married over eight or ten years, has devoted this time to homemaking and child-care services, is of an age or in a physical or emotional condition that may make her unable to work, or that her services contributed to her husband's education, training or increased earning power—in other words, monopolize the factors.

33. In the vast majority of cases, arguments based on the provisions allowing for deviations will be possible on both sides and will, therefore, tend to balance out each other. Attorneys, who perform the function of initial decision-makers in advising their clients about what they predict courts would decide in a specific case, may barter back and forth with each other about the importance of these factors in specific cases, but the presumption affords the standard for predictability. Also, in the small percentage of cases which will actually be litigated, the presumption stands as a seductively simple and fair basis for making decisions which are unlikely to be overturned on appeal.

34. Even if not unduly affected by the presumption of equal distribution, the factors alone are inadequate to guide the trial court or attorneys toward more discriminating decisions based on the specific characteristics of the divorcing parties. They focus on an abstract view of the nature of the relationship between men and women and do not direct attention to the more difficult components of an assessment of need. A woman who has not been victimized by her husband or society may still need more assets than her husband to cope with her postdivorce life as custodial parent. It appears, however, that only the wife-victim can hope to successfully assert need as a basis for inequality. Other women, despite their needs, will be left with the equality model as their sole recourse.

35. *See* Seal, *supra* note 28, at 10. The author's analysis of court records in San Diego revealed that California's rule-equality reform has had an adverse affect on wives. Under the former system, the home and furniture typically were allocated to the wife. After the reform, the home and other assets usually were divided, and the wife was ordered to pay a share of the family debts. Seal also concluded that the actual value of child-support awards tended to be less under the equality mode. The combination of the wife's loss of assets with her increased responsibility for family debts often meant that she had less disposable income and that she would end up contributing more than half to support the children. *Id.* at 13–15.

36. The difficult questions of why one spouse (typically the husband) should absorb an unequal share of the family financial responsibilities or any responsibility for the future financial well-being of his ex-wife deserve more comprehensive treatment than is possible here. The difficulties caused by serial monogamy and ongoing support for prior spouses have been noted. *See* M. GLENDON, THE NEW FAMILY AND THE NEW PROPERTY 87 (1981). Fewer conceptual difficulties are presented, however, if decision making is based on the theory of ongoing responsibility for children. If it is possible to make a distribution of property (i.e., a one-time allocation) which will not seriously impair a man's assumption of new family responsibilities while at the same time allowing his ex-wife and children a better chance for a reasonable economic future, it would seem fair to do so. This result could be achieved if laws focused on specific circumstances such as custody awards in determining appropriate property divisions.

CHAPTER FOUR

1. For a detailed account of the Wisconsin experience in fashioning the marital property concept, *see* Weisberger, *The Wisconsin Marital Property Act: Highlights of the Wisconsin Experience in Developing a Model for Comprehensive Common Law Property Reform,* 1 WISC. WOMEN'S LAW J. 5 (Spring 1979).

2. The Institute for Poverty generates discussion papers, many of which have been instrumental in shaping policy debates. *See e.g.,* Danzinger, *Father Involvement in Welfare Families Headed by Adolescent Mothers,* INST. FOR RESEARCH ON POVERTY DISCUSSION PAPER #856–87; McLanahan and Booth, *Mother-Only Families: Problems, Reproduction, and Politics,* INST. FOR RESEARCH ON POVERTY DISCUSSION PAPER #855–87.

3. *See* Wis. A.B. 277, 82d Sess., 1975 § 1 (adding irretrievable breakdown as a grounds for divorce). The Wisconsin Assembly passed the bill by a 60–30 margin. WISCONSIN ASSEMBLY JOURNAL 1970–73 (1975). *See generally* LEGISLATIVE REFERENCE BUREAU OF WISCONSIN, THE LEGISLATIVE RESPONSE TO DIVORCE: A SURVEY OF NO-FAULT DIVORCE, No. 76–1B-5, at 6 (1976) [hereinafter cited as LEGISLATIVE RESPONSE TO DIVORCE].

4. The senate vote was 17–14 against the Bill. WIS. SENATE J. 1446 (1975).

5. *See* 1977 WIS. LAWS ch. 105.

6. These economic issues were directly related to the no-fault divorce provision, which would make divorce available to either spouse even if he or she had not been "injured," and even if the other spouse did not want the divorce. The possibility of unilateral termination caused some to focus on regulating the economic aspects of divorce to protect an abandoned and possibly dependent spouse.

7. Governor's Commission on the Status of Women, *Fact Sheet* (on file in Wisconsin Legislative Reference Bureau, re: 1977 Divorce Reform Act). One of the Wisconsin reformers described the situation, as she saw it, during an interview: "[In states] just adding a no-fault ground for divorce, women ended up generally in much worse shape than they were under the old law. And as unpleasant and horrendous as the old law was, it did give women a modicum of protection from just sort of being left in the lurch with minimal to no support and a third of the property because that wouldn't happen to them unless they were the person who was wrong and in order to get a divorce most men were going to have to bargain on the economic issues so that they could, in effect, buy out their wives or the wives who would not consent to the divorce."

A comment by Doris Freed, reported by the Washington Post News Service, indicates that this was still a viable perception in the 1980s: "[I]t has been a mistake to give up consent [to divorce] as a trading tool. . . . [U]til the courts give better recognition to the financial needs of housewives, women still need consent as a bargaining chip to defend their interests." Capital Times (Madison, Wis.), 27 July 1982, at 10.

8. In commenting on the national no-fault movement, Freed and Foster cautioned: "The movement for the breakdown ground as the exclusive basis for divorce must and should be resisted unless there are built-in safeguards to protect the economic interests of the parties and the welfare of minor children in the family." Freed & Foster, *Marital Property Reform in New York: Partnership of Co-Equals?*, 8 FAM. L.Q. 169, 195 (1974).

9. *See* WISCONSIN GOVERNOR'S COMMISSION ON THE STATUS OF WOMEN, REAL WOMEN, REAL LIVES: MARRIAGE, DIVORCE, WIDOWHOOD 43–45 (N. Briggs, ed. 1978) [hereinafter cited as REAL WOMEN, REAL LIVES].

10. The new legislation authorized judges to deviate from this standard of equal divisions only after considering specific factors listed in the statute.

11. *E.g.,* Lacey v. Lacey, 45 Wis. 2d 378, 384, 173 N.W.2d 142, 145 (1970) ("[A property] division is not a penalty imposed for fault."); Miner v. Miner, 10 Wis. 2d 438, 446, 103 N.W.2d 4, 9 (1960) ("[A]limony is not decreed to punish the husband. It arises out of the husband's duty to support his former wife.")

12. *E.g.,* Mason v. Mason, 44 Wis. 2d 362, 373, 171 N.W.2d 364, 369 (1969) ("Misconduct of one of the parties does not mean division of property can be used as a means of punishment, yet it is another factor to be weighed by the trial court in determining an equitable property division.")

13. On the value of networking and the use of a preexisting organizational base in reform movements, see Tierney, *The Battered Women Movement and the Creation of the Wife Beating Problem*, 29 SOC. PROBS. 207 (1982).

14. These reforms were referred to as *The Equal Rights Implementation Package* (Jan. 1973). They included 1973 Assembly Bill 21 (relating to marriageable age); 1973 Assembly Bill 22 (relating to equal rights of women: unemployment compensation); 1973 Assembly Bill 23 (relating to eliminating distinctions based on sex in the statute: a comprehensive bill containing all other recommended changes.) The last was referred to as the *Omnibus Bill.* Several of the reformers involved with divorce reform had also been active in regard to these provisions.

15. Values, particularly certain institutionally derived ones such as religious, educational, family, political, and self-actualization, have been described as systematically related to receptivity to ideas of sexual equality. Ball-Rokeach, *Receptivity to Sexual Equality,* 19 N.H. PAC. SOC. REV. 519 (1976). *See also* A. OBERSCHALL, SOCIAL CONFLICT AND SOCIAL MOVEMENTS (1973) ("norm-oriented" reforms, rather than challenges to basic societal goals characterized by "value-oriented" movements, are the most common in nontotalitarian societies).

16. The interviewee continued: "Of course in real life very few people did that. But it caused an awful lot of anger on the part of an awful lot of men, and of course, we would sometimes have men call us up who told us how they were being ripped off or whatever. So it was always a conscious effort on my part as with ERA for instance to say, okay we are going to be really equitable straight down the line. It's going to be sex neutral, and we're not trying to rip off the men, and we're not trying to rip off the women. We are just trying to make it so that you are in as equal a position when you finish as when you began."

17. In particular, the Chair of the Governor's Commission on the Status of Women reported being greatly influenced by the writings of June Menzies on the need for valuing a housewife's work. *See* Menzies, *The Achilles Heel of Women in the Industrial Society,* in 2 WOMEN SPEAKING 18 (Apr. 1969). *See also* Menzies, *The Family, the Homemaker, and the Economy,* in 3 WOMEN SPEAKING 23 (July 1970).

18. The concepts ultimately utilized in the divorce reform were first articulated in the context of the ongoing family. In fact, divorce reform in Wisconsin took place against the background of a consensus among the reformers on the need and desirability of marital property reform, which would include even those in ongoing marriages within the partnership model.

One reformer indicated the relationship between reform of the ongoing marriage and reform in the divorce area: "We were fairly clear on what we wanted to do [with divorce reform]. I mean it seemed obvious to most of us who thought about it a little while that we wanted to start from 50/50 and the factors that we wanted to have considered. . . . But we realized . . . that we had an awful lot more thinking to do on [ongoing marriages]. There were some Commission members who at that time were saying, well, housewives should be paid . . . and then somebody was saying that that would make her the employee of her husband. [But] many husbands couldn't afford to pay their wives. So there was far less consensus and there was zero awareness of community property because we have virtually no attorneys involved. . . . Well we were very aware that we were working on the ideas for marital property when we were doing the divorce [reform] and we knew that we didn't want to have anything that was going to cut across. . . ."

19. University of Wisconsin Extension, *Feminism and the Family* 57–58 (1972) (copies available at the Center for Women's and Family Education, University of Wisconsin Extension) [hereinafter cited as *Feminism and the Family*].

20. Women's Education Resources, University of Wisconsin Extension, *The American Family: Legal Rx for Its Survival* 22–23 (1976).

21. These women recalled being so affected by the conference presentations that they made notes while returning to Madison concerning what types of economic protections would be necessary before no-fault legislation should be established in Wisconsin.

22. One such group was the St. Thomas More Lawyer's Society, which was openly critical of all no-fault proposals partly because the members believed it was impossible to eliminate considerations of fault, and partly because they believed adoption of no-fault would increase immorality and the degradation of the family. *Position Paper of the St. Thomas More Lawyer's Society* (1 Feb. 1977) (on file with the author).

23. 1975 Assembly Bill 277 was the primary no-fault bill considered in 1975. As originally introduced, the bill would have added "irretrievable breakdown of marriage" as a ground for divorce under Wisconsin law. The assembly passed the bill by a 60–30 margin but, after receiving a favorable committee recommendation, the senate defeated it by a 17–14 vote. This vote was the closest Wisconsin had come to approving a no-fault bill up to that date. LEGISLATIVE RESPONSE TO DIVORCE, *supra* note 3.

The feminists did not oppose no-fault but argued that provisions should be added to require courts to recognize the economic value of housework and child care in determining the disposition of marital property. The reformers were responsible for introducing several amendments which were not adopted, providing for the financial security of the wife. See, for example, Sen. Substitute Amendment 1 to 1975 A.B. 277, which provided: "It is the intent of the legislature that a spouse who has been handicapped socially or economically by his or her contributions to a marriage shall be compensated for such contributions at the termination of the marriage, insofar as this is possible, and may be reeducated where necessary to permit the spouse to become self-supporting at a standard of living reasonably comparable to that enjoyed during the marriage. It is further the intent of the legislature that the standard of living of any minor children of the parties be maintained at a reasonable level, so that insofar as is possible, the children will not suffer economic hardship."

The proposed adoption of specific guidelines relative to property settlements was criticized in 1975 on the ground that every divorce case is different, making it impossible to legislate specific property settlements or alimony awards which would be equitable in all instances. LEGISLATIVE RESPONSE TO DIVORCE, *supra* note 3, at 6–7.

24. The key legislator recalled her colleagues' responses when she was ultimately successful in getting through the reform: "They just didn't believe that we had the power to get it across. And this was really the beginning of the political power of the women's movement. I mean the organization that did the work on each legislator was just absolutely critical. They had never done that, you see. The old style legislator here worked on a bill, particularly the advocacy kind of a bill. I mean, obviously, the interest groups have always been here, the economic interest groups and most things that have passed have been bargained out by interest groups. This was an example of something where there was no real strong interest group against it. But there were lots of legislators who were very concerned about the social change involved such as undercutting marriage."

25. As one reformer wrote: "Let us begin our discussion by defining the term *feminism*. Feminism should not be confused with *femininity*, a term that is sometimes complimentary and sometimes derogatory. *Femininity* denotes a state of being, a typically female state of being, whatever that is, usually helpless, or at least dependent, sexually appealing, and more emotional than rational. *Feminism*, in contrast, embodies ideas of action. It advocates a larger role for women; an improvement in the status of women; a demand for greater independence for women." *Feminism and the Family, supra* note 19, at 2.

26. Gender neutrality does not necessarily require a system of a rule-equality, nor does equality, in a broader sense, require gender neutrality. Fairness in predictable results, rather than the appearance of equality on the face of legal rules, would be the goal. *See* Johnston, *Sex and Property: The Common Law Tradition, The Law School Curriculum, and Developments Toward Equality,* 47 N.Y.U. L. REV. 1033, 1035–36 (1972). Johnston also suggested that there are two ways to view a wife's interest in her husband's earnings: "[I]f equality were the touchstone, then either (1) husband and wife would be treated as individuals, and married women would be entitled to fair compensation for their services, or (2) husband and wife would be treated as a marital unit or partnership, and each would share equally in the net income generated." *Id.* at 1071.

27. A Commission publication warned, "The court should presume property is to be divided equally. . . ." Wisconsin Governor's Commission on the Status of Women, *Divorce Reform Legislation* (1978) (on file with the author). This argument for sameness of treatment remains essentially the same in the Commission's later publications. *See, e.g.,* REAL WOMEN, REAL LIVES, *supra* note 9.

28. *See* REAL WOMEN, REAL LIVES, supra note 9, at 42–45. The text of two of the "horror stories" used during the divorce reform movement was set out: "John and Norma Norris were married in 1950. They lived on a farm in Illinois which John had inherited before they were married. At first, Norma was a housewife, caring for their children, performing the usual household tasks, gardening, preserving large quantities of food and cooking five or six daily meals for the hired hands who worked on the farm. Later on, when the children were in school, Norma took on an outside job. She continued to do the traditional tasks, and in addition contributed part of her income for family expenses.

"After 22 years of marriage, John divorced Norma. The court awarded her no alimony. Her share of their marital property consisted of only her own clothing and personal effects, a few household items which she owned prior to the marriage, and an automobile which she had purchased in her own name with her own funds. The house and furnishings, the farm with its machinery and livestock, the savings—all went to John. . . .

"Irene and Jim Murdoch were married in 1943. She owned two horses; he had 30 horses and eight head of cattle. They hired themselves out as ranch hands for several years, saved money, and then invested in a dude ranch. For many years they worked side by side. They saved more money and accumulated more property. She did all the usual household tasks and also did 'haying, raking, mowing, driving trucks, and a tractor, dehorning, vaccinating, branding,' any work that needed to be done.

"For five months a year, while Jim was away from the ranch attending to his duties as a member of the forest service, Irene managed the property alone. To their joint ventures, she also contributed money which she personally earned. In 1968, Jim asked Irene to release her dower rights to a piece of their property so that he could sell it. When she refused, he beat her so severely that she was hospitalized. This led to their separation after 25 years of marriage. Irene Murdoch went to court asking for a legal separation, ownership of the ranch home and the land surrounding it and a one-half interest in the ranch land, cattle, cattle brand, and other assets. The court granted her only $200 a month maintenance. Everything else—land, cattle, assets, family home—went to Jim. The judge justified his ruling this way: 'The land was held in the name of Mr. Murdoch at all times. The cattle and equipment were also held in his name; no declaration of partnership was ever filed . . . and I, therefore, do not form the conclusion that the Murdochs were partners, or that a relationship existed that would give Mrs. Murdoch the right to claim as a joint owner in equity in any of the farm assets.'" Id. at 44–45.

The actual cases reported were Norris v. Norris, 16 Ill. App. 3d 897, 307 N.E.2d 181 (1974) and Murdoch v. Murdoch, 1 W.W.R. 361 (Sup. Ct. Canada 1974); neither was a Wisconsin case. It should also be noted that the reformed law allows deviations based on the amount of property brought to the marriage and excludes gifts and inheritance from the property to be divided, so it is not clear that the reform would produce drastically different results in cases like these. *See* Wis. Stat. § 767.255 (1981–82).

When Real Women, Real Lives, *supra* note 9, was published, the Wisconsin divorce law had been reformed. The horror stories which had earlier been used to illustrate the need for that reform were now being used to illustrate the need for marital property reform. Most of the ongoing marriage horror stories were also from different states: New Jersey, New York and Nebraska.

The Wisconsin horror stories included some Wisconsin cases involving estate law and an unconfirmed letter from a "Northern Wisconsin woman" who wrote to the Commission that her husband refused to put up *jointly* owned property as collateral for a $1,500.00 loan so she could have necessary dental work done. *See also* Wisconsin Governor's Commission on the Status of Women, That Old American Dream & the Reality or Why We Need Marital Property Reform (1977) (repeating the same stories; on file with author).

29. At that time Florida was a common-law property state that adhered to strict title distribution. *See* Freed & Foster, *supra* note 8, at 170.

30. One of the reformers reported how the influence of the few horror stories she collected from women and from casebooks was compounded when the stories did not surprise the audiences to whom she spoke on the need for divorce reform: "[I would tell of] of the woman from northern Wisconsin who couldn't get dental work done because her husband didn't think it was important . . .; that case was unusual because it was so dramatic and the issue was so clear-cut. You can talk about it in two sentences. . . . But her story was not that unusual. In fact it wasn't unusual at all. And homemakers out there were not shocked or surprised when they heard that story. . . . If they needed dental work, if they were married to the right man, they'd get it, and if they weren't, they wouldn't, and

that was life. . . . I was also doing the research on the case law and getting it from that an-
gle too. So it wasn't just that there were ladies out there bitching because they didn't like
their lives. We were finding all sorts of corroboration of their personal experiences in the
few court cases that there were. And of course most of these cases don't ever come to
court. But some of them do in a number of states, and we had to look outside of Wisconsin to get enough of a body of case law to begin to make some generalizations, so we
ended up looking at a lot of separate property states. If we hadn't had both of them at the
same time I think it might have taken us a lot longer to start putting things together and
deciding what needed to be changed."

31. Transcript of Speech, undated (on file with author).

32. The reformers were not too careful about their statements of the law. For example,
the contrast is marked between the survey of the law governing divorce prior to the reform, and the following, presented as "a recent summary of laws affecting women": "[A]ll
income earned by either spouse belongs to that spouse alone, subject to the duty to support a nonearning spouse. This system works a great hardship on the spouse—usually the
wife—who works in the home and does not earn income from an outside job. Despite her
substantial contributions to the marriage partnership, the law does not recognize her domestic and childbearing services as having any economic value. . . . When a marriage
ends, through death or divorce, a wife who has worked beside her husband for years to
build a life together may find that he is or was a wealthy man and she is suddenly virtually
penniless because the assets they have accumulated cooperatively over the years belong to
the person who earned the money to pay the bills. Despite the labor contributed and sacrifices made for her family, the housewife has only a limited legal right to family assets."
Divorce Reform Legislation, supra note 27, at 14–15.

The reformers overstated the law's victimization of women. During the interviews, it
was suggested that the characterization of the solutions contained in the divorce-reform
movement was profoundly influenced at the outset by the reformers' desire to effect marital property reform in ongoing marriages. The divorce-reform legislation was urged as arguing for such reforms. *See* Munts, *Equality in Divorce, But Not Yet in Marriage,* Capital
Times (Madison, Wis., 6 July 1982 (editorial page).

For the further development of the horror story theme see REAL WOMEN, REAL LIVES,
supra note 9, at 4: "Most of these true stories do not have happy endings. In part that is
because in real life few people marry to live happily ever after, as the fairy stories of our
childhood led us to expect. In part it is because most of the stories were chosen to illustrate lesser known points of law still on the books that most fair-minded people today
(when they become *aware* of the law) think should be changed.
The purpose of telling these stories, then, is not to show family life as sour, miserable or demeaning. The purpose is to increase our understanding of how old laws and government policies either succeed in or fail to support the framework of the family when things go wrong.
The purpose in telling these stories is to strengthen our commitment to providing just laws.
There is . . . in family law . . . an imbalance in power. In regard to some decisions, the man,
the traditional head of the family and assumed breadwinner, carries much more weight in law
when he chooses to make a decision than does his wife. So he has much more opportunity to
succeed in being stubborn, unreasonable and unkind. The writers of this book believe that all
human beings—women and men—have a flourishing common sense and feel for what is fair.
They want to move you to work together with them to make marriage an equal partnership
and the family a stable place of refuge for us all."

For other cases of horror stories in different contexts, see Dingwall, *"Atrocity Stories" and
Professional Relationships,* 4 SOC. WORK & OCCUPATIONS 371 (1977). The author

described the way "atrocity stories" are used to communicate, negotiate, or establish norms for behavior, and to voice complaints and draw on common understandings of the world.

Horror stories can also be understood as "rhetorical visions," which are described as composite dramas that can catch up large numbers of people and that may be more persuasive than arguments. World-views are created by such images, and they can be employed by both sides in a dispute. Examples of such powerful images were those used by ERA proponents, who aligned themselves with notions of justice and equality against tyranny and oppression. Anti-ERA people, by contrast, labeled the pro-ERA forces as anti-children and anti-men. The anti-ERA people forged their visions from the American ideals of family and home. *See* Foss, *Equal Rights Amendment Controversy: Two Worlds in Conflict,* Q.J. SPEECH 275 (Oct. 1979). *See also* M. EDELMAN, POLITICAL LANGUAGES: WORDS THAT SUCCEED AND POLICIES THAT FAIL (1977); Arnott, *Feminists and Anti-Feminists as True Believers,* 57 SOC. & SOC. RESEARCH 300 (1973).

33. One looks in vain for alternative horror stories: the working-class woman who struggles with a job (*not* a career) and the housework and children, earning roughly what her husband does, and who at divorce does not have her performance of both roles recognized. Her contribution is greater than the "housewife's," but is nonetheless translated into an equal division that may compel sale of the home. She is left with the children, inadequate child support, and a job. Even if she is able to provide adequately for herself and the children on a day-to-day basis, she will be unable to accumulate the resources for purchasing another home for her family. The horror stories also do not include that of the woman whose second marriage ends in divorce and who, perhaps foolishly, invests her property settlement from her first marriage in a home or other property for herself and for her second husband. She may have to part with half of that property during her second divorce because funds were commingled or are difficult to trace. The stories also fail to tell of the woman who worked and raised children during her marriage, and who will continue to do both after divorce, whose husband is either incapacitated or shiftless and demands that she continue to support him or that he be given a share in the property which her earnings and efforts alone have accumulated. The preceding stories are all based on actual postreform cases in Wisconsin that were reported in questionnaire responses by several attorneys.

Disproving charges of elitism may have been a lost cause. *See, generally,* Cummings, *Class and Racial Divisions in the Female Population: Some Practical and Political Dilemmas for the Women's Movement,* SOC. SYMP. (Spring, 1976), where the author concluded that class issues seem to divide the population, particularly the female population, on many of the central issues championed by the women's movement. The author noted one exception: there was no apparent relationship between class and a person's attitude about equal treatment of women in the work force, although blacks were more supportive than whites. *Id.* at 111.

See also Dixon, *Public Ideology and the Class Composition of Women's Liberation,* 16 BERKELEY J. OF SOC. 149 (1971). Dixon indicated that working-class women and middle-class women, student women and professional women, and black women and white women have more conflicting interests than could ever be overcome by their common experience of sex discrimination. *Id.* at 154.

34. The Wisconsin reformers chose a framework for problem solving in the divorce context that focused on the abstract and symbolic nature of marriage and emphasized the symbolic position of the spouses as partners in a joint venture. This symbolic framework was apparent in their organizational efforts. One reformer recalled that she had organized

"a series of six conferences around the state which we called Homemaking and the Family—Changing Values and Concerns. We thought that was a nice title that wouldn't scare off anybody. Our real working title was the Risks and the Hazards to the Unpaid Homemaker and that's what we talked about. . . . [T]hese were very well and carefully planned meetings."

35. M. MELLI, THE LEGAL STATUS OF HOMEMAKERS IN WISCONSIN, HOMEMAKER'S COMMITTEE, NATIONAL COMMISSION ON THE OBSERVANCE OF INTERNATIONAL WOMEN'S YEAR at V (1977).

36. 120 CONG. REC. 38, 196–98 (1974).

37. See L. HALEM, DIVORCE REFORM: CHANGING LEGAL AND SOCIAL PERSPECTIVES (1980).

38. See Seal, *A Decade of No-Fault Divorce,* 1 FAM. ADVOC. 10, 14 (no. 4, Spring 1979).

39. The data is from FIVE THOUSAND AMERICAN FAMILIES—PATTERNS OF ECONOMIC PROGRESS (1974), at 143–44. See also Smith, *The Movement of Women into the Labor Force,* in THE SUBTLE REVOLUTION (1979), in which the author detailed the sex segregation of women in low-paying, low-status jobs where they earn 60 percent of the wages earned by men. One author noted that few women held union jobs in traditional male fields, and found problems with acceptance by male union members when they were in such jobs. Goldman, *Unions, Women and Economic Justice: Litigating Union Sex Discrimination,* 4 WOMAN'S RTS. L. REP. 3 (1977). In addition, a woman's wage tends to increase much more slowly with age than does a man's wage. In reporting this finding, researchers at the University of Michigan concluded that a forty-year-old man "earns $.70 an hour more than a similar man ten years younger. A forty-year-old woman earns only about $.18 more per hour than a woman who is thirty." *Id.* at 143. In addition, one reformer indicated she knew of Weitzman's preliminary results. Another reformer commented: "[W]e were acutely aware . . . of the difficulties of the California literal interpretation of its equal division of only community assets, and we've had these various horror stories from people where there was no community property and who therefore got 50 percent of nothing. So we wanted to allow a great deal of flexibility, but we were kind of caught in this trap . . . if you give the judges flexibility, they'll use it the way they have always used it."

The reformers were certainly aware that support orders have failed to take adequate care of need. Ms. Griffiths' testimony before the United States House of Representatives stressed both the inadequacy of initial awards of child support and the failure to enforce the large number of awards that were in arrears. 120 CONG. REC. 38 196–98 (1974). In addition, a study in Wisconsin conducted in 1955 indicated that 62 percent of parents under order for child support failed to comply the first year after the court order; 42 percent had not made a single payment.

40. For a system to assess ranking of beliefs when the fulfillment of one prevents the fulfillment of another, see Wegman, *Conceptual Representation of Belief Systems,* 11 J. THEORY SOC. BEHAVIOR 279 (1981). See also NISBETT & ROSS, HUMAN INFERENCE: STRATEGIES & SHORTCOMINGS OF SOCIAL JUDGMENT (1980).

41. Close to a decade after the reform began, the victim imagery was still potent. It was referred to continuously in the interviews conducted with the reformers in the summer of 1982.

42. See REAL WOMEN, REAL LIVES *supra* note 9, at 14–15.

43. THE WISCONSIN COMMISSION ON THE STATUS OF WOMEN, WISCONSIN WOMEN AND THE LAW (1st ed. 1975) (emphasis added).

44. See REAL WOMEN, REAL LIVES, *supra* note 28.

45. The Wisconsin Commission on the Status of Women, Wisconsin Women and the Law 13 (2d ed. 1977) (emphasis added). A third edition was published in 1979.

46. *Id.* It is interesting to note that most community-property jurisdictions provide for *equitable* rather than equal divisions at divorce. Only three jurisdictions ordinarily make equal divisions. Foster, *Equitable Distribution, An Explanation of New York's New Statute,* N.Y.L.J., 24 July 1980, at 1.

It appears the reformers were not well informed about such laws. The executive Secretary for the Commission, one of the principal forces behind the reform, for example, recalled: "I was sort of like the expediter, but I was always sitting in and listening to things that I didn't understand very much and saying 'What do you mean?'and 'Why?' and 'What does that mean?' and all the rest of it. But I thought the role was useful apart from being educative for me. It meant that I became a kind of liaison person translating first for Commission members and then for the other people in the outside groups."

47. The information on which the reformers relied was contrary to this suggestion. They had other information available, but were unreceptive to it. The information upon which their understanding of women's position was based came from states that had rules very different from those operating in Wisconsin. For example, in a memo attached to a notice of a meeting in February 1976 called to "discuss the desirability and feasibility of a partnership marriage model," the following statements were made: "As matters stand now, however, it is both fair and true to say that women in separate property jurisdictions are not as well compensated for their years spent as homemakers as are wives in community property states." This memo cites Freed & Foster, *supra* note 8, and New York case law. At that time, New York was a strict title state, as was Florida, where many of the horror stories of the reformers originated. *See* Freed & Foster, *supra* note 8, at 170. Perhaps the memo was attractive, however, because it espoused the partnership principle quite clearly: "The basic premise of the separate property system is that property is owned by the person who earned it during the marriage. In a community system, the basic premise is just the opposite: regardless of who earned property during the marriage, it is owned equally by both spouses. With such premises as the starting points for courts asked to divide property 'equitably' upon divorce, it seems inevitable that the wife in a community property state will receive a larger share of the property accumulated by either of the spouses during marriage than will the wife in a separate property jurisdiction." This conclusion is unsupported in the memo.

The implementation of the equality model in Wisconsin was also directly related to distrust of judicial discretion.

48. Interview with a reformer who was a member of the Commission.

49. Letter from an attorney to one of the reformers (n.d.) (on file with the author).

50. Letter from an attorney to one of the reformers (22 Oct. 1975) (on file with the author). This concern with assets from a previous marriage was raised by other Milwaukee attorneys.

51. *See* Governor's Commission on the Status of Women, Wisconsin Women and the National Plan of Action: Resolutions Adopted at the Wisconsin State Meeting and the National Women's Conference (1977), which both labels and defines: "DISPLACED HOMEMAKERS: Education, training, and financial aids should be made available for women who have been out of the labor force and wish to return." *Id.* at 5. In a section entitled *Wisconsin Leads the Way* it was noted: "The Wisconsin delegation was proud to be among the states which had already adopted laws remedying some of the discriminatory practices addressed in the National Plan of Action: . . .

HOMEMAKERS . . . [Wisconsin Divorce Reform Law] of 1977 abolished the concept of fault in divorce actions and provided for compensation for a spouse who has been handicapped socially or emotionally through his or her contributions to a marriage (as a homemaker) to ensure that he or she can become self-supporting."

52. There is a great deal of literature on the need for control without destroying discretion. *See, e.g.,* Dawson, *The Decision to Grant or Deny Parole,* in DISCRETIONARY DECISION-MAKING IN THE ADMINISTRATION OF JUSTICE (Atkins & Pogrebin eds. 2d ed. 1982). *See also* DAVIS, DISCRETIONARY JUSTICE (1971) (arguing for structure and confinement, but not elimination of discretion).

Of course and "equitable" statute would have required more individualized decision-making and could be criticized for that reason. For a discussion of the drawbacks and costs of judicial discretion (or individualized justice) versus the fixed proportion, see Rheinstein, *Division of Marital Property,* 12 WILLAMETTE L. J. 413 (1976), at 431–35. Hard-and-fast rules can be criticized for their overinclusiveness, however. *See also* Bardach & Kagan, *Mixing Public and Private Rights,* in REFORMING SOCIAL REGULATION 174–75 (Grayner & Thompson eds. 1982), suggesting that unreasonableness is inevitable when there is regulation and that, even at best, regulation is bound to produce many unreasonable and even deplorable results, even when the results on the whole are quite laudable.

There is also a price for "legal realism." The Uniform Marriage and Divorce Act approach—giving courts standards, not rules, that will allow them by an incremental process to use their "situation sense" to work out the best results over time—may overlook the cost of getting "the right" result. Goodman, *With Equitable Distribution, Divorce Lawyers' Fees Soar,* N.Y. Times, 13 Jan. 1983, at 17, cols. 1–2.

Goodman was commenting on the new New York law, but noted that the old law was certain (though unjust): "Under the old law, whoever had the deed to the house, for example, owned the house. A bank account generally belonged to the one whose name it was in. The result was not particularly fair, but it was not hard to figure out. Now, property is to be 'equitably distributed.' "

The article also pointed out some of the problems involved in presuming equality before the law. In the divorce situation, husbands tend to have better knowledge of the family resources. Wives have to discover the necessary information, and that is a major cost. " 'It is wives who are getting short-changed,' said the lawyer Robert S. Harkfield.

"One reason is that as burdensome as legal fees in divorce are, they are more difficult for women, even wives of very rich men, because they often do not have immediate access to cash. One woman now in divorce litigation put it this way: 'It's like playing poker, but only one player can raise the ante.' Rarely will lawyers take divorce cases without retainers. This is particularly hard on wives, but it is the wife's lawyer who generally has more work to do, since the assets to be uncovered are usually better known to the husband or are in his control, and also because the wife, typically having less, is probably the one seeking support and distribution of the assets. Nor do wives' attorneys like to rely on courts to order the husband to make payment, since a court may award $300 for what the wife's lawyer considers $3,000 worth of work." *Id.*

See also Castillo, *Changed Divorce Law in New York Bringing in Higher Fees to Lawyers,* N.Y. Times, 2 Feb. 1981, at 1, col. 1 (indicating that fees have increased by 25 percent to 50 percent under New York's equitable distribution statute). *See also* Hansen, *Three Dimensions of Divorce,* 50 MARQ. L. REV. 1, 6–7 (1966), in which the author concluded that Wisconsin's 1959 Divorce Reform was a means to make divorce more time-consuming and difficult in order to effect more reconciliations.

A more determinative standard, however, does not ensure that lawyer's fees will not be high. In an unpublished study under a grant from the National Science Foundation, Steve Cox of the Economics Department at Arizona State University examined property division statutes and their effect on the cost of divorce in six cities, including Milwaukee, Wisconsin. Tables supplied by Stephen Smay of the State Bar of Wisconsin showed that of attorneys in the six cities, Milwaukee attorneys charged the lowest fees for a simple will and a will of trust; charged higher fees for uncontested bankruptcy than attorneys of only one other city; *but* charged higher than attorneys of any other city for uncontested divorces— with a mean fee over one hundred dollars more than that of the next most expensive city in the divorce sample.

53. McCabe also correctly predicted that the Wisconsin rule was likely to result in equal divisions: "[The proposed Wisconsin statute] divides the property, beginning with a presumption of equal division, but with consideration of several different factors. The factors relate primarily to contributions. . . . The Wisconsin statute does put the equal division idea into presumption form, although the form is curiously handled and outside the usual concept of legal presumption. That alone may give rise to confusion. However, there is much to bolster the equal division idea and to make it commonly applied. The notion of contribution is one such idea."

One of the commissioners, Herma Hill Kay, a professor at Berkeley who taught family law, had been asked by the reformers to become involved in the Wisconsin reform at its initial stages. She subsequently made a number of trips to the state to speak in favor of the general idea of reform and about the problems confronted by divorcing women, and had to help convince key legislators of the importance of the reform. In a letter to the reformers, she raised another type of horror story: "Your phrase 'the court shall divide the property of the parties' goes far beyond the Uniform Act Provision, since it makes no distinction between property acquired prior to marriage and that acquired afterward. Do you really intend that if, for example, as happened in California, an enterprising young waiter marries an elderly rich women and they divorce soon thereafter, he should have a 'presumption' of entitlement to one-half of all of her previously-owned property?"

The presumption may create additional costs. *See* Friedman, *Legal Rules and the Process of Social Change,* 19 STAN. L. REV. 786 (1967) (*reprinted in* L. FRIEDMAN & S. MACAULAY, LAW AND THE BEHAVIORAL SCIENCES 406–15 (2d ed. 1977): "In the 20th century the cost of using the judicial process, especially if an appeal is made, is so high that it acts as a significant barrier against litigation that does not measure its outcome in the thousands of dollars." *Id.* at 408. In this case, the number of divorces will not drop, nor will more cases be litigated rather than settled, but rather stipulations in accord with the statutory norm of equal division will occur because of the expense involved in challenging the presumption.

54. Letter from John McCabe to a reformer (discussing marriage as a partnership) (on file with the author).

55. *Id.*

56. *Id.*

57. There was, however, some ineffective opposition, such as that expressed in a letter from a state representative (4th Assembly District) to one of the Directors of the State Bar's Committee on Individual Rights: "During the last session of the Legislature, Assembly speaker Norman Anderson and others introduced Assembly Bill 277 which took a somewhat different approach to 'no-fault' divorce reform. That bill, had it passed, would have added to the grounds 'irreconcilable differences.' For a variety of reasons, I believe the Anderson approach is referable to the feminist approach. In addition, I am concerned

that the overriding interests of the feminists in providing for a laundry list of economic protections will run headlong into constitutional problems. If the Board of Directors is to consider this entire subject area, I strongly urge you to look at what I believe to be the more responsible, less revolutionary approach taken by Speaker Anderson's bill." Letter from a state representative to a reformer (15 Dec. 1976) (on file with the author).

58. This may have been because the new act was patterned as much as possible on the old statute and case law, reflecting a conscious political decision by the key legislator: "We never got rid of [the old statute] partly because I made a political judgment that people don't like big change and it seemed that the lawyers who were used to [the old statute], and . . . the family law section [got] more and more involved and . . . nobody saw just starting with a new act here. . . . There was great conservatism in the Wisconsin Bar and in the Bar generally, but I think here more than many places, because in many places they just completely did a whole new chapter. . . . But that wasn't where we were."

59. As noted by the key legislator: "There was lots of newspaper attention on no-fault. People understood no-fault. They really didn't understand it at all, but our bill had the no-fault name just like the [other] bills, and so all we talked about was no-fault. They didn't talk about the rest. And the question of whether you're [just] adding one ground, or replacing ten with one, was barely noticed by the newspapers. So they did us quite a big favor. It was a bill that [the public] expected to pass. [But] a number of [legislators] said on the floor that they wanted to go back to that bill adding one ground. 'We had that nice bill last session. What are we doing here?' "

But see Shoreline Leader, 8 July 1977, at 2, (editorial) which stated: "Most of us realize there is a real need for a change in our divorce laws to eliminate some of the discriminatory provisions and to avoid some of the unnecessary heartache and ill feeling when a divorce is imminent. But the bill says that that no spouse can be found at fault in a divorce proceeding and that's going too far. . . .

"There are some good parts to the bill. These [parts] provided for more equitable settlements between spouses, allowed for the joint custody of children and provided for a more orderly breakup of a marriage when there was agreement between the spouses. The bill recognized the economic value of the homemaker and would provide for a more equitable division of assets. [But] the bill makes a complete mockery of the marriage contract."

The response of one member of the senate to the reform was noted in the same editorial: "Senator Henry Dorman, asked how he would vote on the bill, said that it is a nothing bill and not as good as the present law. He noted that it was written by two women legislators and felt that it should be passed because they claimed that men had always written the divorce laws when a woman should have." *Id.*

60. The key legislator reported receiving the following advice: [D]on't give up on the Catholics. . . . Catholics had supported (because of family conciliation) the original uniform act in California . . . so I just called Wisconsin Catholic Conference and we had several meetings with them and we really neutralized their opposition in a way that was absolutely critical. I mean we were able to say that we had done all the things they wanted. . . . We showed them the draft, you see, before introduction. . . . They did not want divorce made easier, that's the main thing. They really would have liked to have a one-year waiting period. Well, we said, we can't go to the longer waiting period than we've had in this state. You see, I always refused to go further with them, but I went through everything from the standpoint of not doing anything that from their vantage point looked like divorces were becoming easier. And there were still three or four things that they would have wanted, but they wrote a letter that was circulated. We couldn't say we had their support, but we could say that we met almost all of their concerns and that was very important to know. . . . [I]t's a good lesson in general. And

this is my theory about a great many bills—you drown people in input. I mean you just keep working with them and working with them until you know you don't satisfy them about everything. But they get enough in there that they begin to think that gee whiz she's really listened and look how much worse it could have been if we hadn't been involved, and really how much better it was from their standpoint."

61. For a discussion of the importance of legal forms to the future relations of the sexes, see L. KANOWITZ, WOMEN AND THE LAW 4 (1969). The reformers used Kanowitz's articulation of the problem in their brochure on the Equal Rights Amendment: "When men and women are prevented from recognizing one another's essential humanity by sexual prejudices, nourished by legal as well as social institutions, society as a whole remains less than it could otherwise become." Wisconsin Women's Political Caucus, *Wisconsin Equal Rights Amendment Brochure* (n.d.) (on file with the author). What the brochure did not mention, however, was Kanowitz's qualification that laws protecting women from social and cultural disadvantages might be necessary because society has to achieve behavioral modification in role definitions *before* equality in law is imposed as a social norm.

62. K. GRAY, REALLOCATION OF PROPERTY IN DIVORCE—NEWFOUNDLAND FAMILY LAW STUDY 28 n.42 (1977).

63. J. BERNARD, WOMEN AND THE PUBLIC INTEREST; AN ESSAY ON POLICY AND PROTEST 38, 39 (1971), suggests that there are three models of equality: the pluralist model, which allows differentiation of functions among members of a group; the assimilation model, which ignores such differentiations of functions and may make differentiation impossible; and the hybrid model, which involves a radical reassignment of functions.

Bernard claims that women belonging to the National Organization of Women fit within the first or second category of equality, while radical feminists ("new left" or "Female liberation" women) fit within the third. Bernard observes that the more moderate women, by attacking prejudice and discrimination through legal means which are consistent with traditional lines of argument, promote equality in ways that make sense to policymakers. The radical feminists, by contrast, upset those in power by challenging the assumption that "male" standards and values are best.

CHAPTER FIVE

1. The change to custody policy envisaged by challenges to legal rules and standards has as its basis idealistic visions about the capacity of law to transform social behavior. *See generally* Fineman, *Illusive Equality: On Weitzman's Divorce Revolution,* 1986 AM. B. FOUND. RES. J. 781; Fineman, *infra* note 41, at 821–22.

2. *See* N. Polikoff, *Custody and Visitation: Their Relationship to Establishing and Enforcing Support* (on file with author); *see also* M. Raschick, *Wisconsin Non-Custodial Parents' Groups* (16 May, 1985) (unpublished manuscript; primary field research on file with the author). For a discussion of the various ideological strains within the men's movement, see M. Schiffman, *The Men's Movement: An Exploratory Empirical Investigation* 3–4 (26–30, Aug. 1985) (paper prepared for presentation at the 80th Annual Meeting of the American Sociological Association, Washington, D.C.; draft 2.1 on file with the author).

3. *See, e.g.,* Abarbanel, *Shared Parenting After Separation and Divorce: A Study of Joint Custody,* 49 AM. J. ORTHOPSYCH. 320 (1979). The author makes sweeping conclusions based on four cases.

4. *Id.* at 328 (emphasis in original).

5. *See* I. W. BLACKSTONE, COMMENTARIES 435–38 (rev. ed. 1966). In modern practice, this support obligation is fulfilled through child-support payments without the father

having actual physical custody of the children. *See* J. SCHOULER, A TREATISE ON THE LAW OF DOMESTIC RELATIONS 61, 233 (1870).

6. *See* M. GROSSBERG, GOVERNING THE HEARTH 244–47 (1985).

7. *See, e.g.,* Grossberg, *Who Gets the Child? Custody, Guardianship, and the Rise of a Judicial Patriarchy in Nineteenth-Century America,* 9 FEMINIST STUD. 235, 239, 246, 254–55 (1983).

8. For a general description of the development of state supervision of parental duties, *see* Grossberg, *supra* note 7, at 289–91.

9. The phrase *rule of thumb* originated in the common-law rule that a husband could beat his wife without legal sanction if he used a rod not thicker than his thumb. *See* Davidson, *Wife Beating: A Recurring Phenomenon Throughout History,* in BATTERED WOMEN: A PSYCHOLOGICAL STUDY OF DOMESTIC VIOLENCE, 18–21 (M. Roy ed. 1977).

10. For a discussion of the origins of the tender-years doctrine, see Zainaldin, *The Emergence of a Modern American Family Law: Child Custody, Adoption and the Courts,* 1796–1851, 73 NW. U.L. REV. 1038, 1072–74 (1979).

11. Grossberg, *supra* note 7, at 248–49.

12. *Id.* at 237–53. *See also* Levy, *Custody Investigations in Divorce Cases,* 1985 AM. B. FOUND. RES. J. 713.

13. Such indiscretions historically were grounds upon which to base a finding of unfitness and to deny mothers custody under the tender-years doctrine. Under this doctrine, mothers received custody of young children unless they were "unfit" to provide care for them. Common bases upon which to establish unfitness in custody determinations include adultery, cohabitation, and sexual preference. This focus on conduct within the context of custody determinations endures in some jurisdictions today, even though there has been a retreat from fault-based divorce. Some of the states with express statutory grounds require that denial of custody on grounds of conduct be based on a finding that the child is adversely affected by the behavior in question. For data supporting the proposition that women are treated more harshly than men in such instances, see Girdner, *Child Custody Determination: Ideological Dimensions of a Social Problem,* in REDEFINING SOCIAL PROBLEMS, 165, 175–76 (E. Seidman & J. Rappaport eds. 1986).

14. N. BASCH, IN THE EYES OF THE LAW 179–80 (1982). *See also* Olsen, *The Family and the Market: A Study of Ideology and Legal Reform,* 96 HARV L. REV. 1497, 1530–35 (1983). It is also relevant to note that, at this time, there were few divorces, particularly among middle- and upper-class couples, those most likely to be concerned with the content of family laws.

15. *See* Zainaldin, *supra* note 10.

16. For an early proposal of this solution by a judge, see Hansen *Guardians Ad Litem in Divorce and Custody Cases: Protection of the Child's Interests,* 4 J. FAM. L. 181 (1964); *see also* O. STONE, THE CHILD'S VOICE IN THE COURT OF LAW 104–5 (1982) (reviewing the suggestion that family court judges be accompanied by "behavioural science 'judges' " trained in social sciences).

17. *See* Folberg, *Custody Overview,* in JOINT CUSTODY AND SHARED PARENTING (*J. Folberg* ed. 1984).

18. The gender-neutrality debate is also a central focus of British feminism. For a cogent discussion of the historic and contemporary conflict in British feminism between strict or rule equality and special treatment or result equality, see Smart & Brophy, *Locating Law: A Discussion of the Place of Law in Feminist Politics,* in WOMEN-IN-LAW: EXPLORATIONS IN LAW, FAMILY, AND SEXUALITY 1 (J. Brophy & C. Smart eds. 1985).

19. *See, e.g.,* Folberg, *supra* note 17; *see also* Letter from Neal Skrenes, Secretary, Custodial Parents' Rights Coalition, Inc., to Rep. Jeannette Bell, Chair, special Legislative Committee, Custody Arrangements (Wisconsin) (on file with the author).

20. For an analysis of the tender-years doctrine under the equal-protection clause, see *Ex parte* Devine, 398 So. 2d 686 (Ala. 1981), which held that the doctrine constituted unconstitutional gender discrimination. Most state statutes now specifically provide that both parents are "equal," thus forbidding consideration of gender in custody cases. *See State Divorce Statutes Chart and Summary Sheet Introduction,* Fam. L. Rep. (BNA) 5–6 (24 Mar. 1986). For example, the relevant Wisconsin statute reads: "In making a custody determination, the court . . . shall not prefer one potential custodian over the other on the basis of the sex of the custodian." WIS. STAT. ANN. § 767.24(2) (West 1981).

21. A plethora of literature touts the psychological benefits to fathers and children of joint custody. *See, e.g.,* Abarbanel, *supra* note 3, at 320–29 (finding that the benefits of joint custody outweighed the problems it caused for the families studied); Bowman & Ahrons, *Impact of Legal Custody Status on Fathers' Parenting Postdivorce,* 47 J. MARRIAGE & FAM. 481, 481–88 (1985) (arguing that joint-custody fathers are far more active in parenting after divorce then those without custody); Grief, *Fathers, Children and Joint Custody,* 49 AM. L. ORTHOPSYCH. 311–19 (1979) (asserting that fathers with joint custody are more likely to remain active in children's development than those with visitation rights).

22. *See* N. Polikoff, *supra* note 2.

23. *See, e.g.,* M. Raschick, *supra* note 2. For a discussion of the various ideological strains within the men's movement, see M. Shiffman, *supra* note 2, at 3, 4.

24. *See, e.g.,* Everett, *Shared Parenthood in Divorce: The Parental Covenant and Custody Law,* 2 J.L. & RELIGION 85, 85–89 (1984).

25. *See* Chambers, *Rethinking the Substantive Rules for Custody Disputes in Divorce,* 83 MICH. L. REV. 477 (1984) at 482: "[I]n a large proportion of families the differences between parents in the quality of their relationships to their children and in their childrearing skills are more subtle. . . . If the trend toward fathers taking an increased role in childtending continues, it is probable that the incidence of cases in which the differences are subtle will grow [citation omitted]."

Chambers goes on to say, "The broad generalizations about the personalities and behavioral traits of men and women hold up rather poorly when individual adults are studied. While researchers do report some persistent, sex-linked differences in the psychological responses of men and women in general, they also find that large numbers of individual men display traits stereotypically associated with women. The more specific research examining males and females in their interest in children, attentiveness to them, and capacity to understand and respond to their needs—what might be collectively termed their 'responsiveness' to children—is especially inconclusive [citations omitted]." Id. at 518.

Chambers continues, "In the context of custody disputes, the issue of special nurturing traits associated with one sex is posed most purely in cases involving newborns when neither parent has become the primary caretaker for the child and in cases involving preschool children when parents have shared in roughly equal measure the caregiving responsibility. . . . [W]hen fathers and mothers are observed with their own newborns before either has assumed differing caretaking roles, fathers are in general as likely to hold them closely, rock them, talk to them, and look directly at them. New fathers seem as skilled and gentle as mothers with their own children. Observers in the home at later stages, even after differing roles have been assumed, have found that although fathers interact with young children differently than mothers do, with more physical and less patterned, rhythmic play, there still seem to be few differences in the degree of parents' interest in their children or in their capacities to respond to their infants' signals [citations omitted]." Id. at 519–20.

"[T]he issue is not whether 'father's touch' is identical to 'mother's touch' but whether 'father's touch,' whatever it is like, is likely to lead to a less desirable quality of life or less desirable outcome for the child in either the short or long term." *Id.* at 522–23.

"Women have no attributes that so especially suit them for childrearing that they merit a preference in custody disputes simply because of their gender [citation omitted]." *Id.* at 527.

"[T]he weakest part of the case for primary caretakers is not that it exaggerates the importance of attachment in general but that it exaggerates the importance of the bond to the primary-caretaker parent in comparison to the bond with the other parent." *Id.* at 533.

"Some studies have found that at about one year, children more commonly seek out their primary-caretaking mother in preference to fathers for relief when tired or anxious and both parents are present. But, at about the same age, when both parents are present, children more commonly turn to the father for social interaction. Forced to choose, many people would believe that the primary caretaker's relief-giving capacity is more important; yet, there is very little evidence to suggest that when only a secondary-caretaking parent is available, that parent is not fully adequate to provide the needed reassurance [citations omitted]." Id. at 534.

"[Secondary-caretaking fathers] help to establish and enforce rules of conduct; they provide models of appropriate behavior and express expectations for the children's conduct; they concern themselves with the child's physical safety; and they engage in various sorts of reciprocal behaviors such as 'buddy' or 'flirt' [citations omitted]." Id. at 535.

26. Despite their ancillary role, social workers conducting custody investigations were able to affect case outcome in significant ways, including settlement behavior. See Levy, *supra* note 12, at 730–32 & nn. 66–72; *see also id.* at 718–28 (discussing the interventionist philosophy underlying the involvement of social workers in disputed cases).

27. Other authors have observed the significance of the helping professions in the area of custody. See Girdner, *supra* note 13, at 165, 166. ("[Members of the mental health profession] have been critical in defining the custody determination problem and in proposing solutions . . . in the services they offer, in their notions of what is healthy and unhealthy, in their views of what children and parents need, and how families function and change.").

28. California was a pioneer in no-fault legislation. *See* J. AREEN, FAMILY LAW 267–75 (1985). No-fault reforms were the product of various forces. See the discussion in L. WEITZMAN, THE DIVORCE REVOLUTION: THE UNEXPECTED SOCIAL AND ECONOMIC CONSEQUENCES FOR WOMEN AND CHILDREN IN AMERICA 15–51, 366–78 (1985). The central concept was that divorces were "in reality only symptoms of the ultimate failure of the relationship," and not the result of a single party's fault. *See* THE 1966 REPORT BY THE GOVERNOR'S COMMISSION ON THE FAMILY (California), reprinted in part in *id.*

29. Within the context of divorce, the fault standard was initially seen as a central obstacle to attorney/social worker collaboration. *See* Felner, Primavera, Farber & Bishop, *Attorneys as Caregivers During Divorce,* 52 AM. J. ORTHOPSYCH. 323, 324–25 (1982). Conciliation courts and no-fault were viewed explicitly as increasing the potential for social workers' involvement with divorce cases. *See id.* These reforms were also seen as favoring an expanded mental health role in place of the declining role of attorneys. *See id.* at 324;

see also Weil, *Research on Issues in Collaboration Between Social Workers and Lawyers,* 56 Soc. Serv. Rev. 393, 394–95 (1982) (arguing that the declining role of the social worker in juvenile court was accompanied by an increased role for the social worker in family court).

30. The early limited attention to divorce as an emotional event was noted by Freund, *Divorce and Grief,* J. Fam. Couns. 40, 40–43 (Fall 1974). Freund presented divorce as a grieving process with stages akin to those experienced during bereavement. *See id.* at 41–43. J. Louise Despert was one of the early authors to characterize divorce as a series of stages, the first of which was "emotional divorce." *See* Wiseman, *Crisis Theory and the Process of Divorce,* 56 Soc. Casework 205, 205 (1975).

31. *See* Elkin, *Conciliation Courts: The Reintegration of Disintegrating Families,* 22 Fam. Coordinator 64 (1973) (noting that divorcing spouses have the ability to "use the crisis of divorce as an opportunity for personal growth and fulfillment"); Kraus, *The Crisis of Divorce: Growth Promoting or Pathogenic?,* 3 J. Divorce 107 (1979) (discussing scientific studies suggesting that divorce may precipitate beneficial growth); Mumma, *Mediating Disputes* 42 Pub. Welfare 25 (1984) ("The divorcing family must be redefined legally and socially and treated as a family in transition, not as a family in termination. Divorce must be viewed as an opportunity for new growth and success, not defeat and failure.").

32. Some legal scholars have called for the inclusion of the tender-years doctrine in uniform no-fault law. *See, e.g.,* Ellsworth & Levy, *Legislative Reform of Child Custody Adjudication,* 4 Law & Soc. Rev. 167, 202–3 (1969), *quoted in* J. Areen, *supra* note 28, at 432. Although section 402 of the Uniform Marriage and Divorce Act did not ultimately contain such a provision, the Commissioners' comments concluded that "[t]he preference for the mother as custodian of young children when all things are equal, for example, is simply a shorthand method of expressing the best interest of children." Unif. Marriage and Divorce Act § 402, 9A U.L.A. 628 (1970).

33. *See generally* J. Goldstein, A. Freud & A. Solnit, Beyond the Best Interests of the Child (1973), *passim* (advocating a child-placement standard focusing on the child's relationship with her psychological parent and on other criteria related to the child's psychological well-being); Davis, *"There is a Book Out. . .": An Analysis of Judicial Absorption of Legislative Facts,* 100 Harv. L. Rev. 1539, 1547–92 (1987) (describing the psychological parent theory and analyzing its impact in child placement cases). *But see* Radin, *The Psychological Parent Concept in Contested Custody Cases,* 2 J. Psychiatry & L. 503, 512–13 (1983) (arguing that psychological parents may be nonetheless unfit parents and that additional guidelines should also be considered).

34. One commentator has stated: "[A]n analysis of the criteria inherent to the recently enacted [custody] statutes reveal [*sic*] a strong reliance upon factors that can best be evaluated by behavioral science. Among other factors, assessments must be made of the parent's intelligence, morality, knowledge of child development, personality, child-rearing attitudes, emotional ties with the child, and a host of other factors that are of a social and/or psychological nature. The behavioral scientist has essentially been given a societal mandate for involvement and must be prepared to function appropriately in child custody determinations." Woody, *Behavioral Science Criteria in Child Custody Determinations,* J. Marriage & Fam. Couns., Jan. 1977, at 11; *accord* Musetto, *The Role of the Mental Health Professional in Contested Custody: Evaluator of Competence or Facilitator of Change,* J. Divorce, Summer 1981, at 72–74 (promoting a more active role for mental health professionals in disputed custody cases).

35. *See* Polikoff, *Why Mothers are Losing: A Brief Analysis of Criteria Used in Child Custody Determinations,* 7 Women's Rts. L. Rep. 235 (1982); L. Weitzman, *supra* note 28, at 231–35 (1985) (indicating that men succeed in obtaining custody in 63 percent of nego-

tiated cases when they pursue custody—a far different story from the rhetoric of the fathers'-rights movement).

36. J. AREEN, CASES AND MATERIALS ON FAMILY LAW: TEACHER'S MANUAL 122, 124 (2d ed. 1985).

37. A vast body of literature discusses the pros and cons of the courts' use of ancillary personnel to aid in making custody decisions. Lawyers have often been assigned to these roles. For an early proposal by a judge, see Hansen, *supra*, note 16. *See also* O. STONE, *supra* note 16, at 104–05, which reviews the suggestion that family court judges be accompanied by "behavioural science 'judges' " trained in the social sciences.

38. This is not how it is stated explicitly, but it is clearly the basic tenet. Since past behavior is not determinative and other factors are not relevant, biology must provide the key.

39. *See* Everett, *supra* note 24. There is also a growing body of literature which argues that a presumption of joint custody is a constitutional right. *See, e.g.,* E. Canacakos, *Joint Custody as a Fundamental Right,* in JOINT CUSTODY AND SHARED PARENTING, (J. Folberg ed. 1984); Robinson, *Joint Custody as a Constitutional Imperative,* 54 U. CIN. L. REV. 27 (1985).

40. The studies indicate that this has not in fact occurred to any great degree. Mothers still perform not only the vast bulk of child care, but also the majority of housework. *See* Bane, Lein, O'Donnell, Stueve & Wells, *Child Care Arrangements of Working Parents,* 102 MONTHLY LAB. REV. 50, 52–53 (Oct. 1979). A more recent study by the University of Michigan of male and female executives found that women spend more than twice as much time on household tasks, as reported in *Women Executives 'Think Like a Man',* Capital Times, 9 Apr. 1986, at 9, col. 3 (Madison, Wis.). In addition, women seem to plan their careers to accommodate child-care responsibilities in far greater proportions than do men, illustrating that a combination of mothering and professional career is desirable for them. *See* Project, *Law Firms and Lawyers with Children: An Empirical Analysis of Family/ Work Conflict,* 34 STAN. L. REV. 1263 (1982), for a comparison of male and female law students regarding responsibilities for child care. The study reported that women students spend considerably more time than male students in performing child-care tasks and that their job considerations were thus influenced by the availability of on-site child care, opportunities for part-time employment, and provisions for maternity leave. The effect of women's childbearing responsibilities on their market participation is also analyzed by Fuchs, *Sex Differences in Economic Well-Being,* 232 SCI. 459–64 (1986).

41. For an extensive discussion of this point regarding the reform of divorce and property division laws, see Fineman, *Implementing Equality: Ideology, Contradiction and Social Change; A Study of Rhetoric and Results in the Regulation of the Consequences of Divorce,* 1983 WIS. L. REV. 789, 851, 852.

42. For an illustration of the gap between these reform efforts and reality in contemporary custody practice, *see* Girdner, *supra* note 13, at 165, 174–75. Regardless of such empirical data, gender neutrality remains the popular variety of feminist reform. A cogent discussion of the historic and contemporary conflict between strict equality (rule-equality) and special treatment (result-equality) in British feminist thought is provided by Smart & Brophy, *supra* note 18. Within the context of American feminism, see Fineman, *supra* note 41, at 790–96, 811–34, 845, 851, 852.

43. Given the empirical evidence that women are still more likely to be primarily responsible for child-rearing, the debate may be largely theoretical if states adopt, by statute or decisional law, a primary-caretaker preference or presumption. *See, e.g.,* Garska v. McCoy, 278 S.E. 2d 357 (W. Va. 1981). However, as I discuss more fully in this chapter, the

influence of professional opinion at the present time is toward "balancing off" those traits most often identified with gender (like nurturing) against less gender-specific skills like the ability to afford the child social interaction or play by claiming that these traits are not gender-derived or by claiming that both parents possess equal motivation to meet a child's needs. Moreover, the unwillingness to accept the fact of mothers' role in child-rearing within the context of custody policy conforms to the popular gender-neutral focus at the expense of reality. To illustrate, even if the ultimate goal is gender neutrality, the imposition of rules embodying such a view within the context of family-law issues is disingenuous because the effect is detrimental to those who have constructed their lives around "gendered" roles.

In this regard, significant emotional as well as economic costs are risked under re-formed divorce laws. For example, shifting custody policy means the threat of potential loss of children for many mothers at divorce. To most, this risk is too great to contemplate. As a result, many mothers exchange a bargained-down property settlement to avoid a custody contest, because many mothers tend, in contrast to fathers, to consider custody a "nonnegotiable" issue.

44. There is a great deal of literature in this area. *See, e.g.,* Mnookin, *Child-Custody Adjudication: Judicial Functions in the Face of Indeterminacy,* 39 LAW & CONTEMP. PROBS. 226 (1975), where some of the dangers of free will and discretion within an indeterminate system are discussed. For a history of the interplay of discretion and rules in custody proceedings, see Oster, *Custody Proceeding: A Study of Vague and Indefinite Standards,* 5 J. FAM. L. 21 (1965). *See also* Folberg & Graham, *Joint Custody of Children Following Divorce,* 12 U.C. DAVIS L. REV. 523, 535 (1979), where the authors state that "[c]onvenient presumptions, first for the father, then for the mother, are no longer available as a short cut to a court in arriving at the most appropriate custody determination. When parents disagree about custody, judges are now in the perplexing bind of trying to predict, with limited information and no existing consensus, which of two fit parents would best guide a child to adulthood [citation omitted]."

Chambers, *supra* note 25, at 479, states that "[his] search for factors present in all or most custody disputes [. . .] has grown out of an unease with statutes that direct judges to place a child where her interests or welfare will be best served without the guidance of any rule creating a presumption for, or placing a burden of proof on, either party. Such statutes place extraordinary burdens on judges, encourage costly and painful litigation by parents, and probably (though unprovably) lead in many cases to placements for children that do not in fact best serve their needs."

45. A focus on motherhood can take a negative turn, as explored by Chodorow & Contratto, *The Fantasy of the Perfect Mother,* in RETHINKING THE FAMILY: SOME FEMINIST QUESTIONS 54 (1982). Some social scientists have begun to point out that, for many reformers, motherhood is a forgotten issue. In this regard, *see* S. HEWLETT, A LESSER LIFE: THE MYTH OF WOMEN'S LIBERATION IN AMERICA (1986).

CHAPTER SIX

1. *See* Woody, *Preventive Intervention for Children of Divorce,* 59 SOC. CASEWORK 537, 541 (1978) ("Divorce is certainly a process over which children have no control; inasmuch as possible, they should not become its victims.").

2. *See, e.g.,* Mumma, *Mediating Disputes,* 42 PUB. WELFARE, 22, 25 (1984) (stating that "the litigation process is little more than an institutionalized form of emotional abuse to children.").

3. Despite the increased potential for control by men under modern divorce regulation, there has not necessarily been a corresponding increase in responsibilities. Many commentators have noted the negative aspects of the rules designed to give fathers more control. For discussions of the negative impact of joint-custody decisions on the lives of women, see Benedek & Benedek, *Joint Custody: Solution or Illusion?*, 136 AM. J. PSYCHIATRY 1540, 1541–43 (1979) (pointing out the risk of instability inherent in joint custody and stating that "[w]hen the requisite cooperation is not forthcoming, as is often the case following divorce, joint custody can be calamitous"); Schulman & Pitt, *Second Thoughts on Joint Child Custody: Analysis of Legislation and its Implications for Women and Children*, 12 GOLDEN GATE U.L. REV. 538, 570–71 (1982) (concluding that joint custody is only appropriate when both parents desire it and are willing to cooperate); *see also* Neely, *The Primary Caretaker Parent Rule: Child Custody and the Dynamics of Greed*, 3 YALE L. & POL'Y REV. 168 (1984); Fineman, *Dominant Discourse, Professional Language, and Legal Change in Child Custody Decision-making*, 101 HARV. L. REV. 727 (1988).

4. As detailed in chapter 5, one notion articulated within the context of changing custody policy is the assumption that gender-neutral rules are necessary to promote the symbolic ideal of equality between the sexes. Encouraging men to assume more responsibility for home- and child-care tasks promotes various instrumental concerns: most globally, the potential for women to increase their market participation, thus decreasing their economic dependence on men; and, within the context of divorce, relief for the "overburdened" custodial mother, as well as an increased financial commitment by fathers to payment of child-support obligations, owing to the stronger parent-child emotional bond.

5. Wallerstein & Kelly, *Children and Divorce: A Review*, 24 SOC. WORK 468, 472 (1979).

6. In the legal context, *see, e.g.*, WIS. STAT. ANN. § 767.045 (West 1988): "In any action affecting the family in which the court has reason for special concern as to the future welfare of a minor child, in which the legal custody or physical placement of the child is contested, or in which paternity is contested under s. 891.39, the court shall appoint an attorney admitted to practice in this state as guardian ad litem to represent the interests of the child as to legal custody, support and periods of physical placement."

7. This competition among professionals is most evident in the traditional antagonism between social workers and lawyers, as many social workers are uncomfortable with the adversarial nature of legal proceedings. *See, e.g.*, Fogelson, *How Social Workers Perceive Lawyers*, 51 SOC. CASEWORK 95, 99 (1970); Herrman, McKenry & Weber, *Attorneys' Perceptions of Their Role in Divorce*, 2 J. DIVORCE, Spring 1979, at 313, 315 ("The rational logical emphasis of the legal system does not provide an ideal atmosphere for the resolution of interpersonal conflict and, in fact, many serve as a catalyst to increased hostilities."); Oneglia & Orlin, *A Model for Combined Private Practice: Attorneys and Social Workers in Domestic Relations*, J. APPLIED SOC. SCI., Fall/Winter 1978, at 37, 43–44 ("The judge and the lawyer are not qualified to make a determination as to the best placement for a child considering emotional factors. Judges can evaluate financial and physical circumstances—as can almost any layman."). *But see* Charnas, *Practice Trends in Divorce Related Child Custody*, 4 J. DIVORCE, Summer 1981, at 57, 62 (reporting on a study indicating that "there is no interdisciplinary difference in the ability of judges and mental health professionals to select a custodial psychological parent; both overwhelmingly chose as the custodial parent the one which the evaluation reflected as having a more positive and consistent emotional bond with the children.").

8. *See* Girdner, *Child Custody Determination: Ideological Dimensions of a Social Problem*, in REDEFINING SOCIAL PROBLEMS 165, 166, 169 (E. Seidman & J. Rappaport eds. 1986)

(arguing that mental health professionals have had a central role in determining custody decisions: "One assumption underlying the role of mental health professionals in custody determinations is that they are able to make objective, reliable assessments and predictions of parental capacities and children's needs in the context of divorce."). For a skeptical consideration of the expert's role in custody cases, see Okpaku, *Psychology: Impediment or Aid in Child Custody Cases?*, 29 RUTGERS L. REV. 1117 (1976).

9. *See* Elkin, *Conciliation Courts: The Reintegration of Disintegrating Families*, 22 FAM. COORDINATOR 63 (1973).

10. An early proposal was for a "friend of the child" to be assigned. Drinan, *The Rights of Children in Modern American Family Law*, 2 J. FAM. L. 101, 107 (1962). Judge Hansen made the issue into a "campaign." *See* Hansen, *The Role and Rights of Children in Divorce Actions*, 6 J. FAM. L. 1 (1966).

11. *See, e.g.*, Felner & Farber, *Social Policy for Child Custody: A Multidisciplinary Framework*, 50 AM. J. ORTHOPSYCHIATRY 341, 345 (1980) ("One must ask if an adversarial process, in which a child's parents are the adversaries and the child is the prize, is best suited to arriving at a placement that truly serves the child's best interests.").

12. A great deal of literature concerning this crisis exists. *See* chapter 5, note 44.

13. Hansen, *supra* note 10, at 5.

14. Historically, children were the property of their fathers, who upon divorce received custody under the legal doctrine of *pater familias*. *See* J. SCHOULER, A TREATISE ON THE LAW OF DOMESTIC RELATIONS 61, 333 (1870). Such ownership entailed a corresponding duty to support the children, a duty which today is fulfilled through child-support payments without the father having actual physical custody of the children. *See* 1 W. BLACKSTONE, COMMENTARIES 435–38 (rev. ed. 1966).

15. Woody, *Behavioral Science Criteria in Child Custody Determinations*, 3 J. MARRIAGE & FAM. COUNSELING, Jan. 1977 at 11.

16. Watson, *The Children of Armageddon: Problems of Custody Following Divorce*, 21 SYRACUSE L. REV. 55, 66 (1969).

17. Rosenberg, Kleinman & Brantley, *Custody Evaluations: Helping the Family Reorganize*, 63 SOC. CASEWORK 203, 205 (1982).

18. In recent years there has been considerable interpenetration of the legal profession and the helping professions. The members of the helping professions are now, in many respects, far more central to custody determinations than lawyers, while the lawyers are moving more towards the growth area of mediation.

19. *See* Guggenheim, *The Right to be Represented But Not Heard: Reflections on Legal Representation for Children*, 59 N.Y.U. L. REV. 76 100–09 (1984) (making a distinction between the advocate as Champion and the advocate as Investigator).

20. One commentator has pointed out that "an equally crucial issue is posed by the question of the role that the attorney should play—is he a guardian *ad litem* in the traditional sense, or is he an advocate?" Shepherd, *Solomon's Sword: Adjudication of Child Custody Questions*, 8 U. RICH. L. REV. 151, 169 (1974).

21. Genden, *Separate Legal Representation for Children: Protecting the Rights and Interests of Minors in Judicial Proceedings*, 2 HARV. C.R.–C.L. L. REV. 565, 573 (1976) (citations omitted).

22. *See* Guggenheim, *supra* note 19, at 121–26 (arguing that appointing attorneys for children too young to have control over them undermines the legitimate interests of the parents in familial privacy and autonomous decision making).

23. In the words of one writer: "Without a separate advocate, the court may not perceive the existence of the special needs of the child. Even if the court does recognize such

needs, so long as other parties have separate advocates to represent their interests, the court will need an advocate to articulate the child's interest and to marshall the supporting facts." Genden, *supra* note 21, at 573 (emphasis added).

24. *See, e.g.,* Rosenberg, Kleinman & Brantley, *supra* note 17, at 207 ("It is clear that the best interests of the child involve much more than the linear relationships between parent and children. . . . One major consideration often may be the custodial parent's ability to allow an arrangement for an appropriate continuing relationship with the noncustodial parent as well as significant others."). Some states have enacted these so-called friendly-parent provisions. *See, e.g.,* CAL. CIV. CODE § 4600(b)(1) (West Supp. 1988). For a discussion of these statutes, see Schulman & Pitt, *supra* note 3, at 554–56.

25. *See, e.g.,* Kelly, *Further Observations on Joint Custody,* 16 U.C. DAVIS L. REV. 762, 769 (1983) (recognizing some problems of abuse but emphasizing the problem of "emotionally disturbed women who, due to their own pathology, vigorously fight a father's desire to be involved in the children's lives"). *But see* Lemon, *Joint Custody as a Statutory Presumption: California's New Civil Code Sections 4600 and 4600.5,* 11 GOLDEN GATE U.L. REV. 485, 527–31 (1981) (suggesting that the stereotype of the manipulative and vindictive mother opposing joint custody is overstated). The therapist is viewed as having a potentially powerful role in correcting pathological behavior. *See* Abelsohn, *Dealing with the Abdication Dynamic In the Post Divorce Family: A Context for Adolescent Crises,* 22 FAM. PROCESS 359, 365 (1983) (stating that "[t]he therapist delivers this basic message to the mother—you lose, you do not win, if you succeed in keeping your children from their father").

26. Solender, *The Guardian Ad Litem: A Valuable Representative or an Illusory Safeguard?,* 7 TEX. TECH L. REV. 619, 642–43 (1976) (footnote omitted).

CHAPTER SEVEN

1. While psychologists have previously been involved in child-custody cases, this has historically been within the context of specific cases, that is, clinically and not in the formulation of general statutory rules. Even within these narrow confines, there have been criticisms. *See* Okpaku, *Psychology: Impediment or Aid in Child Custody Cases?,* 29 RUTGERS L. REV. 1117 (1976).

2. While my focus in this chapter is on child-custody policy, I believe that the observations and conclusions are generalizable to all areas of legal policy-making where a dialogue with the social sciences plays an important role.

3. For a discussion of criticisms of this aspect of physical and social sciences, see generally T. KUHN, THE STRUCTURE OF SCIENTIFIC REVOLUTIONS (1962); J. BERNSTEIN, THE RESTRUCTURING OF SOCIAL AND POLITICAL THEORY (1976); THEORETICAL PERSPECTIVES IN SOCIOLOGY (S. McNall ed. 1979). Critical theory, in its critique of social science methodology and as a critique of the existence of social science as a cultural institution in postindustrial societies, seeks to be more than abstraction, although abstraction is inherent in any attempt at "bridging the gap between what is and what ought to be. . . ." Sewart, *Critical Theory and the Critique of Conservative Method,* in THEORETICAL PERSPECTIVES IN SOCIOLOGY 318 (S. McNall ed. 1979). Critical theorists differ on how to accomplish a "merger of reason and action, reflection and commitment." *Id.* at 315. In this chapter, I have attempted to incorporate theory with practice by applying a critical-theory approach to uses of social science data in a particular area, child-custody policy. In doing so, I hope to achieve a "critique of society and a critique of the theory of knowledge by which society is known" within the practice context of daily decision making in the custody area, thus fusing the macro and micro levels of analysis. *Id.* at 311.

4. The terms *nonprimary* and *secondary* parent are not mine but are used in much of the literature. *See, e.g.,* Chambers, *Rethinking the Substantive Rules for Custody Disputes in Divorce,* 83 MICH. L. REV. 477, 527–38 (1984). The use of these terms is in part ideological, representing the ideal of gender neutrality, and in part symbolic, reflecting the belief that previous terms like *noncustodial parent* stigmatized the parent without custody. The file of the Wisconsin Legislative Special Committee on Joint Custody, containing material submitted to a committee charged with the duty of evaluating the legislation of a joint custody presumption in the state, is replete with commentary to this effect (on file with author).

5. Social science results may also have influenced the way the research topic was framed and explored and the conclusions that were drawn by the social scientist. The recent criticism of social science literature and positivism is essentially a warning about the difficulty of obtaining and maintaining objectivity.

6. Chambers, *supra* note 4, at 482, seems to adopt this perspective: "To be sure, some cases are easily decided: one parent is severely withdrawn and rarely speaks to his or her child or one parent has been seriously abusive. It appears, however, that in a large proportion of families the differences between the two parents in the quality of their relationships to their children and in their childrearing skills are more subtle, under any view of children's interest. If the trend toward fathers' taking an increased role in childtending continues, it is probable that the incidence of cases in which the differences are subtle will grow [citations omitted]."

Ironically, Chambers himself reviews available data from the United States and Sweden which shows that mere assumption of a "primary caretaking role" by fathers did not mean fulfillment of typically "motherly" or "nurturing" characteristics usually seen as necessary for children's emotional development. *Id.* at 520.

7. It is no less than shocking that the profound changes in custody policy contemplated by contemporary challenges to existing rules and standards have as their basis such idealistic notions about the role of law in transforming behavior. This phenomenon is not uncommon, however, to family law, representing as it does a locus for the debate about equality between the sexes. In this regard, *see* Fineman, *Illusive Equality,* 4 AM. B. FOUND. RES. J. 781 (1986).

8. *See, e.g.,* E. HERZOG & C. SUDIA, BOYS IN FATHERLESS HOMES, 84–85 (U.S. Dept. of Health, Educ. & Welfare, 1970): "Most serious investigators would readily grant that, on the one hand, reality is complex and, on the other, research models often impose an unrealistic simplification. Social scientists . . . are forced to look at small bits and pieces and to construct from them a model of reality. In doing this, they are often forced into taking a kind of shorthand. The problem is that this shorthand tends to become a substitute for reality—in interpreting results, in reporting them, and in making recommendations based on them."

9. As Sewart observes, *supra* note 3, at 311: "There is no generally accepted usage of the notion of positivism [citations omitted]. . . . [In] the practice of social science the term has generally been used to refer to the incorporation of natural science methods into that practice. Three assumptions are implied by this notion of positivism: (1) since the methodological procedures of natural science are used as a model, human values enter into the study of social phenomena and conduct only as objects; (2) the goal of social scientific investigation is to construct laws, or law-like generalizations like those of physics; (3) social science has a technical character, providing knowledge which is solely instrumental. It follows from these assumptions that knowledge is unfinished and relative and, because social science knowledge is neutral with respect to values, that the knowledge has

no inherent logical implications for policy. The categorical distinction between fact and value prohibits the social theorist from taking a normative position or advocating what 'ought to be'; his/her role as a social scientist is confined to formulating and testing propositions about reality, and does not include advocacy or social action."

10. *See id.* at 312, where Sewart notes that "[f]rom a positivist perspective, the task of philosophy is to provide clarity for scientific statements; critical theorists see this as reducing philosophy to methodology. . . . More is involved in this dispute than the issue of proper methodology in the social sciences—the very aim of social science is being questioned."

See also D. Trubek, *Max Weber's Tragic Modernism and the Study of Law in Society* (Institute for Legal Studies Working Paper 1–3, University of Wisconsin Law School) (Dec., 1985).

11. The purpose of this discussion is not to explore in detail the various contemporary criticisms of positivist or empirical methodology. I want to introduce the reader to some of the critics who conclude that "truth is not by nature free—nor error servile—but that its production is thoroughly imbued with relations of power." M. FOUCAULT, THE HISTORY OF SEXUALITY, vol. 1, pg. 60 (R. Huxley, trans. 1978). I believe that knowledge is inescapably linked with issues of control and dominance and that to define, to focus on, or to study a phenomenon is to give it status. For an interesting discussion of law as rhetoric, "failed science," and the telling of stories (hence the telling of "facts") see White, *Law as Rhetoric, Rhetoric as Law: The Arts of Cultural and Communal Life,* 52 U. CHI. L. REV. 684 (1985).

12. G. RUSSELL, THE CHANGING ROLE OF FATHERS 206 (1983). *See also* Oakley, *Interviewing Women: A Contradiction in Terms,* in DOING FEMINIST RESEARCH (H. Roberts ed. 1981).

13. J. PIAGET, THE CHILD'S CONCEPTION OF THE WORLD (1972), *quoted in* Benston, *Feminism and the Critique of the Scientific Method* in FEMINISM IN CANADA: FROM PRESSURE TO POLITICS 60–61 (A. Miles & G. Finn eds. 1982).

14. For a critique of Piaget's own work based on the same criticism, see C. GILLIGAN, IN A DIFFERENT VOICE: PSYCHOLOGICAL THEORY AND WOMEN'S DEVELOPMENT (1982).

15. Alan Ryan, as cited in J.BERNSTEIN, *supra* note 3, at 3–4, has indicated that there are two anxieties among political scientists: first, that they will be viewed as ideologists; second, that they will be accused of hyper-factualism.

16. For an excellent analysis of the political contexts of the construction of social problems, *see* Edelman, CONSTRUCTING THE POLITICAL SPECTACLE (1988). In this regard, consider the observations of economist Victor Fuchs: "[An] . . . important caveat regarding policy concerns the role of *values.* Even if economic theory and empirical research were perfect in their predictions, policy choices must be guided by values as well as by analysis. It is one thing to know that if childcare is subsidized certain changes in fertility and labor force participation will follow; whether or not those changes are considered desirable is another matter. At the root of many policy conflicts are deep-seated value differences concerning the nature of the human enterprise and the vision of a good society.

"Values not only enter at the point of policy choice, but also may influence the process of research. According to the late Swedish economist Gunnar Myrdal, 'Valuations are always with us. Disinterested research there has never been, and can never be. Prior to answers there must be questions. There can be no view except from a viewpoint. In the questions raised and the viewpoints chosen, valuations are implied.' " (Citation omitted). (V. FUCHS, WOMEN'S QUEST FOR ECONOMIC EQUALITY 7 (1988) (Emphasis in original)

17. BERNSTEIN *supra* note 3, is a good source for three such critiques. Feminist critics are an important addition to the articles cited there.

18. Experimentation, of course, is not possible in the social sciences to the extent that it is in the natural sciences. Social scientists must base their conclusions on observations and theories constructed after the fact, and many modern theorists view this as a problem. *See* Baldamus, *The Role of Discovery in the Social Sciences* in THE RULES OF THE GAME: CROSS-DISCIPLINARY ESSAYS ON MODELS IN SCHOLARLY THOUGHT (T. Shanin ed. 1972); DOING SOCIOLOGICAL RESEARCH (C. Bell & H. Newby eds. 1977).

19. *See, e.g.,* J. BERNSTEIN, *supra* note 3.

20. My colleague, Stewart Macaulay, cautioned in his kind critique of an early draft of this section that while "many/most males [may] share norms about power, control, rationality rather than emotion and so on . . . not all men do." Letter from Stewart Macaulay to Martha L. Fineman (Nov. 1986). It is a point well worth making. The use of gendered terms in this context is associated with stereotypical characteristics assigned in this society to men or to women. This is not to say that either gender cannot possess the other's qualities or that progress through selective androgyny is not possible.

21. *See* Benston *supra* note 13, at 62.

22. *Id. See also* E. HERZOG & C. SUDIA, *supra* note 8. Power is an important element that is missing from most social science studies. Feminists are aware of this issue, however, and have demanded that social scientists openly acknowledge their values and their motivations. This does not have the effect of removing the power issues altogether, but it does make them overt and more available to challenge. This fact may mean that feminist demands will meet with some resistance.

23. For a general discussion of these points, see L. STANLEY & S. WISE, BREAKING OUT: FEMINIST CONSCIOUSNESS AND FEMINIST RESEARCH 130 (1983).

24. Vickers, *Memoirs of an Ontological Exile: The Methodological Rebellions of Feminist Research,* in FEMINISM IN CANADA: FROM PRESSURE TO POLITICS (A. Miles & G. Finn eds. 1982).

25. Benston, *supra* note 13, at 54–56. *See also* Vickers, *supra* note 24; Kelly, *Feminism and Science,* in THE SIGNS READER: WOMEN, GENDER AND SCHOLARSHIP (1983).

26. For a fuller discussion of this point, see DOING SOCIOLOGICAL RESEARCH, *supra* note 18. *See also* Oakley, *supra* note 12.

27. Phenomenology, by contrast, is a theory which recognizes that there are "multiple realities." As one commentator writes, "[a]bove all, I am interested in the objects of this world in so far as they determine my own orientation, as they further or hinder the realization of my own plans . . . in a word, in so far as they mean anything to me. This meaning to me implies that I am not satisfied with the pure knowledge of the existence of such objects; but I have to understand them [and therefore interpret them, attaching my own meaning]. . . .

"I cannot understand a social thing without reducing it to the human activity which has created it, and beyond it, without referring this human activity to the motives out of which it springs."

A SCHULTZ, COLLECTED PAPERS II: STUDIES IN SOCIAL THEORY, 9–10 (1964). Phenomenologists realize that categorization is inevitable, but argue that if categories are used, the mere process of formulating and applying them will itself determine what the subsequent observations will be. Acceptance of this position would mean that social science observations cannot independently check the validity of the categories or classifications of a theory. The scientific model, which is based on the natural sciences and therefore presumes extended testing of a hypothesis, cannot apply to information gathered in this manner. Linguistic theory also addresses the issue of subjectivity and concludes that it is inherent in all intellectual endeavors. Beginning with Wittgenstein and ending with deconstruction, linguists have focused on the nature of language, not only as a method of expressing some "thing," but as the "thing" or reality itself.

28. J. HABERMAS, REASON AND THE RATIONALIZATION OF SOCIETY (1981).

29. *See, e.g., id. See also* H. MARCUSE, ONE-DIMENSIONAL MAN (1964).

30. Spender, *Gatekeepers,* in FEMINISM AND SOCIAL POLICY 190 (H. Roberts ed. 1981). This happens in law as well as social science. Feminists have been relatively silent in legal-policy debates, and feminism has not been recognized as a form of legitimate criticism in law as it has in many other disciplines, including political science and sociology. Law, of course, at the academic level, is heavily male-dominated. A recent survey of 103 American law schools revealed that only 15.7 percent of traditional classroom teachers (as opposed to clinical or legal writing instructors) are female. Chused, *Faculty Parenthood: Law School Treatment of Pregnancy and Child Care,* 35 J. LEGAL EDUC. 568, 572 (1985).

31. *See,* Melton, *Developmental Psychology and the Law: State of the Art,* 22 J. FAM. L. 445, 454–56 (1983), where the author candidly admits that theories in psychology are "constructs" which contain "normative notions." Melton distinguishes between the clinical and scientific uses of psychology. *Id.* at 452. In conclusion, he approves of clinical uses, with some reservations, but strongly argues that the "state of the art" does not warrant uses for broad policy conclusions. *Id.* at 472.

32. Again I am indebted to my colleague Stewart Macaulay, who expressed the point in this way: "These various studies talk about men and women doing certain things the investigator wants to call good, bad or indifferent parenting. Think about what an adequate positivist study would require. . . . First, my male parenting involves inputs X, Y and Z (and nothing else that might have an impact). Second, nothing else happens to my children that might affect their personalities that the experimenter cannot control. Third, the study follows my children at ages 5, 10, 15, 20, 25, 30 and so on. That is, I may do something that affects them negatively at 15 but which helps them tremendously at 25. Fourth, at each of these points we have some outcome measure that everyone would accept as evidence of good or bad outcome. Suppose my parenting, for example, produces a lonely kid who writes the late 20th and early 21st century's equivalent to Beethoven symphonies . . . or, in other words, was Mozart's father a good parent? . . . The study is so unrealistic that few would be fooled into thinking it could be done." Letter from Stewart Macaulay to Martha L. Fineman (Nov. 1986).

Of course, less might be viewed as making the case, but the point which should be made and remade any time such lesser studies are employed is that they are inadequate and incomplete and don't begin to tell us most, let alone all, of what we need to know. *See also* Macaulay & Macaulay, *Adoption for Black Children: A Case Study of Expert Discretion,* 1 RESEARCH IN LAW AND SOCIOLOGY 265 (R. Simon ed. 1978) for a description of the way that politics and social criticism might affect the rhetoric and recommendations of the helping professions—those who are often involved in the production and consumption of social science literature on custody or divorce policy-making.

33. J. WALLERSTEIN & J. KELLY, SURVIVING THE BREAKUP: HOW CHILDREN AND PARENTS COPE WITH DIVORCE (1980).

34. Chambers, *supra* note 4, at 507.

35. *See, e.g.,* Robinson, *Joint Custody: Constitutional Imperatives,* 54 U. CIN. L. REV. 27 (1983) at 24. *See also* Abarbanel, *Shared Parenting After Separation and Divorce: A Study of Joint Custody,* AM. J. ORTHOPSYCHIATRY 320 (1979); Rosenberg, Kleinman & Brantley, *Custody Evaluations: Helping the Family Reorganize,* 63 SOC. CASEWORK 203 (1982);

Horowitz & Burchardt, *Procedure for Court Consultations on Child Custody Issues,* 65 Soc. Casework 259 (1984).

36. Wallerstein and Kelly's work has been criticized for lack of clear statistics and for the tendency to use rather vague terms like *substantial, many,* and *a lot of.* This has contributed to the use of the work in support of conflicting viewpoints. For criticisms of this nature, see generally Melton, *supra* note 31, especially at 470–71 nn. 110–11.

37. J. WALLERSTEIN & J. KELLY, *supra* note 33, at 120.

38. *Id.* at 154–55. This substantiates the conclusions of Brown, *A Study of Women Coping with Divorce,* in NEW RESEARCH ON WOMEN AND SEX ROLES 252 (D. McGuigan ed. 1976). Noting that the Chinese term for *crisis* has two characteristics, danger and opportunity, Brown points out that few researchers have investigated the potentially positive consequences of divorce for women. To investigate this possibility, she interviewed twice, with a four-month gap between interviews, 470 divorced women from the general population. She found that the separation was a period crisis, producing a sense of fearfulness about ability to cope. She puts this comment in the context of a marriage structure which, for many, involves loss of autonomy and the assumption of the dependent role. However, she found that the women in her sample had a wide-ranging repertoire of coping strategies, and that the breakdown of the marriage thrust them into a recreation of their self-identity. She states that whereas women are more depressed in marriage, it is men who are more depressed after separation and that men have fewer socially sanctioned ways of managing that distress.

39. *See, e.g.,* Chambers, *supra* note 4, at 507.

40. J. WALLERSTEIN & J. KELLY, *supra* note 33, at 53–54.

41. *Id.* at 207.

42. *Id.* at 208.

43. *Id. See also* Kurdek, Blisk & Siesky, *Correlates of Children's Long-Term Adjustment to Their Parents' Divorce,* 17 DEVELOPMENTAL PSYCHOLOGY 565, 577 (1981), who state, in a discussion of the negative relationship between some children's poor divorce adjustment and the custodial parents' personal competence, "[a] parent who is hard-working, achievement-oriented, assertive, self-controlled, responsible, and dependable . . . may not be able to be receptive to the child's needs and views, a core characteristic of effective parenting [citation omitted] and a key predictor of positive outcome of divorce [citation omitted]."

44. *See* Jones, *The Impact of Divorce on Children,* CONCILIATION CTS. REV. Dec. 1977, at 25; Kurdek, Blisk & Siesky, *supra* note 43, at 565.

45. J. WALLERSTEIN & S. BLAKESLEE, SECOND CHANCES: MEN, WOMEN, AND CHILDREN A DECADE AFTER DIVORCE 295–308 (1989).

46. *Id.* at 295, 308.

47. *Id.* at 295–296.

48. *See* LAMB, *Sibling Relationships across the Lifespan: An Overview and Introduction,* in SIBLING RELATIONSHIPS: THEIR NATURE AND SIGNIFICANCE ACROSS THE LIFESPAN 1–13 (M. Lamb & B. Sutton-Smith eds. 1982); Bryant, *Sibling Relations in Middle Childhood,* in *id.* at 87–118. In her article on middle childhood (the very period when the children would go to the same-sex parent under a scheme developed according to those who make such suggestions), Bryant points out that middle childhood is a "period of active development in which integration of social and effective phenomena are central. . . . We would expect children in the developmental period to be actively engaged with their siblings, struggling to better manage sibling interaction, and [be] attuned to social status within a variety of contexts . . . with siblings playing important roles." *Id.* at 88. She also points

out that siblings provide a means of development of particular social skills and a means of learning skills related to the handling of one's own as well as others' dependency. *Id*. at 104.

49. Chambers, *supra* note 4, at 539–541.

50. *See, e.g.*, Bartz & Witcher, *When Father Gets Custody*, CHILDREN TODAY, Sept.–Oct. 1978, at 2.

51. *See, e.g.*, McCormack, *Toward a Nonsexist Perspective on Social and Political Change*, in ANOTHER VOICE: FEMINIST PERSPECTIVES ON SOCIAL LIFE AND SOCIAL SCIENCES 1 (1975); C. GILLIGAN, *supra* note 14.

52. For a discussion of the need for a reevaluation of object-theory as it pertains to fathers closely involved with child-rearing, see Richards, *How Should We Approach the Study of Fathers?*, in THE FATHER FIGURE 57 (McKee & O'Brien eds. 1982). Richards suggests that the concept of father as representative of separateness and detachment and mother as representative of dependency and passivity will have to be reworked. In a recently published Australian study comparing traditional families with "shared-caregiving" families, Russell begins to address some concerns about different styles of fatherhood. G. RUSSELL, *supra* note 12. In the study, a family was defined as a shared-caregiving family if both parents shared or had major responsibility for the child and if each parent was solely responsible for the child for a minimum of fifteen hours a week. *Id*. at 17. In answer to a question of how parental roles would be defined, Russell notes that the shared-caregiving fathers did not appear to incorporate aspects of the parenting role more clearly identified with mothers, such as caring and affection, but neither did they resort to the extreme stereotyping of traditional fathers. *Id*. at 31–32. On the other hand, both traditional mothers and shared-caregiving mothers gave very similar responses, reflecting their day-to-day responsibility for the child. *Id*. at 33–34. Russell also discusses the type of play in which each parent in a traditional family tends to involve the child. Mothers tend to use more creative play and are more toy-oriented. They are also more likely to read to the child. Fathers, in contrast, are more involved in rough-and-tumble play and in physical and idiosyncratic play. *Id*. at 44. Comparing traditional fathers across several cultures, Russell writes that fathers' "participation levels . . . in physical care and play are considerably lower than those of mothers. . . . 80% of traditional fathers' interactions were associated with play, compared with only 53% of mothers' interactions." It was found that the majority of fathers had never taken responsibility for their children without *the children's mothers* being at home or available. *Id*. at 47. In another work, Russell notes that as parents become more involved on a shared-caregiving basis, the content of their play with the child tends to become similar. Russell, *Shared-Caregiving Families: An Australian Study*, in NON-TRADITIONAL FAMILIES: PARENTING AND CHILD DEVELOPMENT 139, 144 (1982).

CHAPTER EIGHT

1. Much recent academic writing appears to devalue the nurturing ideal or at least to assume that men can nurture children as well as women. *See, e.g.*, the collection of essays in FATHERHOOD AND FAMILY POLICY (M. Lamb & A. Sagi ed. 1984); *see also* some of the articles in JOINT CUSTODY AND SHARED PARENTING (J. Folberg ed. 1984). Initially, the catalyst for these writings was the psychological parent theory advanced by J. GOLDSTEIN, A. FREUD & A. SOLNIT, BEYOND THE BEST INTERESTS OF THE CHILD (1973). Their view, introduced at a time when mothers received custody in the vast majority of cases, was that the psychological parent would retain complete control over the child's upbringing, including decisions about when and whether the child would see the noncustodial parent. *Id*. at 38.

2. This attack on "Mother" seems a strategic maneuver, designed to create enough of a fissure in the mountain of instances where "Mother" assumes or is given custody, to let "Father" pass through. A new, noneconomically based, nonpatriarchal, idealized notion of "Father" has not yet been well defined in mainstream culture. But the list of popular movies, books, and articles dealing with "role reversals" is ever growing. *See, e.g.,* the movies *Author! Author* (20th Century-Fox 1982), *Three Men and a Baby* (1988), *Mr. Mom,* and *Kramer vs. Kramer* (Columbia Pictures 1979). *See also* the television programs *My Two Dads* (NBC) and *Major Dad* (CBS). It is now becoming fashionable for social scientists and others to study fathers, while they have not reevaluated the contemporary understanding of the role that mothers have played in child development, which lately has all too often had a "bad press" from both feminists and social scientists. Presently, the role of father is being promoted as the dominant role. The negative cultural and professional images of "Mother" are, of course, mainly Freudian in origin and tone. There has been some criticism of them for this reason alone. Even feminists seem to have joined the rush to explore fathers' relationships with their children. *See* FATHERS: REFLECTIONS BY DAUGHTERS (U. Owen ed. 1983).

3. In custody decision making neither the equality principle nor no-fault (or contest-free) decision making permits reference to past conduct as a husband or father. *See, e.g.,* Haddad & Roman *No-Fault Custody,* 2 FAM. L. REV. 95 (1979). Mother's conduct seems to always be at issue, by contrast. It is made so by the social construction of her role, which is applied in custody cases. *See* Girdner, *Child Custody Determination: Ideological Dimensions of a Social Problem,* in REDEFINING SOCIAL PROBLEMS (E. Seidman & J. Rappaport eds. 1986).

4. *See* J. GOLDSTEIN, A. FREUD & A. SOLNIT, *supra* note 1.

5. Examples of these studies include: Bartz & Witcher, *When Father Gets Custody,* CHILDREN TODAY, Sept.–Oct. 1978; Chang & Deinard, *Single-Father Caretakers: Demographic Characteristics and Adjustment Processes,* 52 AM. J. ORTHOPSYCHIATRY 236 (1982); Defrain & Eirick, *Coping as Divorced Single Parents: A Comparative Study of Fathers and Mothers,* 30 FAM. REL. 265 (1981); Finkelstein, *Fathering and Marital Separation (Report of Research in Progress),* in NEW RESEARCH ON WOMEN AND SEX ROLES 272 (D. M. McGuigan ed. 1976); Gasser & Taylor, *Role Adjustment of Single Parent Fathers with Dependent Children,* 25 FAM. COORDINATOR 397 (1976); Gersick, *Fathers by Choice: Divorced Fathers Who Receive Custody of Their Children,* in DIVORCE AND SEPARATION: CONTEXT, CAUSES, AND CONSEQUENCES 307 (1979); Greenberg, *Single-Parenting and Intimacy: A Comparison of Mothers and Fathers,* 2 ALTERNATIVE LIFESTYLES 308 (1979); Keshet & Rosenthal, *Fathering After Marital Separation,* 23 SOC. WORK 11 (1978); D. LUEPNITZ, CHILD CUSTODY: A STUDY OF FAMILIES AFTER DIVORCE (1982); Mendes, *Single Fatherhood,* 21 SOC. WORK 308 (1976); Ortner, Brown & Ferguson, *Single-parent Fatherhood: An Emerging Family Life Style,* 25 FAM. COORDINATOR 429 (1976); Santrock & Warshak, *infra* note 21; Schlesinger & Todres, *Motherless Families: An Increasing Societal Pattern,* 55 CHILD WELFARE 553 (1976). Greenberg's study deals with the problems of reestablishing adult intimacy experienced by the solo father. It is limited to an exploration of only this adjustment that men must make after divorce when they have custody of their children. The study compares the response in this regard between divorced men and women and finds that it is the men who experience this as a particular difficulty.

6. Chang & Deinard, *supra* note 5, at 242 (italics and brackets added by author to change the gender of the parent described).

7. Orthner, Brown and Ferguson, *supra* note 5, at 429. *See also* Bartz & Witcher, *supra* note 5, at 5, setting forth the superman concept.

8. D. LUEPNITZ, *supra* note 5, at 133.

9. *See* WALLERSTEIN and KELLY, SURVIVING THE BREAKUP: HOW CHILDREN AND PARENTS COPE WITH DIVORCE (1980).

10. Bartz & Witcher, *supra* note 5; Greenberg, *supra* note 5.

11. Bartz & Witcher, *supra* note 5, at 6; also note that nothing is known about the custodial father who relinquishes custody.

12. Brody & Endsley, *Researching Children and Families: Differences in Approaches of Child and Family Specialists,* 30 FAM. REL. 275, 276 (1981).

13. The single interview's status as the paradigm of social science research has been challenged. See Laslett & Rappaport, *Collaborative Interviewing and Interactive Research,* 37 J. MARRIAGE & FAM. 968 (1975); Oakley, *infra* note 14, at 30–61.

14. *See, e.g.,* Oakley, *Interviewing Women: A Contradiction in Terms,* in DOING FEMINIST RESEARCH (H. Roberts ed. 1981).

15. In particular, see Chang & Deinard, *supra* note 5.

16. Fulton, *Parental Reports of Children's Post-Divorce Adjustment,* J. SOC. ISSUES, Fall 1979, at 126. Perhaps the fathers in the father-custody studies, because they have patently retained their influence, are less perceptive of their children's distress.

17. *See* Chambers, *Rethinking the Substantive Rules for Custody Disputes in Divorce,* 83 MICH. L. REV. 477 (1984) at 539–41.

18. *Id.* In regard to the inherently discriminatory nature of the marriage contract, see Barker, *The Regulation of Marriage: Repressive Benevolence,* in POWER AND THE STATE 239 (1978); Brophy & Smart, *From Disregard to Disrepute: The Position of Women in Family Law,* FEMINIST REV., Oct. 1981, at 3.

19. D. LUEPNITZ, *supra* note 5, at 60, states that over 50 percent of the women in her study had to look for work for the first time.

20. Gasser & Taylor, *supra* note 5, at 397, have observed that the focus of these studies is not all upon the children. Gasser & Taylor also note that the men in their study were most anxious to declare the situation under control and for their families to be seen as functioning smoothly. *Id.* at 400.

21. Santrock & Warshak, *Father Custody and Social Development in Boys and Girls,* J. SOC. ISSUES, Fall 1979, at 313 (citation omitted).

22. Sewart, *Critical Theory and the Critique of Conservative Method,* in THEORETICAL PERSPECTIVES IN SOCIOLOGY (S. McNall ed. 1979) at 312.

23. Chambers, *supra* note 17, at 512–13.

24. Santrock & Warshak, *supra* note 21, at 119–21.

25. Chambers, *supra* note 17, at 513.

26. Santrock & Warshak, *supra* note 21, at 114.

27. *Id.* at 119, 122.

28. *Id.* at 120–21.

29. *Id.* at 120. As reported by Santrock and Warshak, the research of Hetherington does make such a finding. However, the fact that boys in mother custody are doing better on some measures than boys in intact families is often lost. Santrock & Warshak, *supra* note 21 at 121.

30. Santrock & Warshak, *supra* note 21, at 123.

31. *Id.* at 123–24.

32. *Id.* at 123–24.

33. *Id.* at 123.

34. *Id.* at 124.

35. In this regard, see C. GILLIGAN, IN A DIFFERENT VOICE: PSYCHOLOGICAL THEORY AND WOMEN'S DEVELOPMENT (1982), who questions just these sorts of assumptions and conclusions in other psychological studies.

36. White & Mika, *Family, Divorce and Separation: Theory and Research,* 6 MARRIAGE & FAM. REV. 182–84 (1982). Studies discussed herein against which this criticism can be levied include Chang & Dienard, Gasser & Taylor, and Orthner, Brown & Ferguson, *supra* note 5.

37. Gasser & Taylor, *supra* note 5, at 398.

38. Mendes, *supra* note 5, at 309.

39. *Id.*

40. *Id.*

41. Gersick, *supra* note 5, at 322. For a detailed discussion of the way family patterns are repeated intergenerationally, see I. BOSZORMENYI-NAGY & G. SPARK, INVISIBLE LOYALTIES: RECIPROCITY IN INTERGENERATIONAL FAMILY THERAPY (1973). *See also* Keshet & Rosenthal, *supra* note 5, who note that adjustments in the father role go beyond housework to include changes in sensitivity and personal flexibility.

42. McKee & O'Brien, *The Father Figure: Some Current Orientations and Historical Perspectives,* in THE FATHER FIGURE 3 (L. McKee & M. O'Brien eds. 1982).

43. Sutton-Smith, *Epilogue: Framing the Problem,* in SIBLING RELATIONSHIPS: THEIR NATURE AND SIGNIFICANCE ACROSS THE LIFESPAN 384 (M. Lamb & B. Sutton-Smith eds. 1982).

44. Hipgrave, *Lone Fatherhood: A Problematic Status,* in THE FATHER FIGURE 172 (L. McKee & M. O'Brien eds. 1982).

45. Id. at 176.

46. *See* McKee & O'Brien, *supra* note 42, at 4–5.

47. Richards, *How Should We Approach the Study of Fathers?,* in THE FATHER FIGURE 57 (L. McKee & M. O'Brien eds. 1982) at 62.

48. *Id.*

49. Finkelstein, *supra* note 5, at 272.

50. *See* Thompson, *The Father's Case in Child Custody Disputes: The Contributions of Psychological Research,* in FATHERHOOD AND FAMILY POLICY 53 (1983). Thompson advanced the father as the "fun-giving" and experiential parent. The mothering role is portrayed as banal and routine. However, for an appreciation of the importance of the mother's nurturing and caressing roles, *see* A. MONTAGU, TOUCHING: THE HUMAN SIGNIFICANCE OF THE SKIN (1971).

51. Hancock, *The Dimensions of Meaning and Belonging in the Process of Divorce,* 50 AM. J. ORTHPSYCH. 18 (1980) at 23.

CHAPTER NINE

1. *See, e.g.,* CAL. CIV. CODE § 4607(a) (West Supp. 1987), which illustrates changes in procedure (mediation before judicial hearing) and substance (emphasis upon a child's continuing relationship with both parents):"In any proceeding where there is [a contested] issue . . . [of] custody or of visitation with a minor child . . . the matter shall be set for mediation of the contested issues. . . . The purpose of such mediation proceeding shall be to reduce acrimony which may exist between the parties and to develop an agreement assuring the child or children's close and continuing contact with both parents."

Under court-associated mandatory mediation programs, existing institutional actors will more likely than not continue to provide services—the (old) "family court social worker" becomes the (new) "family court mediator." *See, e.g.,* Mumma, *Mediating Disputes,* 42 PUB. WELFARE 22, 26–30 (1984) (describing a court-associated mediation program developed in Virginia Beach, Virginia). In addition, a new market may be created for social workers as mediators in private practice, at least under statutes that allow "opting out" (the satisfaction of the statutory mediation requirement through a private service provider).

2. *See, e.g.,* Canacakos, *Joint Custody as a Fundamental Right,* in JOINT CUSTODY AND SHARED PARENTING 223, 224–25 (J. Folberg ed. 1984) (arguing that a presumption of joint custody is constitutionally mandated); Folberg, *Divorce Mediation: A Workable Alternative,* in AMERICAN BAR ASSOCIATION, ALTERNATIVE MEANS OF FAMILY DISPUTE RESOLUTION (H. Davidson, L. Ray & R Horowitz eds. 1982), *quoted in* KRAUSE, FAMILY LAW CASES, COMMENTS AND QUESTIONS 702 (2d ed. 1983); Robinson, *Joint Custody: Constitutional Imperatives,* 54 U. CIN. L. REV. 27 (1985) (arguing for mandatory joint custody except when a compelling reason for an exclusive award to serve the child's best interest exists); Steinman, *Joint Custody: What We Know, What We Have Yet to Learn, and the Judicial and Legislative Implications,* 16 U.C. DAVIS L. REV. 739 (1983).

3. *See, e.g.,* J. AUERBACH, JUSTICE WITHOUT LAW? (1983); Abel, *The Contradictions of Informal Justice,* in 1 THE POLITICS OF INFORMAL JUSTICE 267 (R. Abel ed. 1982); Delgado, Dunn, Brown, Lee & Hubbert, *Fairness and Formality: Minimizing the Risk of Prejudice in Alternative Dispute Resolution,* 1985 WIS. L. REV. 1351 (suggesting that in cases in which there is a wide disparity in the status or power of opponents, methods of alternative dispute resolution may heighten racial and ethnic prejudice); Menkel-Meadow, *Toward Another View of Legal Negotiation: The Structure of Problem Solving,* 31 UCLA L. REV. 754 (1984) (arguing for a problem-solving approach to negotiation); Rifkin, *Mediation From a Feminist Perspective: Promise and Problems,* 2 LAW & INEQUALITY 21 (1984) (arguing that mediation helps to lessen the problem of dominance).

4. *See generally* Rifkin, *supra* note 3.

5. *See* Engram & Markowitz, *Ethical Issues in Mediation: Divorce and Labor Compared,* 8 MEDIATION Q. 19, 20–25 (1985); Saposnek, *What Is Fair in Child Custody Mediation,* 8 MEDIATION Q. 9, 15 (1985). *But see* Perlmutter, *Ethical Issues in Family Mediation: A Social Perspective,* 8 MEDIATION Q. 99, 103–4 (1985) (suggesting that a solution to the bargaining-power dilemma is to bring lawyers into the mediation process).

6. *See* Greif, *infra* note 13, at 318–19; *see also* Pruhs, Paulsen & Tysseling, *Divorce Mediation: The Politics of Integrating Clinicians,* 65 SOC. CASEWORK 532, 535 (1984) ["Outside the courtroom there is no such thing as sole custody; divorce requires restructuring of the family but will include continued influence by both parents (even in the absence of one parent)."].

7. Abarbanel, *Shared Parenting After Separation and Divorce: A Study of Joint Custody,* 49 AM. J. ORTHOPSYCH. 320 (1979), at 328.

8. Miller, *Joint Custody,* 13 FAM. L.Q. 345, 364–65 (1979) (citations omitted).

9. *See* Pearson, Munson & Thoennes, *Legal Change and Child Custody Awards,* 3 J. FAM. ISSUES 5, 24 (1982).

10. Elkin, *Conciliation Courts: The Reintegration of Disintegrating Families,* 22 FAM. COORDINATOR 63, 64 (1973). The phrase has now become a fathers'-rights cliché.

11. Traditional practice was to award custody to one parent in order to meet children's need for a permanent, stable relationship. *See* J. GOLDSTEIN, A. FREUD & A. SOLNIT, BEYOND THE BEST INTERESTS OF THE CHILD (1973).

12. *See, e.g.,* Ahrons, *Joint Custody Arrangements in the Postdivorce Family,* J. DIVORCE, Spring 1980, at 189, 190 (tracing the gradual downfall of the presumption of maternal

custody); Everett, *Shared Parenthood in Divorce: The Parental Covenant and Custody Law,* 2 J.L. & RELIGION 85, 93–94 (1984)

13. *See, e.g.,* Greif, *Fathers, Children and Joint Custody,* 49 AM. J. ORTHOPSYCH. 311, 319 (1979) (criticizing visitation rights as not maximizing the contact between the child and both parents); Noble, *Custody Contest: How to Divide and Reassemble a Child,* 64 SOC. CASEWORK 406, 411 (1983) (arguing that periodic visitation "does not give sufficient opportunity for the variety and richness of contact that is necessary to sustain complex family relationships"); *see also* Mumma, *supra* note 1, at 25 ("Perhaps the concepts of custody and visitation are obsolete. The words themselves have become so distorted by stereotypical meanings that they may no longer be useful. New terms, or at least new concepts, are sorely needed.").

14. In material presented to a Wisconsin Legislative Committee considering changes in that state's custody laws, William Johnson Everett expressed the social worker's position: "[T]he child is not some indivisible 'thing' over which a person is to have 'custody' or not. Custody is for criminal suspects, not children. Similarly, children are not guests to be 'visited' by their parents. Visitation is for funeral homes and hospitals." Everett, *Shared Parenthood in Divorce: Parental Covenant and Custody Law* 12 (1983) (unpublished manuscript on file with the author).

15. *See* Phear, Beck, Hauser, Clark & Whitney, *An Empirical Study of Custody Agreements: Joint Versus Sole Legal Custody,* in JOINT CUSTODY AND SHARED PARENTING 142, 155 (J. Folberg ed. 1984).

16. *See id.* at 156.

17. Elkin, *supra* note 10, at 71; *accord* Sitkin, *The California Conciliation Court: An Interdisciplinary Effort to Promote Matrimony,* 2 GLENDALE L. REV. 31 (1977).

18. At this time, social workers were experiencing a declining role in delinquency proceedings with the movement away from a therapeutic to a more adversarial model. *See* Scherrer, *How Social Workers Help Lawyers,* 21 SOC. WORK 279, 279 (1976) (remarking on the tension between social workers and lawyers in the juvenile court context); Weil, *Research on Issues in Collaberation Between Social Workers and Lawyers,* 56 SOC. SERV. REV. (1982) at 394–39 (contrasting the trend toward adversarial proceedings in juvenile and dependency courts with a "countertrend . . . in the area of divorce and child custody").

19. *See* Elkin, *supra* note 10, at 63.

20. Reducing or managing conflict is a clearly stated goal in many instances of divorce, regardless of the ultimate outcome. For example, in an early and influential writing, the ambitious scope of the social workers' task at divorce was clearly set forth: "We do not have as a goal the saving of all marriages, but we are concerned with the tragedy of the unnecessary divorce. . . . A conciliation court serves families. If in the course of such service a family does not reconcile, this does not mean that the counselor's concern and responsibility to the family is at an end. In such cases, we still offer a very important and worthwhile service in our counseling efforts to help the family close the book gently rather than bang it shut in anger; to help the family terminate the marriage with dignity, minimal trauma, and without the need to strike back—a need which is often responsible for much of post-divorce litigation."

21. *See* Kraus, *The Crisis of Divorce: Growth Promoting or Pathogenic?* 3 J. DIVORCE 107, 108–11 (1979) (describing and critiquing the "pathogenic" perspective on divorce); *see also* Girdner, *Child Custody Determination: Ideologized Dimensions of a Social Problem,* in REDEFINING SOCIAL PROBLEMS (E. Seidman & J. Rappaport eds. 1986) at 169–70 (noting that "[t]he ideological definition of divorce as pathology was pervasive until the 1970s").

22. *See, e.g.,* Girdner, *supra* note 21, at 169–71.

23. *See* Elkin, *supra* note 10, at 64; Kraus, *supra* note 21, at 108; Mumma, *supra* note 1, at 25.

24. A family systems approach focuses on the ways that a group of individuals affect and are affected by each other. Divorce, therefore, is a process through which the unit or system moves, not an event that happens to individuals. *See* Mumma, *supra* note 1, at 24–25.

25. *See generally* Counts & Sacks, *The Need for Crisis Intervention During Marital Separation,* 30 Soc. Work 146 (1985) (outlining factors that increase stresses of separation and presenting strategies for intervention by mental health professionals).

26. *See* Durst, Wedemeyer & Zurcher, *Parenting Partnerships After Divorce: Implications for Practice,* 30 Soc. Work 423 (1985) (describing five types of continuing parental partnerships in postdivorce families).

27. Everett & Volgy, *Family Assessment in Child Custody Disputes,* 9 J. Marital & Fam. Therapy 343, 348 (1983).

28. Although common sense might indicate both that no mediation or therapy is needed by divorcing spouses who handle their divorces without protracted, acrimonious litigation, and that spouses in strong opposition to one another will not be transformed into conciliatory shared-parenting partners by any amount of mediation or therapy, the advocates of therapy recognize few exceptions. One commentator has stated: "Virtually all divorcing parents need help in minimizing and managing stress. For this sample, no immunity to stress was afforded by age, sex, socioeconomic status or other background factors. Besides the passage of time, only one other factor led to a significant decrease in stress—the parental use of valued helping resources in coping with the divorce." Fulmer, *A Structural Approach to Unresolved Mourning in Single Parent Family Systems,* 9 J. Marital & Fam. Therapy 259, 268 (1983); *accord* Counts & Sacks, *supra* note 25, at 149 ("Few people caught up in the process of separation are equipped to deal effectively with the considerable and unique stresses [involved]. . . . This is especially true of children and adolescents. Thus, intervention is important and should be the rule, not the exception."). Legal authors, by contrast, characterize the same situation not as a treatment opportunity but as a situation raising questions about the appropriateness of state intervention. For documentation of potential abuses, see Levy, *Custody Investigations in Divorce Cases,* 1985 Am. B. Found. Res. J. at 769–70, 771–75.

29. *See* Pearson & Thoennes, *Mediation in Custody Disputes,* 4 Behav. Sci. & L. 203, 203–5 (1986).

30. *See* Scherrer, *supra* note 18 (suggesting six areas—interviewing, evaluation, crisis intervention, short-term case work, negotiation, and referral—in which the social worker can make a significant contribution).

31. For amplification of the partnership ideal as expressed in 1973, see Elkin, *supra* note 10, at 63. Later mediation literature, however, suggested a complete displacement of attorneys: "At the close of mediation, with a legally binding settlement agreement, either party may obtain an uncontested, no-fault divorce at a nominal cost." McKenry, *Mediation Eases the Split,* Prac. Dig. Dec. 1979, at 8, 9.

32. Elkin, *supra* note 10, at 70. Social workers have frequently expressed their discomfort at working in the legal system because law and social work are perceived as encompassing contrasting frameworks. Whereas both professions "help" clients—lawyers with the client's rights, social workers with the client's emotions—social workers believe their values and principles are compromised by the adversarial model. *See, e.g.,* Fogelson, *How Social Workers Perceive Lawyers,* 51 Soc. Casework 95, 99 (1970); Pruhs, Paulsen & Tysseling, *supra* note 6, at 537; Scherrer, *supra* note 18, at 279. For example, several authors

found that "[t]he rational-logical emphasis of the legal system does not provide an ideal atmosphere for the resolution of interpersonal conflict and, in fact, may serve as a catalyst to increased hostilities." Herrman, McKenry & Weber, *Attorneys' Perceptions of Their Role in Divorce,* 2 J. DIVORCE 313, 315 (1979).

33. *See* Pruhs, Paulsen & Tysseling, *supra* note 6.

34. *See, e.g.,* Felner & Farber, *Social Policy for Child Custody: A Multidisciplinary Framework,* 50 AM. J. ORTHOPSYCH. 341, 345 (1980) ("One must ask if an adversarial process, in which a child's parents are the adversaries and the child is the prize, is best suited to arrive at a placement that truly serves the child's best interests."); Mumma, *supra* note 1, at 25 (stating that "the litigation process is little more than an institutionalized form of emotional abuse to children"); Woody, *Prevention Intervention for Children of Divorce,* 59 SOC. CASEWORK 537, 541 (1978) ("For the average family, divorce constitutes a serious crisis situation, and it is likely to be a 'psychological emergency' for the children."). Children were considered the innocent victims of the increasing divorce rate. *See id.* at 541 ("Divorce is certainly a process over which children have no control; inasmuch as possible, they should not become its victims.").

35. Haynes, *Divorce Mediator: A New Role,* 23 SOC. WORK 5, 5 (1978).

36. Rosenberg, Kleinman & Brantley, *Custody Evaluations: Helping the Family Reorganize,* 63 SOC. CASEWORK 203, 205 (1982).

37. *See* Oneglia & Orlin, *A Model for Combined Private Practice: Attorneys and Social Workers in Domestic Relations,* J. APPLIED SOC. SCI. Fall/Winter 1978, at 37, 39.

38. *See supra* note 28; *see also* Herrman, McKenry & Weber, *supra* note 32, at 321 (stating that "[i]t may be necessary in some circumstances for one or both lawyers to undertake the temporary role of listener, but the ultimate goal should be to get the client into the hands of a trained therapist." [citation omitted]). For discussions concerning the role of the therapist in child-custody disputes, see generally Counts & Sacks, *supra* note 25; Everett & Volgy, cited in note 27 *supra;* Sprenkle & Storm, *Divorce Therapy Outcome Research: A Substantive and Methodological Review,* 9 J. MARITAL & FAM. THERAPY 239 (1983); and Woody, Colley, Schlegelmilch, Maginn & Balsanek, *Child Adjustment to Parental Stress Following Divorce,* 65 SOC. CASEWORK 405 (1984).

39. *See, e.g.,* Wiseman, *Crisis Theory and the Process of Divorce,* 56 SOC. CASEWORK (1975) (stating that "[l]awyers do little to lessen the anger that naturally arises; . . . often they appear to heighten it").

Some have viewed the nature of legal training as the cause of attorneys' inadequacies. *See* Oneglia & Orlin, *supra* note 37, at 39 ("Training in contracts, torts and the doctrine of the 'reasonable man' does nothing to prepare the lawyer to handle the human being who is behind the legal problem. . . . [T]he lawyer has no time for non-legal 'trifles'— ironically usually most of the major grievances of the suffering client.").

Others gave advice as to how to handle the attorney involved in the social worker's case: "[A]n early meeting or telephone contact with the attorneys involved [. . .] may begin to reduce the adversarial nature of the process [. . .]. The legal process often seems to have a life and energy of its own; active and repeated attempts [. . .] are needed to diminish the pressure on the parents to continue their adversarial stance." Rosenberg, Kleinman & Brantley, *supra* note 36, at 205.

40. Oneglia & Orlin, *supra* note 37, at 43–44.

41. Noble, *supra* note 13, at 407 (footnote omitted).

But see Charnas, *Practice Trends in Divorce Related Child Custody,* J. DIVORCE, Summer 1981, at 57, 62 (reporting on a study indicating that "there is no interdisciplinary difference in the ability of judges and mental health professionals to select a custodial psychological parent; both overwhelmingly chose as the custodial parent the one which the evaluation reflected as having a more positive and consistent emotional bond with the children").

The competition between the social worker's role and the lawyer's role (as defined by social workers) becomes apparent: "The pain, anger, and frustration of divorce are frequently exacerbated by the legal process as it presently works. Frequently, the social worker who has been involved with the family during the period leading up to the decision to divorce is excluded from the proceedings, and the clients are passed onto [*sic*] a person in another profession. However, it is at precisely this time that the special skills of the social worker are most needed." Haynes, *supra* note 35, at 5.

42. *See* L. WEITZMAN, THE DIVORCE REVOLUTION: THE UNEXPECTED SOCIAL AND ECONOMIC CONSEQUENCES FOR WOMEN AND CHILDREN IN AMERICA (1985), at 16–17 (discussing reformers' objectives); Elkin, *supra* note 10, at 69.

43. Pruhs, Paulsen & Tysseling, *supra* note 6, at 532.

44. *See id.* at 532–33.

45. *See* Derdeyn, *Child Custody Consultation*, 45 AM. J. ORTHOPSYCH. 791, 796–97 (1975); Mumma, *supra* note 1, at 24 (stating that "[t]he adversarial court proceeding and the social worker's investigation and report did not reinforce cooperation and agreement, but rather seemed to generate conflict"); Rosenberg, Kleinman & Brantley, *supra* note 36, at 207.

46. Pruhs, Paulsen & Tysseling, *supra* note 6, at 532 (emphasis in original).

47. Haynes, *supra* note 35, at 5.

48. With half of all first marriages ending in divorce, courtrooms are jammed with hostile parents prepared for battle over the custody or visitation of their mutual children. These parents and children face a destructive adversarial process that will activate a network of court personnel, social workers, and other professionals in a consuming, costly, and stressful human drama that frequently endures for years. For most of these parents the wrangling ends only when one or both litigants become financially or emotionally exhausted and can no longer continue the legal battle. Judges' orders do not seem to settle things, at least for very long. Children suffer and parents blame each other, fueling the conflict and maintaining the tragic cycle.

"What can be done to help? Parents can voluntarily seek out a mediation center . . ." Mumma, *supra* note 1, at 22.

49. *Children and Divorce: A Review*, 24 SOC. WORK 468, 472 (1979).

50. *See, e.g.*, Musetto, *The Role of the Mental Health Professional in Contested Custody: Evaluator of Competence or Facilitator of Change?*, J. DIVORCE, Summer 1981, at 76, 78. Even if some valid reasons for custody disputes were recognized, they were considered "exceptional." *See* Noble, *supra* note 13, at 407.

Conflict in other areas might also be viewed as indicative of pathology: "Struggles over property may be necessary but they are frequently a manifestation of, if not a metaphor for, security needs. Each parent has a right to have these needs met to the extent of the available resources. It is in the best interest of each parent to see that the other spouse's needs are met." Pruhs, Paulsen, & Tysseling, *supra* note 6, at 535; *accord* Johnston, Campbell & Tall, *Impasses to the Resolution of Custody and Visitation Disputes*, 55 AM. J. ORTHOPSYCH. 112 (1985) (proposing that interpersonal conflict reflected in the decision to divorce manifests itself in a variety of continuing battles between former spouses).

51. *See* Rosenberg, Kleinman & Brantley, *supra* note 36, at 204, 207; Wallerstein & Kelly, *Children and Divorce: A Review*, 24 SOC. WORK 468 (1979).

Even though the child is characterized as the ultimate beneficiary (as he or she must be for obvious reasons), sometimes it is clear that others are also winners: "Rather than support the imposition of legal visitation restrictions, we should do everything in our power to maximize contact between the child and both parents. One clear way of doing that is through joint custody arrangements. As suggested by this study, structural arrangements such as custody and visitation are crucial to the postdivorce *adjustment of fathers and, ultimately, of their children.* A different quality of psychological involvement grows out of the opportunity to take care of (*i.e.,* be a parent to) one's child, rather than 'visit' with one's child." Greif, *supra* note 13, at 319 (emphasis added).

52. Ahrons, *The Continuing Coparental Relationship Between Divorced Spouses,* 51 AM. J. ORTHOPSYCH. 415, 415 (1981).

53. The debate among mental health professionals over the form of the postdivorce family was perhaps engendered in 1973 by the publication of J. GOLDSTEIN, A. FREUD & A. SOLNIT, BEYOND THE BEST INTERESTS OF THE CHILD, cited in note 11 above. The thesis of the work was that custody-placement questions should be resolved according to who was the child's "psychological parent." Perhaps more controversial, however, was the authors' suggestion that the custodial parent be given complete decision-making power in relation to the child, including whether the noncustodial parent had visitation privileges. *See id.* at 38.

54. *See, e.g.,* Mumma, *supra* note 1, at 30 ("We attempt to base recommendations on the desired changes in the relationship. For example, we may recommend custody be given to the parent who is most likely to allow the most frequent or flexible contact with the other parent and extended family.").

55. Some states have enacted so-called friendly-parent provisions. *See, e.g.,* CAL. CIV. CODE § 4600(b)(I) (West Supp. 1987). For a discussion of these statutes, see Schulman & Pitt, *Second Thoughts on Joint Child Custody: Analysis of Legislation and Its Implications for Women and Children,* 12 GOLDEN GATE U.L. REV. 539, 554–56 (1982).

This version of the shared parenting ideal is being implemented even without statutory authority, as I discovered during my primary research in family-court counseling units in Wisconsin during 1984–85. These court-associated social workers were engaged in implementing the shared-parenting ideal through the informal adoption of a friendly-parent provision and a joint-custody norm.

Sometimes these generous-parent innovations are justified by the custodial parent's perceived need for assistance from the noncustodial parent: "[P]arents, like children, benefit from two-parent families. The burdens of being a single parent are unfair not only to the child but also to the parents." Pruhs, Paulsen & Tysseling, *supra* note 6, at 535.

At other times, the children's perceived needs seem paramount. "It is clear that the best interests of the children involve much more than the linear relationships between parent and children. . . . One major consideration often may be the custodial parent's ability to allow an arrangement for an appropriate continuing relationship with the noncustodial parent as well as significant others." Rosenberg, Kleinman & Brantley, *supra* note 36, at 207.

56. The following quotation shows the way in which the helping professions assert this preference for mediation: "The role of the divorce mediator is to assist the parties to reach a fair settlement in a way that enables them to separate the economic issues from the emotional ones. In the process, he performs the function of helping the clients focus on the future rather than the past. The mediator has another important role. At this critical moment, he may be the only person in the couple's lives who is nonjudgmental and interested in their needs." Haynes, *supra* note 35, at 6.

57. See the quotation from Haynes at the beginning of chapter 4.

Mediation is often presented as the solution to all sorts of family problems created by the adversary system. *See, e.g.,* Mumma, *supra* note 1, at 24.

This change in procedure is viewed as likely to effect a change in the dynamics of the divorce process: "Managing the process not only provides the instrumental assessment, planning, and ongoing reinforcement of the mediation, but allows the mediator to role-model the 'how to' of cooperative conflict resolution, so that when the parties leave, they can emulate the system for their future needs." Barsky, *Strategies and Techniques of Divorce Mediation,* 65 Soc. CASEWORK 102, 105 (1984). Even these idealized presentations, however, recognize that some hostility is inevitable: "Some ventilation of hostility may be necessary so that the individual can move beyond the emotional feeling and not be held back by it. Thus, permitting a display of anger may be useful, if the mediator keeps in mind its effect on the other spouse." *Id.* at 106.

58. Edelman, *The Political Language of the Helping Professions,* 4 POL. & Soc. 295, 296 (1974).

59. *See, e.g.,* Herrman, McKenry & Weber, *supra* note 32, at 314–15.

60. *See* Blinder, *Marital Dissolution and Child Custody: A Primer for Family Therapists and Divorce Attorneys,* 9 FAM. THERAPY I, 5 (1982).

61. *See, e.g.,* Noble, *supra* note 13, at 407 (arguing that lawyers are naturally biased in favor of their clients and that the exercise of judicial discretion is a product of the judge's temperament, background, interests, and biases).

62. *See, e.g.,* McKenry, *supra* note 31, at 8; *accord* Barsky, *supra* note 57, at 105 ("When the man and woman first entered mediation, their conflict-resolving styles may have consisted primarily of the withdrawing, smoothing, or forcing procedures; by the time their agreement is reached, they have learned the mediator's managerial skills of confrontation and compromise.").

63. *See* Deis, *California's Answer: Mandatory Mediation of Child Custody and Visitation Disputes,* 1 OHIO ST. J. ON DISPUTE RESOLUTION 149, 163–66 (1985) (discussing the advantages of mandatory mediation); Pearson, *Child Custody: Why Not Let the Parents Decide?,* 20 JUDGES' J. 4, 6 (1981) (outlining the argument "that the adversary system is simply inappropriate for the resolution of many marital disputes," including child custody).

64. Parsloe, *The Interface of Law and Social Work,* 4 CONTEMP. SOC. WORK EDUC. 183, 184 (1981).

65. *See id.*

66. *See, e.g., supra* note 48.

67. A large body of literature on family mediation exists in both social work and legal publications. For an understanding of the development of family mediation and how it contrasts with what are typically known as *therapy,* and *how-to* techniques, see Folberg, *A Mediation Overview: History and Dimensions of Practice* 1 MEDIATION Q. 3 (1983).

There is some debate among mediation practitioners about the extent to which they perform "actual therapy." They analogize private mediation to settlement negotiation, although there is a trend toward viewing child-custody mediations—particularly among court-associated services—as more therapy-oriented. *Compare* Haynes, *supra* note 35, at 6–8 (urging the distinction between mediation and therapy) *with* Mumma, *supra* note 1, at 23 (stating that there is no distinction between mediation and therapy in the court-associated program in which Mumma is involved). The process itself, however, is considered "therapeutic" because it uses different procedures and philosophies from the legal model. *See* Haynes, *supra* note 35, at 7–8. Similarly, because its agreements are touted as the product of self-determination, they are considered preferable to those imposed by the court or produced via reliance on third-party advocates (attorneys). *See id.* at 5–8. Paradoxically, although mediation involves a third-party mediator, it is not viewed as relying on outsiders; the process is characterized as the product of each spouse's individual self-determination.

68. O. COOGLER, STRUCTURED MEDIATION IN DIVORCE SETTLEMENTS 97 (1977), *quoted in* Winks, *Divorce Mediation: A Nonadversary Procedure for the No-Fault Divorce,* 19 J. FAM. L. 615, 646; *accord* CAL. CIV. CODE §§ 4351.5, 4607 (West 1983 & Supp. 1985) (requiring that court-appointed mediators hold a master's degree in social work, marriage counseling, psychology, or a related field).

69. "Our goal is to divert families from continued litigation, to help them resolve the current issues of dispute by agreement, and to assist them in establishing a more successful way of resolving future disagreements. Our brief intervention is designed to create an environment in which parents and children can disengage themselves from conflict and get on with their lives. . . .

"We were [helping] families negotiate their own custody and visitation arrangements, and they were staying out of court. Children who were displaying symptomatic behavior often began to show improvement—sometimes dramatic—when their parents began to cooperate. It became increasingly clear that parental agreement and cooperation had a greater effect on children than the actual custody or visitation arrangement. . . .

"The goal [of child custody mediation] is to shift the group from its preoccupation with negatives to a rediscovery of positives, from incompetency to themes of competency, and from conflict to cooperation." Mumma, *supra* note 1, at 24, 26.

70. See, for example, the primary field research of M. Raschick, *Wisconsin Non-Custodial Parents' Groups* 17 (May 16, 1985) (unpublished manuscript on file with the author); *see also Priorities for Dads PAC* (Sept. 1984) (on file with the author). For a discussion of the various ideological strains within the fathers'-rights movement, see M. Shiffman, *The Men's Movement: An Exploratory Empirical Investigation* 3, 4 (paper prepared for presentation at the 80th Annual Meeting of the American Sociological Association, Washington, D.C., 26–30 Aug. 1985).

71. Some argue that increased power in the form of mandatory joint custody will inspire fathers to pay their child support. *See* text accompanying *supra* note 8; *Suggestions from Julilly Kohler for Changes in Child Custody Law* [Kohler] 4 (2 Nov. 1984) (Submitted to Special Legislative Comm. on Custody Arrangements (Wisconsin) (on file with the author). *But see* Bartlett & Stack, *Joint Custody, Feminism and the Dependency Dilemma,* 2 BERKELEY WOMEN'S L.J. 9, 35 n.109 (1986) (suggesting a lack of causal link between custody arrangements and compliance with child-support orders).

72. *See, e.g.,* Bruch, *Making Visitation Work: Dual Parenting Orders,* FAM. ADVOC. Summer 1978, at 22, 25–26.

73. One example of direct control over the custodial parent's life is found in "permission to leave the state" statutes, which have become popular. These require a custodial parent to get consent of either the noncustodial parent or the court before moving out of the state. *See, e.g.,* WIS. STAT. ANN. § 767.245(6) (West 1981). These statutes have been criticized. *See* Sheehan, *Post-Divorce Child Custody and Family Relocation,* 9 HARV. WOMEN'S L.J. 135 (1986).

74. *See* Zolla & Alexander, *Report of the Family Law Mediation Program of the Los Angeles County Superior Court (Western District),* 14 BEVERLY HILLS BAR ASS'N J. 87, 88–90 (1980).

75. *See, e.g.,* J. HEINZ & E. LAUMANN, CHICAGO LAWYERS: THE SOCIAL STRUCTURE OF THE BAR 90–94 (1982) (showing "divorce" and "general family" as the two areas ranking lowest in a "Prestige Ranking of Thirty Fields of Law").

76. *See, e.g.,* Folberg, *supra* note 2.

77. *See, e.g.,* Benedek & Benedek, *Joint Custody: Solution or Illusion?,* 136 AM. J. PSYCHIATRY 1540, 1541–42 (1979). (pointing out the risk of instability inherent in joint cus-

tody); *see also* Schulman & Pitt, *supra* note 55, at 570–71 (concluding that joint custody is only appropriate when both parents desire it and are willing to cooperate).

78. *See* Benedek & Benedek, *supra* note 77, at 1543. (stating that "[w]hen the requisite cooperation is not forthcoming, as is often the case following divorce, joint custody can be calamitous").

79. This anecdotal information comes from lawyers and legal academics working in the area. *See, e.g.,* Neely, *The Primary Caretaker Parent Rule: Child Custody and the Dynamics of Greed,* 3 YALE L. & POL'Y REV. 168 (1984).

Women and men seem to view the custody issue differently, with women regarding it as more central. *See* L. WEITZMAN, *supra* note 42, at 310–12 (concluding that "[w]omen . . . draw a line when it comes to custody"). Joint custody has also been the focus of fathers'-rights reformers.

80. *See* J. GOLDSTEIN, A. FREUD & A. SOLNIT, *supra* note 11, at 12 (noting that children "become prey to severe and crippling loyalty conflicts" when parents are hostile to each other); *see also* Chambers, *Rethinking the Substantive Rules for Custody Disputes in Divorce,* 83 MICH. L. REV. 477, 550–57 (1984). (cautioning that research on joint-custody arrangements is incomplete and suggesting possible problems with such arrangements); Felner & Farber, *supra* note 34, at 343–44 (questioning the wisdom of joint custody when parents cannot resolve important issues concerning their children).

81. *See, e.g.,* Pruhs, Paulsen & Tysseling, *supra* note 6, at 537 ("Comprehensive mediation is a *superior absolute system* which with careful nurturing *may ultimately supplant the adversarial process* in the majority of divorce cases" [emphasis added]). *See also* Sprenkle & Storm, *supra* note 38, at 240, 252 (describing mediation as superior to traditional adversarial methods for resolving custody and visitation disputes, and citing "an increase in joint custody arrangements" as one of the favorable results of mediation).

82. *See* Abarbanel, *supra* note 7, at 321; Greif, *supra* note 13, at 318–19; Noble, *supra* note 13, at 411; Wallerstein & Kelly, *supra* note 51, at 471. Social workers are aware that the operative legal standard in a given jurisdiction constrains the extent to which they can implement their ideal postdivorce family structure of shared parenting. Many jurisdictions still require the selection of a custodial parent when, for example, no statutory authority exists for joint custody. Even in those instances, however, social workers' rhetoric suggests ways to achieve postdivorce shared parenting in fact if not by law. Commentators have described social workers' responsibility to achieve postdivorce shared parenting in such situations as follows: "Clinical research in the area of the divorce process is pointing to the importance of the child's need for a continuing relationship with both parents; legal systems are shifting to accommodate this recognized need. . . .

"The end result of [the] painful procedure [of a court-ordered custody evaluation] is a recommendation regarding which parent is the 'best' or the 'psychological parent' and therefore the one who should have custody of the child. . . .

"Professionals must use the evaluation and subsequent recommendations to convey [the value of not terminating the relationship with the noncustodial parents] to the family and to attempt to shift the focus from a contest over the 'best' parent to a redefinition of roles and a restructuring of the children's family. Such a use of custody evaluations goes beyond the legal process, for which any therapeutic outcome is irrelevant. . . .

"Thus there are dual goals in the evaluation process—prompt resolution of custody issues and the restructuring of the children's family with continued contact with both parents." Rosenberg, Kleinman & Brantley, *supra* note 36, at 203–4.

83. After a traditional divorce, if one party wants to change custody or visitation arrangements, he or she may do so in cooperation with the other parent or may apply to the

courts for changes. If the route is through the courts, doctrines such as the "substantial-change-in-circumstances" test operate to deter noncustodial parents from using the legal process to harass custodial parents continually. *See, e.g.,* UNIF. MARRIAGE & DIVORCE ACT § 409, 9A U.L.A. 197 (1979) (precluding modification of custody decrees for a two-year period unless evidence is presented that the current arrangement may endanger the child's health).

84. Compare Edelman's discussion of the public's tendency to adopt the point of view of professional experts: "The lay public by and large adopts the professional perspective; for its major concern is to believe that others can be trusted to handle the problem. . . . This public reaction is the politically crucial one, for it confers power upon professionals and legitimizes their norms for society generally. The public reaction, in turn, is a response to the language of the professions and to the social milieu that gives that language its authoritative meaning." Edelman, *supra* note 58, at 304.

85. *See, e.g.,* Lefcourt, *Women, Mediation and Family Law,* 18 CLEARINGHOUSE REV. 266, 269 (1984) (concluding that the unequal financial and social power of men and women makes mediation an unfair process); Woods, *Mediation: A Backlash to Women's Progress on Family Law Issues,* 19 CLEARINGHOUSE REV. 431 (1985) (arguing that mediation fails to protect battered women and produces unequal financial results).

86. For an example of the presentation of conflict as "illegitimate," see Wallerstein & Kelly, *supra* note 51.

87. *See, e.g.,* Kelly, *Further Observations on Joint Custody,* 16 U.C. DAVIS L. REV. 762, 769 (1983).

88. The characterizations in this paragraph are based in part on interviews with social workers conducted by the author. In addition, the negative image of mothers is reflected in the literature. Sometimes the formal characterizations are gender-neutral, although it is clear that it is the primary caretaker or custodial parent who is being criticized. *See* Musetto, *supra* note 50; Wallerstein & Kelly, *supra* note 51. Others, however, are more explicit in their gendered view of the situation. *See* Abelsohn, *Dealing with the Abdication Dynamic in the Post Divorce Family: A Context for Adolescent Crisis,* 22 FAM. PROCESS 359, 364–66 (1983); Greif, *supra* note 13; Hancock, *The Dimensions of Meaning and Belonging in the Process of Divorce,* 50 AM. J. ORTHOPSYCH. 18 (1980); Kelly, *supra* note 87; Lerman, *Mediation of Wife Abuse Cases: The Adverse Impact of Informal Dispute Resolution on Women,* 7 HARV. WOMEN'S L.J. 57 (1984).

89. The prospect of continued contact is especially troubling in cases of spousal or child abuse. *See, e.g.,* Lerman, *supra* note 88, at 107; Schulman & Pitt, *supra* note 55, at 555–56 (pointing out the danger of continuing contact with an abusive father).

90. *See, e.g.,* Kelly, *supra* note 87, at 769 (recognizing some problems of abuse but emphasizing the problem of "emotionally disturbed women who, due to their own pathology, vigorously fight a father's desire to be involved in the children's lives"). *But see* Lemon, *Joint Custody as a Statutory Presumption: California's New Civil Code Sections 4600 and 4600.5,* 11 GOLDEN GATE U.L. REV. 485, 527–31 (1981) (suggesting that the stereotype of the manipulative and vindictive mother opposing joint custody is overstated). The therapist is viewed as having a potentially powerful role in the process of correcting pathological behavior. *See* Abelsohn, *supra* note 88, at 364–66 (stating that "[t]he therapist delivers this basic message to the mother—you lose, you do not win, if you succeed in keeping your children from their father").

Although the bulk of the literature discussed in this chapter presented the recent scholarly and professional focus on fathers as a "natural" evolution, some authors have argued that this shift has not necessarily been the product of neutral, detached observation or analysis: "In my five years of professional experience in an academic pediatric hospital, divorced women with children occasioned little comment, other than negative. They were dealt with routinely, given appointments without asking about their schedules, handed instructions imperiously without a thought as to how they would carry them out amidst the conflicting demands of work and child care. Yet when any father with custody of his children appeared, the staff went out of its way to praise his efforts and laud his heroism. They agonized over the conflicts he must face in the exigencies of caring for his child and managing his life. In both situations, one adult had sole responsibility for parenting and work. What differed was the way the parent was viewed." Hancock, *supra* note 88, at 23.

CHAPTER TEN

1. L. WEITZMAN, THE DIVORCE REVOLUTION: THE UNINTENDED SOCIAL AND ECONOMIC CONSEQUENCES FOR WOMEN AND CHILDREN IN AMERICA (1985).
2. The fact that women face such economic complications and the fact that they will be compounded after divorce as they are forced to assume primary economic responsibility for themselves and their children are not reflected in laws which treat them the same as their husbands. See Justice Abrahamson's dissent in Johnson v. Johnson, 78 Wis. 2d 137, 159, 254 N.W.2d 198, 209 (1977) in which she stated: "We cannot proceed in a divorce case on the assumption of 'legal equality of employment' beyond the extent to which it appears that such an assumption is justified in the particular case, that is, the individual woman in the case at bar has attained access or can obtain access to the job market to be self-supporting. Equality of men and women means eliminating sex stereotypes and looking at the individual. *Just as it is unacceptable for the law to force all women into the mold of homemaker, it is similarly unacceptable to treat all women upon divorce as per se self-sufficient breadwinners in an open, full-employment job market.*" (Emphasis added.)
3. See Seal, *A Decade of No-Fault Divorce,* 1 FAM. ADVOC. 10 (Spring 1979). The author's analysis of court records in San Diego revealed that California's rule-equality reform has had an adverse affect on wives. Under the former system, the home and furniture typically were allocated to the wife. After the reform, the home and other assets usually were divided, *and* the wife was ordered to pay a share of the family debts. Seal also concluded that the actual value of child-support awards tended to be less under the equality model. The combination of the wife's loss of assets and her increased responsibility for family debts often meant that she had less disposable income and that she typically would end up contributing more than half to support the children. *Id.* at 13–15.
4. V. FUCHS, WOMEN'S QUEST FOR ECONOMIC EQUALITY 146–47 (1988).
5. *Id.* at 145–46.
6. The concern for women's economic welfare emerges and is articulated in terms of their rights based on the concept of contribution. Consider the statement of legislative intent in the Wisconsin Family Code: "It is the intent of Chapters 765 to 768 to promote the stability and best interests of marriage and the family. It is the intent of the legislature to recognize the valuable contributions of both spouses during the marriage and at termination of the marriage by dissolution or death.
. . . Under the laws of this state, marriage is a legal partnership between 2 equal persons, a husband and wife, who owe to each other mutual responsibility and support. Each spouse has an equal obligation in accordance with his or her ability to contribute money or services or both which are necessary for the adequate support and maintenance of his or her minor chil-

dren and of the other spouse. No spouse may be presumed primarily liable for support expenses under this subsection." Sec. 765.001(2), Wis, Stats. (West Supp. 1989).

7. Reynolds, *The Relationship of Property Distribution and Alimony: The Division of Property to Address Need*, 56 FORDHAM L. REV. 827 (1988), at 849–854.

8. *See, e.g.*, Moore, *Should a Professional Degree be Considered a Marital Asset on Divorce?*, 15 AKRON L. REV. 543 (1982); Note, *Domestic Relations: Military Retirement Fair and Equitable Division in Divorce Courts*, 34 U. FLA. L. REV. 280 (1982); Comment, *Family Law: Ought a Professional Degree be Divisible As Property Upon Divorce?*, 22 WM. & MARY L. REV. 517 (1982); Comment, *Property Theory of Future Earning Potential in Dissolution Proceedings*, 56 WASH. L. REV. 277 (1981).

There are objections to language that characterizes women as being in need in many areas other than divorce. The objection is also raised that disguising need in an attempt to give status to nonworking women may hurt some other groups of women. For example, one author objected to the present label for spouse benefits under social security, *dependent benefits*, as "degrading." Mayers, *Incremental Change in Social Security Needed to Result in Equal and Fair Treatment of Men and Women*, in A CHALLENGE TO SOCIAL SECURITY: THE CHANGING ROLES OF WOMEN AND MEN IN AMERICAN SOCIETY (Burkhauser & Holden eds. 1982). *See also* Fierst, Discussion, in *id.* at 66, 71: "[I am] offended philosophically by [proposals for] homemaker credits and increased child-care drop-out years because they increase the rewards of not being employed. Fair play requires that the woman who works and pays taxes should get more for her efforts than the one who does not. Much as I want the homemaker to be secure in old age, I do not want to give her preference [over] the working woman."

9. L. WEITZMAN, *supra* note 1.

10. *See* Fineman, *Illusive Equality: On Weitzman's Divorce Revolution*, 1986 AM. BAR FOUND. RES. J. 781.

11. L. Weitzman, *supra* note 1, at 30.

12. *See generally* Mnookin, *Child-Custody Adjudication: Judicial Functions in the Face of Indeterminacy*, 39 LAW & CONTEMP. PROBS. 226 (1975) (arguing that psychological theories cannot accurately predict the effects of alternate custody determinations and arguing for less discretionary custody-award standards).

13. *See, e.g.*, Chambers, *Rethinking the Substantive Rules for Custody Disputes in Divorce*, 83 MICH. L. REV. 477 (1984); Neely, *The Primary Caretaker Parent Rule: Child Custody and the Dynamics of Greed*, 3 YALE L. & POL'Y REV. 168 (1984); Polikoff, *Why Are Mothers Losing: A Brief Analysis of Criteria Used in Child Custody Determinations*, 7 WOMEN'S RTS. L. REP. 235 (1982).

14. *See* Chambers, *supra* note 13, at 527 (confirming the application of the primary-caretaker rule to children of "tender years"); Neely, *supra* note 13, at 180–82 (advocating application of the primary-caretaker rule unless the children are old enough to decide for themselves who should be the custodial parent).

15. A version of this test was set forth in Garska v. McCoy, 278 S.E.2d 357 (W. Va. 1981). One commentator has hypothesized that such a standard would encourage fathers to co-parent during marriage. *See* Polikoff, *supra* note 13, at 241–43. Which party is the primary caretaker would be established by "lay testimony by the parties themselves, and by that of teachers, relatives, and neighbors. Which parent does the lion's share of the chores can be demonstrated satisfactorily in less than an hour of the court's time in most cases." Neely, *supra* note 13, at 181. Thus, this test is very different from the one for determining the psychological parent, which relies heavily on expert testimony.

16. V. FUCHS, *supra* note 4, at 4.

17. The potential drawbacks of expert testimony were well demonstrated in the recent Baby M. case. *See Nothing Surrogate About the Pain,* N.Y. Times, 9 Mar. 1987, at A14, col. I (noting potential class biases in testimony by experts in the case).

For a scholarly discussion of the use of expert testimony in child-custody decision-making, see Okpaku, *Psychology: Impediment or Aid in Child Custody Cases?,* 29 RUTGERS L. REV. 1117, 1144–50 (1976).

18. *See* Weitzman, *The Economics of Divorce: Social and Economic Consequences of Property, Alimony and Child Support Awards,* 28 UCLA L. REV. 1181, 1251 (1981). The Weitzman study found that in the first year after their divorces under the equal-division rules, men in California experienced a 42 percent increase in their standard of living, as measured by income in relation to needs. Divorced women, by contrast, experienced a 73 percent decline. This postdivorce economic analysis indicates how marriage masks the subordinate economic position of women.

19. *See* Neely, *supra* note 13, at 180 (noting that the situation in which neither parent is clearly the primary caretaker is rare).

20. Moreover, women experience parenthood differently than men in the sense that they are more willing to arrange their lives, even in the anticipation of motherhood, to accommodate child-rearing responsibilities. *See* Project of *Stanford Law Review, Law Firms and Lawyers with Children: An Empirical Analysis of Family/Work Conflict,* 34 STAN. L. REV. 1263, 1274 (1982).

21. *See* Neely, *supra* note 13. Judge Neely anticipates that the evidentiary hearing on who is the primary parent would only cost a few hours and that the witnesses will be neighbors, teachers, and so on, not experts. *Id.* at 181.

22. *See* Fineman, *Implementing Equality: Ideology, Contradiction and Social Change: A Study of Rhetoric and Results in the Regulation of the Consequences of Divorce,* 1983 WIS. L. REV. 789, 832–42 (describing the gender-specific impact of the gender-neutral equal property division reform in Wisconsin); *see also* Neely, *supra* note 13, at 180–81 (arguing that the unequal impact of the rule on fathers is justified because women are in an unequal bargaining position and often trade economic advantages because they fear losing custody). In any case, many family-law rules have a gender-specific impact; joint-custody norms certainly have gender-specific implications.

23. For a discussion of the coin-flip approach that includes some indication of why we as a society would view this as inappropriate, see Mnookin, *supra* note 12, at 289–91. *Compare* Elster, *Solomonic Judgments: Against the Best Interest of the Child,* 54 U. CHI. L. REV. 1, 41 (1987), which argues that random custody decision making minimizes the harm done to children by protracted litigation and appeals to equity concerns.

24. For a fuller exposition of these ideas, see Sampson, *Scientific Paradigms and Social Values: Wanted—A Scientific Revolution,* 36 J. PERSONALITY & SOC. PSYCHOLOGY 1332 (1978).

25. *See* JOINT CUSTODY AND SHARED PARENTING (J. Folberg ed. 1984).

26. Even when the mother works, it is typical for her to assume control of the child. *See* Maret and Finlay, *The Distribution of Household Labor Among Women in Dual-Earner Families,* 46 J. MARRIAGE & FAM. 357, 360 (1984).

27. Lempert, *Grievances and Legitimacy: The Beginnings and End of Dispute Settlement,* 15 LAW & SOC. REV. 707 (1980–81), noted this relationship between legal action and legitimacy in producing *prima facie* neutral decision making. He suggested that neutrality is questioned, however, when the ideological underpinnings of the law or rule are open to attack. If a rule is attacked successfully, it can no longer be viewed as neutral and so must be discarded for a "legitimate" (ideologically supported) rule, so that neutral legal action is again perceived as possible.

Index

Academic literature, its impact on professional discourse, 117
Adversarial model of divorce, 151, 153–54, 159, 161, 165
Affirmative action, and feminism, 23, 25, 26
Alimony, 82, 176, 178; relationship to custody decisions, 178
Areen, Judith, 91–92
Behavioral scientists, "disinterested" role at divorce, 102
"Best interest of the child" test, 82–85, 86, 87, 90, 92–93, 155, 180, 183, 185; attempts to redefine, 111; how determined, 102, 103, 105
Career choices, gendered, 23n
Child advocacy, 84, 86, 92, 95–96, 98, 99; political implications of 100–101, 103, 107–8
Child advocates, 97, 99, 184; role of, 100, 103, 104–5, 107–8
Child custody, 34; changes in legal policy, 109; conceptualized from a child-oriented perspective, 119–20; rules governing awards of, 112
Child support, 43, 48, 49, 180; and custody determination through mediation, 162n; enforcement of, 68n, 81, 88
Children: as fathers' property; as social investment, 82–83; "Bill of Rights for," 101; "independent legal clients," 99–100, 103–4, 107–8; in the best interest of, 96–97, 98, 99, 100, 103, 107–8; isolation from the family unit, 96–97, 100; state involvement with, 97, 101; victimization of, at divorce, 95–96, 98, 101–2, 103
Civil Right's Movement, 27
Conciliation courts, 151n

Contract, marriage as, 19, 24, 39
Contribution as a defining concept at divorce, 63, 67, 68
Contribution versus need in property division, 52, 67, 74–75; as factors influencing property division, 40–42, 44–46, 48–50
Custodial mothers, desire for sole custody, seen as pathological, 106; political powerlessness of, 146
Custodial parent, economic status of, 91–92
Custody, father custody, 81, 89; father- and mother-custody, comparisons of 132–33, 134–35, 141; joint 37, 52; maternal custody, helping professions' opposition to, 148; maternal custody norm, professional attack against, 111; maternal custody, resilience of, 112
Custody battles, helping professions' view of, as pathological, 151, 153, 167
Custody orders, modifiability of, 184
Custody policy: 79–94, 144–69; and economic bargaining at divorce, 161; equality ideal applied too, 144, 148; helping professions' view of, as discriminatory against men, 148n; history of, 82–85; and struggle between law and social work professions, 150, 164
Custody reform, 5–6, 20, 27
Displaced homemakers: 71, 73
Divorce: as crisis, 187; as feminist issue, history, 57–59; costs of, for women versus men, 175–76, 180; economic aspects of, 36–52; impact of no-fault on custody decisions, 84, 90; impact of no-fault on role of social workers in divorce, 89–90; legal model versus therapeutic model of, 150–54, 161, 164;

Parenthood after divorce, legally recognized ideal of, 109–10

Partnership metaphor (for marriage), 4, 18, 29, 40, 42, 43, 45, 49, 50, 52, 72–73, 174

Pater familias doctrine: 82, 88; alteration and perpetuation of, 169

Paternal visitation, its decline over time, 123

Positivist research: controversy over, 113; elevation of, 114; qualitative date, as a valid form of social science research, 116; rationality, the elevation of, 114–15; Russell, 114; self-reported questionnaires, the inaccuracy of, 131; single interviews, methodological problems with, 131; technical focus of, 116–17

Postdivorce family, state intervention in, 79–80, 83, 86, 92, 184–85

Poverty reform, Wisconsin, 54n2

Primary caretakers, 129, 138

"Primary caretaker" rule, 180–85, 187; and economic bargaining at divorce, 182–83; susceptibility to legal analysis, 181

Professional norms, recognition of by policymakers, 109

Property: contribution versus need as determining factors in, 178; division of at divorce, 18, 33, 34, 39, 62, 70–73, 175–76; "horror stories" influence on reformers, 63–65, 68–71; impact on custodial parent, 40, 45, 49, 52; influence on reformers, 63–65, 68–71; relationship to custody decisions, 177–78, 179; rhetoric of, 52, 67, 74–75

Psychological research, use of as systems theory, 139

Result equality, in family sphere, feminist objection to, 21, 26; compared to progressive era "special treatment," 22

"Revolution" in divorce reform: 31–33

Rhetoric in child custody, political nature of, 146, 158; fathers' interest and, 150; political ramifications of, 150; effect on sole-custody mothers, 150

Rhetoric in divorce, reformers, 95; as crisis versus legal problem, 153; emotional versus legal, 152–53, 154, 168

Rule equality versus result equality, 3–4, 20–22, 25, 27–29, 32, 45–46, 47–48, 50, 52, 54, 68, 70, 72, 79–81, 85, 92–93, 94, 176; failure of, 27, 34–35; feminist embrace of, 52, 67, 74–75

Shared parenting: emergence of, 149–50; helping professionals and development of, 150; ideal of, 146–47, 164; ideal of imposed, 106; ideal versus actual, 176, 187–88; potential problems of, 162; social workers' bias for, 146–47; social workers' insistence on, as norm in custody decisions, 145, 154;

Single-fathers, great reliance on support systems, 135–36

Single mothers, the social stigmatization of, 130

Smart, Carol, 7

Social science data, 9, 87, 109; methodological flaws in, 117; methodology used, 134–35; misuse of, 112–13, 118, 124–25; political nature of masked, 112; political use of, 117, 121–22, 124; subjectivity of, 114; use in custody policy, 186; the use and misuse of, 134–36, 137, 143; use of, by law professors and legal policymakers, 110, 112–13, 118, 121, 124; use of, to enhance fathers' rights, 112, 121–22; use of, to maintain status quo, 114

Social science methodology: critical theorist, critique of, 114; feminist critique of, 114–16

Social science studies: as a collaborative endeavor, 116

Social science studies by: Brody & Endsley, 131; Chang & Deinard, 129; Elkin, 152; Gasser & Taylor, 138; Gersick, 139; Hipgrave, 140; Kleinfeld, A., 95; McKee & O'Brien, 140; McKenry, 160; Mendes, 138–39; Piaget, 114; Rosenberg, Kleinman & Brantley, 103; Santrock & Warshak, 133–37; Wallerstein & Kelly, 97, 118–22, 156

Social workers/mediators/helping professionals: alliance with legal profession, 160–62, 163n; conflict with legal profession, 150, 154–55, 157, 159; custody discourse of, 161; dominant role